LET

TO A S ⌐ER

BR

BLOOMSBURY READER

Discover books by Rose Macaulay published by
Bloomsbury Reader at
www.bloomsbury.com/RoseMacaulay

Orphan Island
Personal Pleasures
They Went to Portugal
Told by an Idiot

LETTERS
TO A SISTER

ROSE MACAULAY

Edited By
Constance Babington Smith

BLOOMSBURY READER

LONDON · NEW DELHI · NEW YORK · SYDNEY

This edition published in 2013 by Bloomsbury Reader

Bloomsbury Reader is a division of Bloomsbury Publishing Plc,

50 Bedford Square, London WC1B 3DP

ISBN: 978 1 4482 0760 2
eISBN: 978 1 4482 0729 9

Visit www.bloomsburyreader.com to find out more about our authors and their books
You will find extracts, author interviews, author events and you can sign up for
newsletters to be the first to hear about our latest releases and special offers
Printed and bound by CPI Group (UK) Ltd, Croydon, CR0 4YY

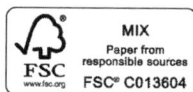

MIX
Paper from
responsible sources
FSC
www.fsc.org   FSC® C013604

Contents

v

Preface

Most of the letters which Rose Macaulay wrote to her sister Jean were preserved, so at the time of Dame Rose's death in 1958 Miss Macaulay possessed a large accumulation. She reread all of them, destroyed quite a number, eliminated parts of others, and then invited me to edit the remainder for publication.

The series now published covers a period of thirty-two years, beginning in 1926 when Rose Macaulay was forty-five. It represents her side of the correspondence only, for after her death, in accordance with her wishes, Miss Macaulay destroyed all the personal letters in her flat. As this included all those which had been kept of the series written to Dame Rose by Miss Macaulay herself, no question of publishing both sides of the correspondence has arisen.

In editing the letters I have made more extensive cuts than in those from Dame Rose to Father Johnson (published as *Letters to a Friend* and *Last Letters to a Friend*) because the originals contain many references to ephemeral matters such as the weather, arrangements for meetings, passing ailments, and family comings and goings. This editing policy may, however, give a false impression of brusqueness, and I would like to emphasize that the manner in which certain of these trivialities are discussed shows a touching solicitude—for example there are repeated warnings against overwork. In addition to the passages just mentioned, I have omitted only those which are repetitious or which might cause embarrassment to living persons.

Many of the letters are not fully dated, but I have been able to establish the dates, nearly all to the day, from information in the letters themselves. Some of the originals are typed but many are handwritten, and in these I have expanded most of the contractions. I have also corrected occasional typing errors and mis-spellings, and punctuation which might be misleading. In general, however, I have not amended incorrectly written quotations etc., nor have I rectified slips of grammar when the meaning is clear. I have indicated the occasional cases where there is no signature.

The Introduction to this book is intended to give as much background as is needed for an understanding of the letters. More detailed accounts of Rose Macaulay's life have been given in the Introductions to the two volumes of her letters to Father Johnson.

The surviving fragments of *Venice Besieged,* the novel Dame Rose was writing just before she died, are published in this book as an Appendix. They consist of a complete first chapter, the beginning of a second, and some rough notes which give indications of the shape the book might have taken. The first chapter exists in two separate versions, one handwritten and the other typed. The latter is published as it stands, except that where Dame Rose had been experimenting with different Christian names for some of the characters I have adjusted occasional discrepancies, using the names which recur most often in her latest corrections. (It is clear she had also been considering various different titles for the book itself; *Venice Besieged* was apparently her most recent favourite.) The rough notes are a medley of transcriptions, random ideas, and scraps of dialogue. A certain amount of rearrangement was imperative, and I have also omitted a few of the jottings which appear to be no more than reminders.

Throughout the work of editing I have received constant encouragement and assistance from Miss Jean Macaulay. I have turned to her continually with every sort of problem, and her keenness, good sense, and good humour have been an inspiration as well as a unique help. To her, and to certain of Dame Rose's dearest friends, who have also given unwavering support to the project of publishing the letters, I am inexpressibly grateful.

I am much indebted to Miss Dorothea Conybeare for help in tracking down information for various footnotes; to Professor Bruce Dickins, whose interest in the problems of my editing has been a great encouragement; and also to Mr A. F. Scholfield, who has most kindly helped me in numerous ways. Many others, too, have taken special trouble in replying to my enquiries (chiefly in connection with footnotes) and I would like to express my thanks to all of them, particularly the following: Miss Doreen Berry, Mrs R. Cavenagh, Rev. Mother Clare, D.S.S. C.S.A., Mr Peter Fleming, Miss L. Joan Gray, Rev. Gerard Irvine, Rev. Hugh Johnston, Mr David Ley, Rev. Canon Fenton Morley, Mr F. A. Richardson, Mrs Paul Roubiczek, Rev. W. G. Sinclair Snow, Rev. Canon Charles Smyth, Miss Lucy Sutherland, Rev. E. K. Taylor, Rev. Cyril Tomkinson, Mr David Trevor, Prof. H. Trevor-Roper, Rt Rev. R. P. Wilson, and Miss Ruth Young. I would also like to acknowledge the kind permission given by Professor C. S. Lewis to quote from his letter concerning *Till We Have Faces*.

For expert assistance in deciphering the handwritten letters I am very grateful to Miss M. F. McKnight. My thanks are also due to the Cambridge University Librarian for permission to make researches at the Library, and I would like to add a special mention of the unfailing courtesy and co-operation of the staff of the Periodicals Department.

Finally, as regards the illustrations in this book, I gratefully acknowledge the permission of Mr Cecil Beaton to reproduce his photograph of Dame Rose, that of Mr Victor Glasstone to reproduce his of Miss Jean Macaulay and that of Topix Picture Service to reproduce their picture of Dame Rose typing.

Constance Babington Smith

Cambridge, 1963

Introduction

There were many different sides to Rose Macaulay. Her gift for being all things to all people made her much beloved, but she could be elusively reticent, and most of her friends knew her only in the setting which was also theirs. Few realized, for example, how lovingly she cherished family ties; even remote cousinships were delightfully compelling bonds to her. Filial loyalty, concentrated towards her adored father, had always been a fundamental of her life, and her affection for brothers and sisters counted for almost as much. During childhood they had been inseparable playfellows, and although, as they grew older, their lives led them far apart they remained a closely united family. So it is not surprising that as time went on, and one after another of them died, Rose's relationship with her remaining sister Jean became increasingly intimate and fond.

She had always enjoyed corresponding with 'Jeanie', who on her side delighted to hear Rose's latest news, also her candid running commentary on books, broadcasts, sermons, politics, and topical questions of religion and ethics. Jean's lively sense of humour and energetic, logical mind made her a stimulating correspondent; their exchanges were like fast rallies between a couple of well-matched tennis players. At the same time Jean's innate simplicity of character—she was much more matter-of-fact and less sophisticated than Rose—provided an excellent complement to her sister's adventurous intellect, imagination, and wit.

Their correspondence flowed steadily on throughout their lives, irrespective of where they happened to be, nor did it diminish when they were meeting more often—rather it increased in volume, as shown by the letters in this book, which were written during three successive periods, each involving somewhat different circumstances. Between 1926 and 1939, when Jean's work as a nurse kept her out of easy reach of London, letters were their chief means of communication. Then during the war and after it, the time that brought Rose into a wilderness of sorrow, illness, and distress, they met often but wrote constantly as well. Lastly, during the 1950's, when Rose's return to the Anglican Church, after a lapse of thirty years, had removed an unspoken barrier between herself and Jean, they wrote more profusely than ever; this in addition to weekly talks and many interminable chats by telephone.

The letters between the sisters naturally take for granted the whole family background, with its Evangelical traditions of service, its churchgoing and family prayers and Bible-reading, its learning and scholarship, its Liberal politics, its life in country parishes and University towns. Also taken for granted, of course, are the characters of the immediate family circle, especially of all the brothers and sisters. Jean was the nearest to Rose in age, so near that they sometimes called one another 'Twin', for they had been born within the same twelve months. But as children their companionship had been subsidiary to that of 'the five', as the elder Macaulays called themselves, in the days when they played together on the beach at Varazze, the fishing village near Genoa which was their home for nearly seven years. The childhood of the Macaulay boys and girls was an idyllic one, with freedom and sunshine instead of the restrictions of Victorian England that would have been their lot if their mother's doctor had not insisted that she should live in a warm climate. For a time Rose and Jean, with their elder sister Margaret, went to an Italian convent school, but this was not a great success. The nuns frowned on 'the little heretics' at prayer-time, and they were nicknamed 'Long Legs' by the other children because their skirts were considered too short. Margaret, 'the quick-tempered one', Jean, 'the stubborn one', and Rose, 'the good one', much preferred their mother's inspiring Sunday-school lessons and their father's reading aloud from Herodotus and the English classics.

George Macaulay, a dedicated academic, was worshipped by Rose, though she came to realize that he was not, in worldly terms, a success. It was from him she first acquired a respect for sound scholarship; she also shared with him an attitude which was a haunting burden. Sensitive and conscientious, with a strong tendency towards depression, he had always been convinced that he was destined for Hell, a belief which in turn seeped into the imaginations of his three elder daughters. In the mind of Rose's mother, on the other hand, there had never been any such terrors. Grace Macaulay believed that Heaven could and should be anticipated with joyful confidence. Born a Conybeare, she was gifted with originality and imagination along with a flair for story-telling; she also possessed a quick intuition which swayed her towards unbalanced enthusiasms and prejudices. She had been spoilt as a child and also as an attractive young wife threatened by tuberculosis. Accustomed to having her own way without question, she treated her children according to whim. As her daughter Jean has put it, 'You never knew whether to expect kindness or a scolding.'

When the family returned to England in 1894 the three Macaulay girls, then in their teens, attended the Oxford High School. Paralysed by shyness they clung together and did not make any friends. Their gauche misery continued after leaving school, aggravated by the puritanical ideas of their mother. Jean, after attending one dance at the invitation of her brother Aulay, resolved never to go to another and never did. Her decision to abstain from alcohol also dates from about this time.

There were two Macaulay boys, Aulay and Will, both of them younger than Rose and Jean. Aulay was mathematically inclined and joined the Royal Engineers, later serving in India, where he died tragically in 1909, murdered by thieves on the North-West Frontier. Will, who as a curly-headed little boy had so closely resembled Rose that the two of them could deceive their parents by dressing up in one another's clothes, was quite different in temperament from the others. Placid, optimistic, and lowbrow, he studied at an agricultural college and then emigrated to Canada and settled happily on a farm in Alberta.

The bond of affection between these five—Margaret, Rose, Jean, Aulay, and Will—stood for all that Rose valued most in family life. The other two Macaulay children, Eleanor and little Gertrude (who died as a small child in Italy) were much younger and were never regarded as equals by the elder ones.

As Rose and Jean grew up their paths diverged entirely. Rose, thanks to the generosity of her well-to-do Macaulay godfather, Uncle Regi, went up to Oxford, where she blossomed at

Somerville, and for the first time made friends outside the family. Soon afterwards she published her first novel, and thenceforward her activities centred more and more on London.

Jean too had longed for a University education, but this would have been beyond the family's means, and at twenty-three she left home to become a nurse. For the next thirty-four years, until just before the second world war, her work more or less cut her off from the family. She did, however, share with Rose in one or two holidays abroad, and there were occasional family reunions. These took place first at Great Shelford outside Cambridge, where their father held a University Lectureship in English for some years before his death in 1915; then, for the ten years their mother survived him, at Beaconsfield; and finally with their sister Margaret in Hampshire. Jean's vocation as a nurse bound her to a life of service, both in England and abroad, which demanded every scrap of her time and energy. (The main work of her career was in District Nursing—she was one of the pioneers—though she also served with the French Army during the 1914–18 war.) But however exhausted, she made a point of writing regularly to her 'Darling Twin'. Not only affection prompted her; through Rose she could keep in touch with the interests of which she was starved in her non-stop professional life.

Rose's world was indeed a contrast to Jean's. In 1926, the year when the first of the letters in this book was written, and her fifteenth novel, *Crewe Train*, was published, she was already well established as a literary celebrity. Almost every year she was writing a new novel, portraying with detached amusement the vagaries of contemporary society. Meanwhile her controversial articles in the daily press and her witty broadcasts helped to keep her well in the public eye. London was her home, and each summer she travelled abroad, usually gravitating towards the Mediterranean, though she made one trip to America with her sister Margaret. Surrounded by friends she was not tied to any one set, and she revelled in a kaleidoscopic life which she believed in enjoying to the full, as testified in her *Personal Pleasures.* By now she was no longer *pratiquante,* but church topics never ceased to fascinate her, and 'sitting under' a good preacher gave her as much pleasure as ever; 'Anglo-agnostic' was how she later described the ambivalent state of her religious feelings at this time. She worked extremely hard at her writing, and her relaxations were strenuous too: swimming, long country walks, bicycle rides—she thought nothing of pedalling twenty miles. But she had a tendency to faint, and in the '20s her doctor advised her to have her heart checked. Rose, with much amusement, reported the depressing findings to Jean, and then continued to live her usual active life. By nature she was exceptionally strong, with a spirit that dominated her body.

Rose and Jean shared many of the same tastes, notably a great love of books. For fun they would compile rival lists of their first hundred favourites, then embark on interminable debates as to the pros and cons. 'Listening in' was an intriguing new hobby for both of them, which later became an established habit; they took enormous pleasure in listening to the same programmes and discussing them by letter afterwards. Both always followed the front-page news of the day: murders, scandals, everything. Political events, too, provided endless food for discussion, and Rose was often able to pass on titbits of news and opinion, from her vantage point among those in the know. Thus Jean, alias Nurse Macaulay, bicycling hurriedly from patient to patient, could ponder on what Sir William Beveridge had told Rose about the crisis in the Coal Industry, or smile to herself at the secret knowledge of what the *New Statesman* was going to say next week. Pacifism, the League of Nations, Abyssinia, the psychology of Hitler, the Cliveden set, the leakage of Budget secrets—Rose had plenty to say about all of them. And personalities like Chesterton, Shaw, and Wells, who would otherwise have been mere names to Jean, became real people in the light of Rose's outspoken comments. Perhaps, however, the most satisfying of all the pleasures which Jean and Rose loved sharing together were their arguments over the rights and wrongs of ethical problems. Generations of Conybeares before them had doted on just such battles of wits. Their to-and-fro had all the warmth and seriousness of a fray at a debating society, often with one of them spontaneously playing the part of devil's advocate. If a popular daily posed the question 'Should one tell a lie to shield a murderer?' Rose and Jean were as happy as terriers after a rabbit. What matter which came off victorious? The whole point was in the chase itself.

There were other enthusiasms, too, to Jean all-important, though less so to Rose, who nevertheless took a sisterly interest in them. One was a strong loyalty to missionary work, a loyalty which in three cases actually shaped the lives of Rose's sisters. Margaret had become a Deaconess in 1913, devoting herself to parish work in the East End of London; Eleanor became a missionary in India with the Society for the Propagation of the Gospel; to Jean the greatest fulfilment of her life was the few years' work she did in South Africa as a missionary nurse just before the second world war. Rose herself, after the shock of her brother Aulay's death, had also volunteered as a missionary. But this rash offer was declined and she never repeated it.

Charitable giving was another activity that was very close to Jean's heart—a good deal closer than to Rose's. Both sisters made regular donations to Charities as a matter of course, but their attitudes towards money were different. In childhood they had both been accustomed to a standard of living that was frugal by necessity; their father's income could barely meet the expenses of educating a large family. Rose had been rescued from this financial struggle first by her rich godfather and then also by her own earnings. And although there was always a certain Spartan independence about her she valued comfort, especially warmth, and liked being surrounded by a mass of belongings. Jean, on the contrary, had plunged into a life of real austerity in her chosen work among the poor, and gave herself enthusiastically to the practice of self-denial. With a minimum of possessions (books were almost her only indulgence) she habitually gave away much of her inadequate income. In the 1930's she also began to organize a campaign for 'planned giving' to Charities, which she named the League of Stewards. With Rose's help this project was brought to the attention of Canon 'Dick' Sheppard in 1936 and he was keen to help in launching it. But before there was time for this Jean was given the opportunity of working in South Africa; when she returned Sheppard was dead. Then the war came and the project was dropped. Jean's inspiration was twenty years too soon: the Christian Stewardship campaigns which are now the fashion are based on exactly the same idea.

It was in 1939 that Jean returned from South Africa. She had worked herself to a standstill at the Jane Furse Memorial Hospital in the Transvaal, and eventually had to come home on doctor's orders. She then took an appointment as a District Nurse at Romford, on the Essex side of London (in company with her lifelong friend, Nancy Willetts, a fellow-nurse from Birmingham). This meant that Rose and Jean were now only fifteen miles apart, and Rose was soon going every week to see Jean on her day off. Both set great store by these meetings though at the time they were often a strain for Jean. She had always taken Rose's lapse from the Church deeply to heart. It was never mentioned, but against this background of silence Jean's feelings were painfully vulnerable to the shafts of ridicule which Rose often aimed at the ideals of Christianity. Jean believes that Rose was quite unaware of the pain she caused, but it was none the less acute, and sometimes after Rose had left to return to London she would give way to tears. She was far too busy to brood, however, and when the time came for Rose's next visit she was as eager as ever for their usual talk.

And there was much to talk about, much to share, as week by week the daily life of both became enmeshed in the machinery of war. Long before war actually began, Rose had made up her mind that in the event of the evacuation of women and children from London, she herself was not going to be banished from home. According to Jean it was largely this that led 'Emily Macaulay' to volunteer as a part-time driver with the London Auxiliary Ambulance Service. 'Emilie' was the first of Rose's two baptismal names, and she made use of 'Emily' when she did not want to be recognized, though of course everyone at the Ambulance Station soon knew who she was. Anyway, it was delightful that driving about in her faithful Morris was now important war work. War was utterly abhorrent to Rose, but when it came—especially when the bombing came—she met its impact with her usual capacity to find enjoyment in almost everything. And in spite of it all she was still getting a little writing done; seeing dear friends—Gilbert Murray, Harold Nicolson, Victor Gollancz; relishing the game of trying to find out, despite propaganda and censorship, what was really happening in the war. Every week she sent on to Jean the King-Hall news-letter, as well as any cuttings that had interested her—usually with a few tart comments.

All in all, the surge of events during the first eighteen months of the war brought more stimulation than distress to Rose. But enjoyment fled away after the Spring of 1941, when she was gradually overwhelmed by a rising tide of personal sorrows and disasters. Illness and death came to one after another of those she loved; first of all her sister Margaret died of cancer. There had always been a close affinity between Rose and Margaret, and her death, though not unexpected, was a severe shock. Then when Rose was away in Hampshire making arrangements for the sale of Margaret's house and furniture, her flat in Marylebone was bombed. Before this she had never realized how much she cared for her belongings. When she found them gone she was more grief-stricken than she could ever have imagined. Yet in her sorrow she discovered anew the kindness of her friends, who hastened to her support with every kind of gift, including books to replace some of those she had lost; the destruction of her library had caused her an agony of grief.

She found a new flat in Hinde Street, off Manchester Square (her home for the rest of her life) but after settling there she collapsed into illness, and early in 1942 had to give up her ambulance work. It was then that she first began to depend on Jean, who, with her friend Nancy Willetts, nursed her through several illnesses.

Before the war ended, and during the years just after it, the sunshine of Portugal and Spain restored her natural eagerness for life and work, though spiritually she was still wandering lost among ruins, like Barbary in *The World my Wilderness*. Then in 1950, the year when that novel was published, she received from

America the letter which was to initiate her return to faith. It was an appreciation of her historical novel *They Were Defeated* from her one-time confessor Hamilton Johnson of the Cowley Fathers.

When Rose first started corresponding with Father Johnson she did not say anything about it to Jean. Not until she was well established as a regular worshipper at Grosvenor Chapel did she mention the fact, quite casually, and Jean tactfully accepted it without much comment. Thenceforward the barriers of reserve fell gradually away, and their mutual love became ever more understanding and strong.

As they reached their seventies, the death of their sister Eleanor in India meant that they were the only survivors of the last generation of Macaulays. When July and August came round each year, bringing the birthdays which they observed as faithfully as when they were children, they were recurrently reminded that there was no younger generation to carry on this branch of the family; that they and their brothers and sisters, in failing to marry and produce offspring, seemed to have failed in a joint responsibility. But it was comforting to Rose, and also to Jean, to be able to discuss old age, as it advanced, with a sister who was not only loving but had courage and a sense of humour. Jean's many infirmities, including failing sight and hearing, forced her more and more to accept the role of an old woman. Rose, fully active till the end, never thought of herself as aged, and in spirit she never was.

The last thing in the world that either of them would have sought after was public recognition, but when Jean, after her retirement in 1956, was awarded the M.B.E. for her exceptional service as a District Nurse, Rose was naturally delighted, and accompanied her to Buckingham Palace for the investiture. Jean believes that this may have helped Rose to make up her mind to accept the D.B.E. when it was offered to her two years later. She recalls that in the past Rose had declined a C.B.E., because she felt she would thereby be under an obligation to conform to conventional standards in her work. In 1958 no such scruples held her back, and she became Dame Rose Macaulay, slightly to her own embarrassment and to the joy of her numerous friends.

During Rose's last years many treasured friendships developed for her, especially among fellow Anglicans, and in her letters to Jean she wrote with affection of John Betjeman, Trevor Huddleston, Gerard Irvine, and Susan Lister, as well as the clergy at St Paul's, Knightsbridge, and at Grosvenor Chapel, the two churches she attended regularly. Often too, during those years, she liked to discuss with Jean her latest thinking on religious matters. Paradoxically—since high-church ritual appealed to her so strongly—she became a champion of Intercommunion, and made a point of taking part in the worship of various Nonconformist churches. Towards the end of her life, as these letters show, she was also becoming rather more tolerant towards Roman Catholicism. She even went so far as to write to Jean, on a gay holiday postcard, that if she were an atheist she would feel strongly tempted to join the Roman Church, 'but not in England; it would have to be in Italy, and preferably Venice'. Rose's holidays still drew her irresistibly to 'dear abroad'—to Cyprus and the Middle East, to Turkey, to Venice, to the Aegean Islands and the Black Sea. But she now also enjoyed staying quietly with friends in the country, often with Raymond Mortimer in Dorset, or visiting the Isle of Wight with Jean and Nancy Willetts.

These final years of Rose's life brought radiant fulfilment to her in many ways. Her spiritual 'exile' and the torments of remorse and contrition were left behind, and in profound thankfulness for the Christian life with its 'new dimension', as she called it, she longed to share with others her blessed experience of forgiveness. In this frame of mind she wrote *The Towers of Trebizond*. Its resounding success caused her intense joy. Many greeted it as the best novel she had ever written, while perceptive readers prized its deeper meaning.

But its message was in some ways cryptic, and much of its light relief invited misinterpretation. Among Rose's closest friends were several who delighted in *Trebizond,* but found its end unsatisfying, and they urged her to write a sequel. Yes, she would write again of the conflict of good and evil in the human heart. There would be a different set of characters but again the story would begin in England and then move southwards, this time to her beloved Venice. Perhaps it was Rose's mermaid blood, like that of Ellen Green—the willowy heroine of *And No Mans Wit*—which inevitably made her such an ardent Venice-lover. Her first enchantment had been as a little girl in 1892, when she was taken there for a visit with her sisters Jean and Margaret. Staying in Venice more than sixty years later was still 'like living in some lovely poem'. Rose was on the crest of the wave of *Trebizond*'s success when her new novel began to take shape in her mind. When she died, in October 1958, only one chapter of *Venice Besieged* had been written, but there was also a notebook of rough jottings. How tantalizing! Yes, but a challenge to the imagination that the finished 'Venice-book' could never have been.

In the complete first chapter, which begins with a road accident near Stonehenge on a midsummer night, one gets to know the characters. The notes take them on to Venice, and show the wealth of scholarship and fantasy and wit Rose would have interwoven with the ingenuities of the plot. How would it all have ended? These fragments do not provide a definite answer, though there is just a hint that eventually catastrophe and chaos would have been superseded by redeeming love. Unavoidably one is left with many unanswered questions, but with a unique glimpse behind the scenes at the process of Rose Macaulay's art.

CONSTANCE BABINGTON SMITH

1926–1936

In the train
Easter Day [4 April], 1926

Dearest Jeanie,

... I am en route for Petersfield,[1] going by train to Godalming, and bicycling the last 20 miles from there. It is lovely country from there, and a perfect day, so it should be a nice ride, especially as I have left lots of time to loiter and explore by the way....

I went to Grosvenor Chapel on Good Friday, where Mr Underhill[2] gave quite good addresses, very practical. He seems a good man, on the whole, I think; I'd never heard him before....

Another advantage of the wireless, according to an article I

---

[1] To stay with R.M.'s elder sister Margaret, who had recently retired from working as a Deaconess in the East End of London. After their mother died in 1925 she had established a family home at Petersfield.

[2] Rev. Francis Underhill, cousin of Evelyn Underhill.

read yesterday by the Editor of the *Church Times*, is that it is saving family life from boredom and irritation. No longer, he said, does the husband have to sit in the evenings and listen to inanities from his wife about the neighbour's baby or the servants; he and she can now both sit in silence, with the phones on their ears. I quite agree…. I'm not sure if you meant that wireless or work was the most splendid invention that has ever been, you put it ambiguously. If you meant work, I don't agree (I'm not sure about wireless, either, though I love to have it—but it's a better idea than work, anyhow!). Of course it all depends on the work. There is dull, and interesting work. Mr Underhill was saying on Friday that the dullest lives he had ever seen were those of working mothers, always at some dull household chore from morning till night, and scarcely ever getting out, and never going away. He worked in a poor parish for 25 years, so knows about it. I'm sure they wouldn't agree with you about work being a good invention. I read a rather interesting novel the other day, by a friend of mine, called *The Question Mark*.[3] It is about the world some thousands of years hence, when everything gets done by machinery, so no necessary work is left to do. Consequently work is only done by the intelligent and highly educated, and the others, the 'normals', concentrate on sport, sensation, and sex interest, and get generally demoralised. This person agrees with you, apparently….

Very much love.

R.M.

---

[3] Muriel Jaeger, *The Question Mark* (1926).

[2,] St Andrew's Mansions,[4] Dorset St, W.1
18 April, [1926]

Dearest Jeanie,

… I am glad you have got a member into the Have-Not League.[5] Is she the only one besides you? I'm sorry you can't get any of your own family to join: I feel we ought, but also that we shan't. When the moment comes to decide whether to go a walking tour in the Pyrenees (or whatever our form of luxury may be at the moment) or to give the money away, I feel I always decide on the selfish side. It is very bad; I feel rather like St Augustine, that perhaps I shall be better when it matters less, at some future date, perhaps when I am too old to go about etc.

This day last year was our first day at Soller, I believe—I mean the day after the first night. Do you remember how exquisite it was, waking to the sound of bells, and going out on the terrace with the wistaria to the lavatory (tho' perhaps the less said of the lavatory itself the better) and coming down to coffee and *ensaimada*,[6] then going out into the town. I forget if we climbed the Puig Mayor that day or another, but everything we did was lovely. Possibly we drove to Miramar….

Much love.

R.M.

---

4   *R.M.*'s flat at this time.

5   This was an idea of Jean Macaulay's to facilitate charitable giving, inspired by Fr Waggett's preaching on 'the Haves and the Have-Nots'. It later developed into her League of Stewards, see below p. 73n.

6   A Majorcan 'croissant' pastry shaped like a Bath bun.

Thursday [22 April, 1926]

Dearest Jeanie,

... I still am rather fevered and coldish—hope not flueish.... I stay in, and listen to the wireless. Those horrid Australians[7] were speaking this afternoon, about what a 'pure' and noble game cricket is. They didn't say how or why it was purer than football, hockey, tennis or golf. Cricketers are conceited.

Then I heard the Archbishop of Canterbury[8] at some meeting Eleanor is at[9]—less offensive but equally dull. At least, as a Christian, he knows that it's not true that 'Britishers always play the game, in life as well [as] on the field'. I wonder if people who say that ever read the papers, and see what Britishers do in the way of fraud and wickedness. But of course I don't really know what 'playing the game' means. Much love.

Your loving *R.M.*

2, St Andrew's Mansions, Dorset St, W.1
3 May, [1926]

Dearest Jeanie,

... The strike is over my head, and I don't think anything sensible about it, except that it seems inevitable now.[10] A man I

---

[7] An Australian Test Team was then in England.

[8] Abp Randall Davidson.

[9] R.M.'s sister Eleanor (a missionary in India) was home on leave, and was attending an Annual Meeting of the Society for the Propagation of the Gospel.

[10] The General Strike was due to begin at midnight on 4 May.

know[11] who was one of the recent Coal Commission spent ½ an hour a few nights ago explaining the position to me, and if I were to try and pass what he said on to you it would take many sheets of paper. It would take less time to tell you what Mr Trowles, my char's husband, thinks, as the thoughts of the poor & simple are shorter than those who know more of the subject. *He* doesn't see why the miners who are only pushing trucks and ponies about above ground should get so much more than other working men as they do, though he thinks that those of them (a small proportion) who go down into what Mrs Trowles calls 'the bowels of the earth' should not have any reduction of wages or increase of hours. The proposal, isn't it, is to lower wages to only 20% above prewar level, instead of 33⅓% as it now is. But I forget if this means purchasing power or actual coinage—so little do I know of the subject, even after Sir William Beveridge's exposition.

But I must say I do object on principle to general strikes to settle questions concerning a particular industry.

I suppose the chief thing about the mining question is, where is the money to come from? At present coal isn't paying its way at all, but [is] being worked at a loss, until the new improvements can be carried out. I don't think it would be a good thing to continue the subsidy, it's such a heavy burden on tax-payers. I wish the Union would consent to the 8-hour day, which would, they say, make all the difference to production. But they seem firm on the 7 hours …

Much love.

E.R.M.

p.s. What do you do with mawkish female admirers who vent their passion by leaving you expensive flowers and begging you

---

[11] Sir William Beveridge.

to have meals etc. with them? I get them through my books, and they are becoming (one in particular) a problem. I don't like being rude, yet it bores me to see her, and I haven't time either. Yet, as she says, I must have lunch somewhere, and can she join me at it. I think I must pretend to have gone abroad or something. She asks if she may become, if possible, one of my friends. *What do I say?* She mayn't, but I must convey this politely if possible. So far I've not answered the letter. She called to see me, with lilies of the valley, and I went out to lunch to get rid of her, and she had it with me. Writing books is a terrible magnet for such as her. They are so very boring, as a rule. I suppose no-one who wasn't would force their way into people's lives like that. Now that she has seen me, she is *worse* than ever. Do you have them too, or is everyone you know too busy? I'm really too busy myself, but one's own busyness doesn't deter people. Anyhow I have enough friends already, and I do resent people thinking they can become friends merely by pushing their way in. As a matter of fact I select my friends with great care, and only have those who please me a great deal. There must be a way out of these problems, I wish I could hit on it. I must ask other novelists what they do.

2, St Andrew's Mansions, Dorset St, W.1
17 May, [1926]

Dearest Jeanie,

   … I wish I understood more about the strike … I mean, the miners' strike—I do understand the other,[12] I think, and don't

---

[12] The General Strike.

approve at all. The men didn't want to come out a bit, so every-one says, but they had to obey their Unions or get into trouble with them, which they can't afford. To make it more palatable, the Union leaders spread the quite untrue report that the lower-ing of miners' wages was a prelude to an attack on other wages. I saw this in a leaflet that was being sold. The question was raised in Parliament, and [J. H.] Thomas didn't attempt to deny that it had been a fabrication for propaganda purposes. I do dislike that man. I heard him in the House the other day, and thought him *very* cheap and insincere and unfair.

According to Mr Trowles (my char's husband) the story was widely believed, but even with it he said he knew very few work-ing men who wanted to come out. It was obviously wrong of the Unions to tell them to, as most of them broke contracts to do so. It would have been thought very wrong if employers had broken their contracts with their men by sacking them without due notice for no fault of theirs, just because they disapproved of the way some other men in another trade were behaving, and this was just as mean, I think, and quite as illegal. Also very silly, of course, as it could do no good.

Of course the miners' is a quite different question, and far more difficult. In fact, too difficult, unless one is a coal expert. The agreement of 1921, by which they got these wages, automatically ended on May 1st 1926, and trouble was bound to come. Last year the Government spent 23 million pounds, which the country can't afford, on subsidising the coal industry, and obviously that can't go on indefinitely, though I think it should for a time. The fact is that it is not at present, under present condi-tions and with present wages and hours, a paying industry, and mine after mine will have to be closed down unless the men can produce more somehow. Also if the present wages continue, there will be more unemployment, as so many can't be employed. Of course the reductions don't affect the lower-grade men; no-one under £2:5 a week is reduced at all, and these not much. The cuts only seriously affect the £3:18 to £4:15 men—i.e. those who do the actual deep pit work, and some of the high-grade men on the surface. These could lose about 10/- a week, which is hard on them, but they would probably re-win it when coal paid better. A Welsh girl I know whose family are all miners says her father and 3 brothers each earn about £4, & share a house, so get £16 a week; but this is exceptional luck, of course. Of course the whole wages question seems to me so difficult, because *I* don't see how anyone can raise a family on under £3 a week, and yet they do. I mean, I would raise *all* wages, if industry would allow, not especially to miners, who are better paid already than most, in the high grades. When this agreement was made, in 1921, cost of living was 268%. Now it is reported to be 168% (above pre-war cost, this is, of course). So, a man who was now reduced from £4 to £3: 10, would actually in buying power be better off than in 1921—he would lose ⅛ of what he earns, but has gained more than that in purchasing power. But still, no-one wants to lose any money, and one can't help feeling they have a good case and are wise to fight it. The only possible end is more Government subsidy, I think. I believe it's true that the coal-owners are going bankrupt and can't pay more.

Of course we hate governments, because they make us do what we don't like, it's what they're for. They're all silly, too. I hated the *British Gazette*, horrid little paper. I prefer a Liberal government on the whole. But no gov. can solve the coal question well …

[The end of this letter is missing]

Dearest Jeanie,

… I disposed of my admirer by, when she insisted on lunching with me, arranging with some other friends of mine to turn up and lunch with us, so that there could be no private conversation and so that it must have been obvious to her I didn't mean to be alone with her. She has taken the hint, and subsided into silence— I am so glad, because I began to fear her skin was too thick for any hint, and that I should have to be unkind straight out, which I never like. If one *can* settle an affair politely, so much the better.

The coal strike is dreadful. It seems we are losing thousands of pounds a minute by it, at a time when the country can't afford, if it's to pay its debts and keep up, to lose anything at all. It seems at present a hopeless impasse—first the miners reject the terms, then the owners do—so, as Mr Bennet said of Elizabeth and Mr Collins, it seems a hopeless business. Meanwhile the Government, like Mrs Bennet, is all of an uproar trying to bring them together.

By the way, I asked a man I know[13] who works for the T.U.C. how anyone came to be getting only 30 or 35 shillings, and he said it must be in one of those pits where all the men don't work the full week, but are only allowed to work some days and [are] paid accordingly, which is very hard on them. The minimum for the full week is more than that, of course.

There seems to be a wide-spread fear, according to this man,

---

[13] H. B. Usher, who during the General Strike worked in a temporary information and intelligence section at the T.U.C. headquarters.

(who is standing Labour for Leicester and was up there a good deal during the strike) of a general lowering of wages if the miners' are lowered. It is quite unreasonable, of course, as the coal question is all by itself, and the lowering only follows an artificial raising, but it has got about. I wish it were possible to have a national minimum in each industry, that couldn't be lowered. Or else profit-sharing. Only this wouldn't help coal, which is yielding no profits at present except to the coal-shop-men who are getting much more than they should compared with what the workers and owners get.

I hear that miners' wives in some places threaten a rebellion, on account of wash-houses being put up at the pits, which enable their husbands to clean themselves and doll up and go into the town without coming home first. They threaten to pull them down. This seems reasonable, tho' one sees the poor miner's point of view too. What a complicated world it is! Perhaps the Bishops are right when they say that mutual charity is the only solution, though it always sounds silly in face of a question which is as difficult as coal and seems to need mainly brains to solve it....

Very much love.

R.M.

10, St Andrew's Mansions,[14] Dorset St, W.1
28 January, [1927]

Dearest Jeanie,

... I think a bicycling tour is a v.g. idea. But I don't see how it's

---

[14] *R.M.* had moved to another flat.

going to take you a week to get from Deal to Petersfield unless you spend most of each day at the places you pass. I should have thought 2 or 3 ordinary days' bicycling, not at all fast or much, would do it. If I were doing it, I should avoid the coast road, which is very crowded and ugly, and also the seaside inns are full, and bicycle inland, through Kent and Sussex, through quiet lanes & country villages—much prettier and more country and quieter and also the inns wouldn't be so full. I dislike watering-places always; however, perhaps you want to keep by the sea. As to sleeping out, I'd rather sleep on a hay-stack than on a crowded beach. However, that is all a question of taste, and anyhow a bicycling expedition is fun, however one does it, if only the weather is good and the winds favourable, which is *most* important; in fact, if a wind is against me I don't bicycle at all....

Did you listen last night to the debate between Lady Rhondda and G. K. Chesterton, on Leisured Women?[15] I was there, and it was quite amusing, without saying much sense on either side. Shaw, in the chair, was the best. But I agree with Lady Rhondda; Chesterton's glorification of an exclusive home life seems to me quite a wrong and silly idea, and, as Lady R. said, probably very bad for the children on whom excessive attention is concentrated. Chesterton said that the home is now the only place where a man can call his soul his own and say and think what he likes. Shaw said he mustn't speak of '*the* home', he must say what home, and that in most cases people's homes were the last places where they could say what they thought—e.g. Socrates. Chesterton said he had meant the Chestertons' home. I'm sure he is right about that,

---

[15] A broadcast debate on 'The Menace of Leisured Women'.

as he has in it only the admiring Mrs C. and a meek secretary.
But I imagine Shaw is right about most homes ...

> Very much love.
>
> *E.R.M.*

10, St Andrew's Mansions, Dorset St, W.1
16 February, [1927]

Dearest Jeanie,

... Shall you try and guess the objects shown to the telepathic subjects to-night?[16] I shall if I get back from the theatre in time. The Society for Psychical Research is unfair, as usual, in saying that if no one guesses any of them it will prove nothing adverse to telepathy, but that if anyone does it will prove that telepathy exists. Anyhow, with thousands of guessers, some of the objects are almost bound to be hit on. I expect the *Daily News* is right in saying that we shall each think of what we like ourselves—the child of doughnuts, Mussolini of portraits of himself, etc. I am broadcasting on Saturday night, two essays, 'On questions and answers', and 'Travelling by Train', from *A Casual Commentary.* I see in some paper that 'Miss R.M. will intersperse her reading with some pungent remarks that occur to her at the moment', but this is not so. I don't know what pungent remarks are, but I certainly shouldn't be

---

[16] There was to be a broadcast programme entitled 'An Experiment in Telepathy', in which selected 'agents' at the office of the Society for Psychical Research were to concentrate on a series of objects shown to them. Listeners were invited to record on paper their impressions, 'if any', of each of the objects shown.

allowed to make any on the spur of the moment …

Much love.

E.R.M.

10, St Andrew's Mansions, Dorset St, W.1
Thursday [14 April, 1927]

Dearest Jeanie,

… I quite agree that the mind is the *important* part of the human affair—the only question is, which causes which. However, as you say, we shall never know. Your argument is weak about importance. Love (between man & woman) is the important part of their desire for each other, but the originator of it, which called love into being in man, is mere animal desire. I mean, the important factor often comes chronologically second. Similarly (as Socrates used to put it) the important part of an electric lamp is the light it gives, but the light is a function of the physical structure, and operates strictly within it, and would perish if the lamp were smashed. However, I am myself uncertain about body and soul!

… Your loving *E.R.M.*

[This letter was probably written in September, 1927.
The first part of it is missing.]

… Kenneth Mozley[17] turned up yesterday and took me to the Falkland naval battles film[18]—a very good film indeed, but too

---

[17] Rev. J. K. Mozley, D.D. (1883–1946).

[18] *The Battles of Coronel and the Falkland Islands.*

sad and full of ships going down, which I hate. A bright spot, however, was the way the German Commander uttered the same noble sentiments as the English, about sinking rather than surrendering, and went down with flag flying, and the audience cheered them as loudly as they cheered the English for doing and saying the same, which showed a very good spirit. Afterwards Kenneth and I had tea, and he told me how he was the only true Augustinian in the church, much to the interest of the neighbouring tea tables. 'I have no use at all, my dear Rose', he said, getting very loud and shrill, 'for your weak, striving, well-meaning God, who has to rely on our encouragement of him for his success'. Everyone looked at me with scorn, for having a God like that. I like to see a man so animated about religion.

Very much love …

Your loving *E.R.M.*

24 October, [1927]

Dearest Jeanie,

… I thought the Archbishop's letter to Barnes very good didn't you.[19] I'm afraid he won't be tried for heresy. Though it would be a good entertainment, it would be very unedifying, and I fear we should become laughing-stocks, like Tennessee.[20] Besides, his

---

[19] Rt Rev. E. W. Barnes, Bp of Birmingham, had defined his position as a Modernist, and his hostility to the doctrine of Transubstantiation, in an open letter to the Archbishop of Canterbury, published on 20 October 1927. Abp Davidson rebuked him in a reply published four days later.

[20] The State of Tennessee had passed an 'anti-evolution' law in 1925, by which any teaching inconsistent with the Genesis account of man's creation (taken literally) was forbidden. The American Civil Liberties Union

remarks about the Sacrament, though not very intelligent or at all polite, weren't heretical. The old Canon who thought they were is obviously dotty.[21] I'm glad all the bishops are snubbing him. But he wrote a very conceited reply to London,[22] saying how many congratulations he had received. I think *he* should be tried, for brawling; only that he'd enjoy it so. He obviously thinks he has lit a candle that will never be put out. I'm glad they've all made it clear that evolution has nothing to do with the quarrel, the press was so silly about it. Even now it is making a heading of 'Gorilla Sermons',[23] though the Archbishop said they had nothing to do with the case.

Very much love.

E.R.M.

29 October, [1927]

Dearest Jeanie,

... Have you enough time to follow the great Church squabble? I thought Inge had a very good and convincing article in the

---

offered to defend any teacher who would 'personally test the constitutionality of the statute'. John T. Scopes, a science teacher, 'formally violated the law', and was then tried and convicted. The case received world-wide publicity.

[21] Canon G. R. Bullock-Webster (d. 1934) had led a protest against Bp Barnes' preaching in St Paul's Cathedral on 16 October.

[22] Rt Rev. A. F. Winnington-Ingram.

[23] A nickname for the sermons on anthropology and sacramental theology recently preached by Bp Barnes.

Evening Standard the other day[24], for which I see the *Church Times* this week is furious with him. It attributes anger to him, after the habit of people who are angry themselves, but his article was actually quite calm, though annoying, no doubt. But I don't know why the *C. T.* should defend Jesuits with such fervour; however, of course it would, against Inge.[25]

I was sorry Barnes repeated his foolish proposal of a test of consecrated bread against unconsecrated.[26] He ought not to have gone on about it, after the Archbishop had told him to shut up. He is a tactless man.

Did you listen in last night to Shaw & Chesterton?[27] I thought Shaw rather good on the Church controversy. I expect the B.B.C. were angry with him for referring to it, as they don't encourage people to be 'controversial', which, he said, was why he selected the most controversial subject he could think of to allude to. I wonder if, on the whole, it's done good or harm to the Church—the brawl, I mean, and subsequent discussion. Good, I should think. Anyhow I hope the Archbishop's letter has killed for ever any Anglican folly (if there was any) about the origins of man. As to the sacramental question, people take it so oddly that it's difficult to say whether public discussion is good

---

[24] 'The Latest Heresy Hunt' *(Evening Standard, 26* October, 1927). Dean Inge advocated a progressive attitude in religious education, and disparaged a recent newspaper article by a Jesuit.

[25] An editorial in the *Church Times* (28 October) criticised Dean Inge for 'sneers … positively outrageous in their bad taste'.

[26] On 26 October Bp Barnes had addressed a second open letter to the Archbishop of Canterbury.

[27] 'Do we Agree?', a broadcast debate between G. B. Shaw and G. K. Chesterton.

or bad. All these people who write to the press and say they are 'wounded' by Barnes' view and its expression—can they really be wounded by someone else's opinion, or is it all humbug? People *are* such humbugs often that one can't tell. I can't myself imagine being hurt or offended or wounded by any publicly expressed views, however different from mine, even on the matters most sacred to me. What is all this being hurt that seems to go on—does it really? I half believe they invent it, to get people who differ from them rebuked by Archbishops. I feel they should try and be harder-headed, more intellectual and abstract, and less touchy and sensitive …

Very much love …

E.R.M.

10, St Andrew's Mansions, Dorset St, W.1
Whit Sunday [27 May, 1928]

Dearest Jeanie,

… Whom do the Esquimaux missionaries convert? Other Esquimaux? I wish them every possible luck! Ought I to send them money? I enclose an article by an actress recommending all women to spend their money on beauty-improvement. What can we do about this? I am writing an article, and I think we should all **SPEAK** about it, it is too degraded and fearful. With all these unconverted Esquimaux and unsupported hospitals and penniless old people—and this woman says she would rather go hungry than be plain—and what she means is she would rather other people went hungry than that she were plain. Sometimes I wish I were a clergyman, a bishop, or a pope, or a dean, to speak out from a pulpit. When the clergy do preach on beauty culture they do it all wrong, saying it is ungodly and immodest, instead of attacking its selfishness and imbecility. This actress says it is a sign of brainlessness *not* to spend money on beauty culture. What a world!

… Very much love.

E.R.M.

10, St Andrew's Mansions, Dorset St, W.1
4 June, 1928

Dearest Jeanie,

… I am expecting Margaret here for to-night on her way home.[28] St David's must be a lovely place, but obviously there is far too much house-work—she says they keep on dusting and washing up, even when there are no Retreatants staying, and waste all the day at it instead of being out, and she doesn't like to leave them at it. It must be [a] maddening waste of time. *My increasing purpose is to save time for the things I most want to do in it.* I fail hopelessly, as most of my time goes on things I don't want to do at all, but it remains a purpose. Perhaps this is a pity, as it makes a discord in my life and makes me cross and discontented. But I should go quite insane in a house where I had to waste much time on washing up and dusting things that seemed to me as well undusted or only dusted once a week—or at least not so important to dust as to go out into the country (which is as

---

[28] Margaret Macaulay had been staying at the Diocesan Retreat House at St David's, Pembrokeshire.

bad as a Hutchinson sentence,[29] but this subject makes me lose control of grammar, as perhaps his subject did him). But people's sense of values are so different that I suppose the Sisters really do like best to live that way. Another lesson against sharing other people's lives without being able to sit quite loose to them, which one can seldom do …

I have to write an article for the *Daily Herald* on What most Interests Me. I think of saying country walks (involving the preservation & restoration of foot-paths, and the protection of the country from increasing motoring and building), and also the study of words and their derivations and meanings, and language in general. What would you say, I wonder? People, I expect. And possibly religion? Apropos of religion, I am sending you (partly because you might enjoy it, partly to help its sale) a rather nice book on the Anglican Tradition, by Mr Carpenter.[30] I think it is very good and clear, and I hope lots of people will read it, and correct their muddled ideas on the Prayer Book etc. before they get the new book.[31] Joynson-Hicks' book[32] is most unfortunate and ill-timed and tiresome. He is a silly little creature. By the way, I see Inge has been denouncing Dr Voronoff and monkey glands, as 'unholy'.[33] Is there anything in this? I mean, does it really add an ape-like quality to those who have it done? If so, it is certainly a serious business, and may lower the level of the human race, which can little afford it….

---

[29] The novels of A. S. M. Hutchinson abound in long meandering sentences, and his syntax is often unorthodox.

[30] S. C. Carpenter, *The Anglican Tradition* (1928).

[31] The 1928 revision of the Book of Common Prayer.

[32] W. Joynson-Hicks, *The Prayer Book Crisis* (1928).

[33] This was in a sermon in Westminster Abbey on 3 June.

Are you following 'Where are the Dead?' in the *Daily News?* They've none of them yet answered the question.[34] I am thinking of writing to them to say I know where the dead are, and will tell for a high enough fee.

Very much love.

E.R.M.

10, St Andrew's Mansions, Dorset St, W.1
28 June, [1928]

Dearest Jeanie,

Our letters crossed the other day; I suppose telepathy worked. Many thanks for yours. This is a supplement to mine, to answer your questions as to (a) how I am (b) where the dead are.

(a) My health is excellent. I've no bad symptoms of anything, and haven't fainted for ages.

(b) I can't imagine where the dead can be. As it seemed that the *Daily News* writers could not imagine either, and never said (except the R.C.,[35] as you say, and I knew already what he would think) I gave up the *D.N.* I can imagine what Robert Lynd would have said (if he's said it yet).[36] He would say they are in heaven. He is a kindly man, and is also almost the only layman I know well (except R.C.s) who believes in survival after

---

[34] Contributors so far had been Bp E. A. Knox, Arnold Bennett, and G. K. Chesterton.

[35] G. K. Chesterton.

[36] Robert Lynd said *(Daily News,* 27 June, 1928) that he believed in Immortality, 'but not by any process of reasoning'. He took it for granted because he 'had never met an argument on the other side that undermined it'.

death. At least, he gives it the benefit of the doubt. I couldn't even guess, myself. I should like very much to believe in it, but am not able to, so am divided between wish and actual belief. I couldn't possibly have written about it. I feel I really agree with Sir Arthur Keith and Julian Huxley and the other scientists,[37] but would so much rather think we somehow go on that I don't like to write about it.

Very much love.

E.R.M.

10, St Andrew's Mansions, Dorset St, W.1
10 November, 1928

Dearest Jeanie,

… The *Well of Loneliness* case yesterday was quite amusing.[38] Half literary London had turned up, by request, as well as social workers, clergy, teachers, etc. to say what they thought of the book, but the magistrate[39] ruled out their evidence as inadmissible, as he said it was his business alone to decide whether or not the book was immoral. So only a Police Inspector gave evidence, and Desmond MacCarthy, the first literary witness called, wasn't allowed to speak, and all the talking was done by the lawyers and the magistrate. I enclose what I had

---

[37] Julian Huxley wrote *(Daily News,* 5 June): 'I can think of our personalities being lost, blended, taken up into some general reservoir of mind and spirit'. Sir Arthur Keith gave his opinion on 7 June: 'For me life is a web and is immortal'.

[38] The publishers of Radclyffe Hall's book *The Well of Loneliness* had been prosecuted on the grounds that it was obscene.

[39] Sir Chartres Biron.

written,[40] when asked my view of the book by letter. They sent me this copy of it, so that I should remember to say the same in court, but I was glad I didn't have to. For one thing, with the author sitting in the court, it would have seemed rude to say this, but I should have wanted to say it, so as not to seem to be supporting the book at all on literary grounds. No-one but the lawyers for the defence (and the author) admire it as literature, I imagine. My only reason for consenting to give my opinion was that it is definitely not 'obscene' in any sense, and that it is rather important that the police should not be able to destroy books on their own ill-considered judgment. I mean, there *is* pornographic literature, and pictures etc., I believe, which are watched for and destroyed continually in England (though unfortunately they do a free trade in France); and it is absurd to confuse with these an ordinary quite respectable book, merely because it deals (quite without impropriety) with the subject of unnatural relations. So little is it indelicate that one lawyer[41] took the line (though he abandoned it later) that the friendship between the women was merely intellectual. However, obviously he had been better instructed by the author over lunch, for after lunch he retracted this.

The book doesn't mention any physical harm coming from the relationship. Does it actually? I wonder why. I know nothing about these people really, or what kind of terms they are on with each other—extremely silly is the only thing it seems to me, but no doubt they lead some kind of queer life outsiders don't know anything about, among themselves. Anyhow, I do feel this book

---

[40] This enclosure was not preserved with the letter.
[41] Norman Birkett, K.C.

24

is a warning, as I said in my Opinion.

Julian Huxley, as a scientist, is to be allowed to witness. He quite approves of the book, I believe.[42] So does the Rev. Mr Fry, the rather nice little clergyman who married Sheila Kaye-Smith.[43] But it *is* a silly and tiresome book. I wish they didn't go on in court as if it was a great piece of literature. People *are* silly about books.[44] I am reading a paper to-morrow at Cambridge[45] about Literary Tastes and Standards, from the earliest times up to now.

I have obviously roused a hornets' nest by my *Daily Mail* article on 'What I Dislike'.[46] I enclose two angry anonymous letters. How wonderful people are, aren't they. They must think I have a lot of influence. I like the pink one best, the opening is so good. She obviously thinks not liking cats is an Unnatural Vice. Also I enclose an explanation by someone of why I don't like cats, which may be correct …

Very much love.

E.R.M.

---

[42] Sir Julian Huxley comments that he disapproved of the censoring of *The Well of Loneliness*, though this does not mean he approved of the book itself.

[43] Sir Penrose Fry, Bt (formerly Rev. T. Penrose Fry) comments that he and his wife knew and liked Radclyffe Hall (d. 1943), but he cannot recall having expressed either approval or disapproval of *The Well of Loneliness*.

[44] The magistrate's judgment in this case, given on 16 November, was that the book was an obscene libel, and that it would tend to corrupt those into whose hands it should fall. He made an order for copies of the book to be destroyed.

[45] Probably to the Heretics Society.

[46] 'Why I dislike Cats, Clothes and Visits', *Daily Mail*, 2 November, 1928.

10, St Andrew's Mansions, Dorset St, W.1
23 November, 1928

Dearest Jeanie,

   … I was quite hurt about your thinking I don't attend in church. Of course I know there is religious teaching in church services, but what I mean is, it's not definite or detailed enough. I mean, talking about new hearts and clean hands and love and charity etc. is not enough. What my ideal church would have is explicit teaching about what we are to do to express these things, and would suggest lots of ways, such as visiting so-and-so in the parish who is ill, giving money to this or that cause, being honest in business, kind to relations, avoiding unkind gossip, parents not nagging children, children being considerate to parents, telling the truth, working hard, not being vulgar or nasty, etc. etc. I mean, all detailed and concrete, instead of leaving general admonitions to people to interpret for themselves which may be all right for educated and intelligent people, but is too difficult for the simple and unimaginative. If you have prayers about these things in your new church, I shall approve, and I hope the lantern slides will point the morals,[47] and *not* be just Bible pictures, which I feel sure are quite out of date as moral instruction. Here is a little book I got about the Church by Dr Major,[48] but it seems rather commonplace. Don't send it back …

Very much love.

E.R.M.

---

[47] Jean Macaulay was very keen on the idea of using a magic lantern in church services.

[48] Probably H. D. A. Major's pamphlet, *Modern Problems of the Church* (1928).

Dearest Jeanie,

I am just back from Petersfield, and keeping Margaret's birth-day. We read the poem about 'Seven times',[49] as she was 7 times 7 to-day, but the lady in the poem had been very unfortunate, and had lost her husband and *all* her children and was bewailing an empty nest and looking towards her end. M. is luckier. But I always thought that woman had a discontented nature. She was happy at 7 x 1, but at 7 x 2 was pinning all her hopes on the future instead of enjoying her birthday; she was tolerably cheerful (being excited by love) at 7×3, but more or less worried by 7×4, and a miserable widow at 7×5, and at 7×6, when she was getting a daughter married, she could only think how she had given up all and was now losing her child and getting no thanks …

I've just written, to oblige Mr Duncan-Jones, an article on 'A Church I should like if it existed', for his new magazine.[50] It has wheels, and roves about the countryside from one beautiful scene to another, according to weather and seasons, so that it always commands a nice view and attractive sounds and scents from outside (besides the incense inside). Don't you think this is a good idea? And really stimulating preachers, lay and clerical, not allowed to refer to early Jewish history, but always dealing with ethics and problems of the present moment and the individual

---

[49] 'Songs of Seven' by Jean Ingelow (1820–97).

[50] R.M.'s article, 'A Church I should Like', was published in the first issue (May 1929) of the *St Paul's Review, The London Diocesan Quarterly*, which was edited by Rev. A. S. Duncan-Jones.

person. And lovely music, and very good windows and Early English (i.e. lancet) architecture, about 1250 in date.

'The Leaders of Thought' (including me) have been writing in an Evening Paper[51] on Hell. Shall I send you the Series? They are not very enlightening, I fear.

26 March, [1929]

Dearest Jeanie,

… Here is … my article in the Hell series.[52] The Ideal Church one isn't out yet. You are wrong about your preachers being so absorbing that you wouldn't notice what the church was like; they wouldn't be preaching (I hope) all the time, and you would have a lot of the prayers-and-reading-aloud-time to look about in. It would be no good finding a car outside, as this would take you away from the church, whereas my moving church would provide changing scenes of beauty while you worshipped. I believe in sensation as a stimulus to religious feeling: hence incense and music. You provide the food for thought, and then the emotional stimulus to make people more inclined to act on the thoughts they have had. I have laid great stress on first-rate preaching in my church. I am inclined to think that bad and stupid and useless preaching is one of the worst faults in all churches as it is. My preachers (clerical & lay) would be a carefully trained body of thoughtful and intelligent

---

[51] The *Evening Standard*.

[52] 'Where are the Fires of Yester Year', *Evening Standard*, 25 March, 1929, R.M. maintained, somewhat wistfully, that the views of the Christian Church on Eternal Punishment had of late become less 'robust'.

and eloquent people, all morally keen, and all trained to use the voice skilfully …

Very much love.

E.R.M.

Heathlands,[53] *Petersfield*
5 May, 1929

Dearest Jeanie,

I came here on Friday, and am staying till Tuesday … I am quite recovered. Dr R——[54] took me on Friday morning to a heart specialist, to be examined and electrocardiographed—i.e. you have your heart's motions photographed by an electric machine. The specialist examined my heart and said it was a poor kind—'a low-grade, C3, tubular heart with a rough patch', probably damaged by past bronchitis. All I can say is that if mine is like that, what must a high-grade, *A1*, globular heart be like? I should probably, if I had that, be like Grandpa in the Kruschen advertisements, leaping over pianos. No doubt it is as well to know what kind of heart one has, but I don't feel it makes much practical difference to me. Dr R. said that when I come back they would give me a Rule of Life, but I expect it will be a very foolish one and not to be taken much notice of. Really I can do all I want with my heart as it is, so I shan't bother about it. The specialist said don't get tired except when necessary. I shall take this as a pretext for not doing things that tire me, except when I want to. Doctors have their uses …

---

[53] *Margaret Macaulay's house.*

[54] R.M.'s general practitioner.

10, St Andrew's Mansions, Dorset St, W.1
24 July, 1929

Dearest Jeanie,

Very many happy returns of the day. The day we turn 47 is a very significant day in our lives. So is the day we turn 48, I believe, but shall know more as to this next week. I am making a lot of new resolutions, such as to organise my life better, thus getting more done that I really think is worth doing, and not to mind being rude by leaving letters unwritten. It has taken me nearly 48 years to learn that both to answer letters and to do anything else in life without too much strain is impossible, so the letters (outside 3 or 4 people including the family) must go, and postcards take their place in future. Heaven grant me strength of mind to pursue this course! Or else I must keep a secretary, who will deal with correspondence. I hope you have made some equally useful plans …

Very much love,
Your loving twin[55], *E.R.M.*

During the winter of 1929 Rose and Margaret visited America. They joined their brother Will on the West Coast, and then shared in a motoring holiday to the South-West and Mexico, returning by way of Florida and the South.

---

[55] Because Jean's birth (in 1882) had taken place less than twelve months after her own, R. M. liked to call her 'Twin* in birthday letters.

Nearly at Portland [Oregon]
8 December, [1929] 6.0 p.m.

Dearest Jeanie,

We are in the last lap of our train journey, and shall meet Will and the car at Portland, Oregon, at 7.35. Wonderful thought, to have all converged on Portland from so far and actually to be meeting there. The train journey has been splendid—such marvellous scenery ever since we got up into the Rockies, and across the Divide and down the western slopes, where the snow & frost has changed to mild English rain, which I hope won't go on after today, though they all say the North-West is perishing of drought, and needs it. I expect Margaret has told you about our crossing (rather trying, on the whole, tho' not too bad) and New York, where we spent one night; what I liked best there was the beautiful Jamaican hotel-boy, who told us he was a British subject, and about the 'tropic splendour' of Jamaica. We didn't have time to see anything of N.Y., as we got there very late, and were kept hours by the Immigration Officers questioning us all as to why we had come, how much money we had (he didn't think much of what M. and I had, but said he supposed we should help each other out) etc. etc. Luckily we passed the judgment; some were turned back and told to go to Ellis Island. Fortunately all his searching enquiries failed to reveal any reason why we shouldn't land (we said we did no work, which disarmed him and prevented his suspecting us of competing with American workers in any field). I didn't feel safe till we were off the boat. The train journey has been very agreeable; the people are very charming, and the black Pullman porters delightful. Our Pullman was rather Fundamentalist on the whole; it had a loquacious minister, who once, it seemed, had 'lived in sin', but now quite the contrary, ever since the Lord had spoken to him while he was getting theatre tickets at a box office and said 'Touch not the unclean thing'. Since then he hasn't. He and his wife were having a dispute about dancing with some other passengers, who thought it comparatively innocent. The minister condemned it utterly, and said that 90% of the criminals in the U.S. gaols attributed their downfall to dancing, according to a recent questionnaire. It must obviously be prison etiquette to put that, when asked such a foolish and impertinent question. Anyhow, they were all most religious & scriptural; the very porter (a black) had found the Lord. In fact, I expect the only passengers who hadn't were us and a couple of Japs who played cards all day; and one negro waiter who told M. he was Episcopalian. Everyone is very much interested in M.'s clothes[56]; the porters and waiters etc. ask what she is. The man who sells candy on the train asked me this morning; he thought we must be coming out to do mission work, and tried to sell us religious books, though I told him we had only come motoring. They are also interested in where we come from, because of the way we talk. I like the western voice—it is attractive, especially the negro. They are very friendly people everywhere …

New Orleans
23 January, [1930]

… We got here to-day, after a very interesting few days across the old negro sugar-plantation country. It is fascinating watching the changing panorama unwind itself, as if we were seeing a film.

---

[56] Margaret Macaulay always wore her Deaconess habit, even after she retired.

We left Spain behind us about three days ago, in Texas; ever since San Antonio the people in shops and restaurants and streets have stopped speaking Spanish and looking Mexican, and negroes abound everywhere instead, with their nice soft southern drawl. And now we are in the old French part, of course. New Orleans is mixed French and Spanish, and American from 1803 on. We are staying in the old French quarter, but haven't seen much of it yet. It's not French in the sense that Texan & Californian towns are Spanish—I mean one doesn't hear it talked much—but one sees houses with green shutters etc. and I believe the market is very French. It is a fine city, a good deal modernised, of course.

Mexico was wonderful—I *do* wish we could have had longer there. If only they had let M. in,[57] and if only the roads had been better. Still, we have been in it and seen it. My heart still pants after it, and I feel almost moved to take a step across the Gulf of Mexico to Tampico. However, Florida will be lovely too …

The Southern people are very frank about their attitude towards negroes—they say they can't help it, as they are Southerners. Quite an intelligent woman talked to us about it, also a nice farmer. They quarrel with their Northern friends about it, they say, so don't raise the subject. It is very queer in such nice kind people.

Very much love.

E.R.M.

---

[57] Margaret Macaulay was not allowed to enter Mexico because at this time a violent conflict between Church and State was proceeding, and the authorities would not believe she was not a Roman Catholic nun.

1 June, [1930]

Dearest Jeanie,

... I quite agree about Time. Dorothy Brooke[58] rang me up this morning and said she was wanting to start a League about it. The first rule is that no-one is hurt when told that a friend has no time to see them at present. She thought of this independently, I mean I hadn't mentioned it, so it looks as if it was in the air. At present only she, I and you belong, I believe. I expect Margaret would join. Her second rule is that we speak the truth to those who want our time, whether they are prepared to keep Rule 1 or not. (In fact, if they didn't belong to the League, I suppose they wouldn't keep Rule 1.) I must make all my correspondents join it, if possible. Shall I write an article about it? But at present I have no Time for that ...

Did you hear Dr Gann on Guatemalan ruins he had found, the other day on the wireless?[59] Very thrilling. He is organising another expedition this year to excavate further. There may be treasure hidden there, it seems. How I wish I could go & see!

> Very much love.
> *E.R.M.*

---

[58] Dorothy Brooke, *née* Lamb, wife of Sir John Brooke (d. 1937), later Lady Nicholson.

[59] 'Further Adventures in Search of a Treasure Temple', a broadcast talk given by Dr Thomas Gann on 31 May, 1930.

18 March, [1931]

Dearest Jeanie,

… Last night I went to a party at Maisie Fletcher's,[60] and saw crowds of the young generation of Fletchers, Aclands, Trevelyans, Ritchies, etc. etc.—I felt like a mother myself. Eleanor Acland[61] was also there—very handsome still. She and her husband and her son Dick[62] are going to stand as Liberals in 3 Devon constituencies next election. It would make a very nice family party if they all get in, but, being Liberals, they no doubt none of them will. I like these gatherings of relations and primeval friends and their offspring. But, dear me, what a sadly sterile family we have been ourselves! I do think it is rather a pity. I do wish Will would do something about it before it is too late; it is so much more interesting to produce some young and see what they will do. I felt quite ashamed of my egotistic, aloof life, with nothing to show for it. I think it is quite different for you, who are busy doing things for people all the time. But still, I expect it is all fancy that it is better to continue the race; anyhow, there are plenty of people doing it, and it doesn't always work out very well, so perhaps we have acted for the best.

Much love.

R.

---

[60] Mary ('Maisie') Fletcher *(née* Cropper), wife of Sir Walter Fletcher (d. 1933).

[61] Eleanor Acland *(née* Cropper, d. 1933), wife of Sir Francis Acland, Bt.

[62] Later Sir Richard Acland, Bt.

Dearest Jeanie,

... Here are two Quandaries,[64] in your line. The answer to both is obvious; only in the case of the baby, I should wait till the nurse was out of the room, for fear of gossip.[65] I wonder if any-one will say they would let the baby live. It would have been more interesting if they had made it a less extreme case—paralysis of all arms and legs, as well as deformity and imbecility and strait-ened means, seems rather piling it on ...

The Sunday Films Bill debate is very interesting to read.[66] It always surprises me how many people there still are who con-sider Sunday occupations quite apart from the question of forced employment for workers. It reads very medievally when people like Sir Basil Peto begin to talk about it. He thinks the

---

[63] R.M. had moved to another flat.

[64] The *Evening Standard* was then running a series of 'Quandaries', one each day, with comments from readers on the previous day's problem.

[65] The 'Quandary' for 27 May, 1932 was as follows: 'A doctor has one minute ago assisted at the birth of a severely deformed baby. In addition to the deformities the child has paralysis of both arms and legs and the shape of its head shows that, mentally, it can never be better than the worst type of imbecile. It may live for a few hours, or for a few years. The father has previously been warned that the child is likely to be abnormal and has expressed the hope that it will not survive, especially as the mother has two other young children, and recently the family's circumstances have been much straitened. The mother is still under chloroform. The nurse is discreet. What should the doctor do?'

[66] The Sunday Entertainments Bill had been debated in the House of Commons on 27 May.

secularization of Sunday has led to our economic evils, which were sent the world as a punishment. How interesting people are!

Very much love.

R.M.

Are you near Birchington-on-Sea? If so, you should take a trip to the Mysteries House, where veiled women have lived unseen for 13 years, and the *Sunday Express* man could get no answer when he called.[67]

11 June, [1932]

Dearest Jeanie,

    … I will enclose to-day's Quandary and answers … *Do* be a Mr Johnston when you retire.[68] M. should drop her 'Sister'[69] and be merely 'X', as the non-religious would fight shy of a sister …

Very much love.

E.R.M.

P.S.… Here is a quandary which I met when out at lunch in a shop to-day. I sat at a table with an unpleasant looking woman,

---

[67] See 'The Weirdest House in Britain', *Sunday Express*, 29 May, 1932.

[68] This refers to Rev. Hugh Johnston, Curate at St Martin-in-the-Fields from 1923 to 1931, who was allowed by the Vicar, Canon Sheppard, to open what was called the 'Quest Room'. Anyone could come, without giving a name, and ask any question. 'Ask Mr Johnston' became a Macaulay family joke.

[69] Since Margaret Macaulay became a Deaconess she had been known as 'Sister Margaret'.

who took and ate 3 cakes from the dish before her. She then, instead of waiting for the waitress to come and give her her bill, as is usually done, got up and went a little way off (so that I shouldn't hear, I think) and told the waitress in a low tone, which however I heard, that she had had one cake. The waitress gave her her bill accordingly, without coming to look at the plate, and she paid it and went out.

What should I have done? Got up and intervened, in time to make her pay for the cakes? Told the waitress later, when I paid my own bill? Or said nothing at all? The third is (as you will guess) what I did do. The situation was not complicated by fear of being suspected of having taken the two other cakes myself, as I go there often and they know me quite well; if I had been a stranger to them, I should have mentioned it, I think. As it was, they lost their money and the thief got off.

What would Mr Johnston advise? The obviously easiest line is not to make a scene or interfere—though of course I should interfere if it was a question of more money than that, or objects of more value. But I don't like to see shops cheated, even of a few cakes, and I never like to see thieves get away with it.

7, Luxborough House, Northumberland St, W.1
23 July, 1932

Dearest Jeanie,

… I met a film king, very fat, with a large cigar, who wants to film *Orphan Island*, but I don't expect he will. If he does, he will increase and concentrate on the love interest; he seems also to think the clash between 19th and 20th century very important, and that he must introduce a very modern girl who comes to the island. As a matter of fact his scenario would be very different from mine, but I said he could do what he liked. He said (looking very common) that it was very sad how vulgar popular taste, both in films and newspapers, was. I said (in effect) 'it is people such as you who make it so, by your pandering to it', but he thought not. The public will have their Barney case[70] etc, he said, and a newspaper has to be vulgar before it pays its way. I suppose the remedy is to forbid any of them to be vulgar, then the refined ones wouldn't have to suffer competition. But, as to films, I don't know if he's right …

[The end of this letter is missing.]

7, Luxborough House, Northumberland St, W.1
7 September, [1932]

Dearest Jeanie,

… I am *so* glad you like my book.[71] What is the Church history you have been reading? It was a very stormy and interesting time in religion. The worst time for the Church was the Commonwealth, when all the sects broke out, and the Anglican service was forbidden. And the worst of *that* was that the Church returned, at the Restoration, more persecuting than ever, and gave the Conventicles a far worse treatment than they had ever had themselves. And the Papists too. And then James II came in,

---

[70] The murder trial of Mrs Elvira Barney.

[71] *They Were Defeated.*

and wanted to persecute everyone except Papists, and made them hated worse than ever. And the poor Quakers, beaten and cropped and imprisoned by everyone. The one thing no-one thought of, but a few Congregationalists, was toleration. But it is all an interesting story.

I see Inge has been lecturing[72] on the attraction of Catholicism (Roman and Anglo) and on how many literary people in England become R.C. He says, what everyone says, that the Church is losing more adherents in R.C. countries than it is gaining in Protestant ones. It would be curious if, in another century, England should be the great R.C. country, surrounded by a heretic continent! It is just possible, I think. But England will always have plenty of heretics of her own, if so, both Protestant and other ...

Very much love.

E.R.M.

7, Luxborough House, Northumberland St, W.1
25 September, [1932]

Dearest Jeanie,

... Yes, I think Germany does well to turn on us. But our Note in reply was unsatisfactory.[73] However, the leading articles in

---

[72] At the opening of the 19th Conference of Modern Churchmen at Bristol on 5 September.

[73] After Germany's withdrawal from the Disarmament Conference at Geneva, the British Foreign Secretary (Sir John Simon) had suggested a compromise between the continuing disarmament of Germany and her equality with the other nations.

both the two important Sunday papers to-day take Germany's side; the *Sunday Times* even takes the unusual step of commenting adversely on the remarks of its own Geneva correspondent about the situation—Wickham Steed, who is, I always think, rather a dangerous man, and who says to-day that any disarming would mean war, probably! Just what they used to be saying before the Great War. Apropos, I enclose a rather good picture of the man who suggested disarming at a Disarmament Conference. I'm afraid he is shrinking so small with shame that he will soon shrink quite away. There are some other jokes on the same page, which I throw in gratis, but that is the best …

I have just been reviewing a Life of Mary Kingsley.[74] She was a most charming adventurer in West Africa—went exploring and trading in the 1890's, all alone, among cannibals and traders, and never shot wild beasts, as she didn't think it ladylike, but let them out of snares instead and then ran. You should read it sometime. She is not, I think, quite just to missionaries. She disliked the hymns they taught the blacks, with such refrains as 'A little talk with Jesus, Makes it right, All right'. Also she didn't think they understood West African negroes, and they forbade polygamy, which annoyed the wives, who didn't care to run the house and husband all alone. How complicated missionary work must be!

> … Very much love,
>
> *E.R.M.*

---

[74] Stephen Gwynn, *The Life of Mary Kingsley* (1932).

7, Luxborough House, Northumberland St, W.1
24 November, [1932]

Dearest Jeanie,

… This is not another letter to be answered, but an answer to yours, and to enclose a cutting about the Buchmanites at Oxford which may interest you, and show you how right I am not to approve of them. I have heard worse tales than this from those who have been at the meetings. I believe it [public confession of sin] does *not* replace sin, but encourage [s] it, as they want new things to confess and make a stir with. I don't like all that laughter, it is affected.

Shall I write a novel about it, after attending some meetings? No, you will reply, suspecting nasty cuts. But there would be none of those; I should treat it very respectfully, though with some regret. My hero or heroine, seeking religion, would try it, but retire after a time, debauched by and the worse for the experience. But I should need to know plenty about it first, and, in learning about it, I might get converted and stay to pray, you never know.

As to the obscenity, of course the obscene will be obscene anywhere, *so long as they are allowed to be.* The trouble is, the Groups do not only allow but encourage it, at least they did. There was some trouble about it, and they may censor the confessions more now, perhaps …

Much love.
E.R.M.

Between this letter and the next—written more than a year later—there is a gap in the surviving correspondence. During this interval Rose finished her short Life of Milton, travelled in the Basque country (the setting for her satire on the Oxford Group, 'Going Abroad'), and compiled her anthology 'The Minor Pleasures of Life'. At this time she also started writing the 'Marginal Comments' column for 'The Spectator'. Rose was a loyal supporter of the League of Nations, and her pacifist sympathies were much in evidence at the time of the Abyssinian crisis.

Sunday [probably during May, 1934]

Dearest Jeanie,

... I have been *very* busy lately, and not able to do scarcely anything beyond my Anthology,[75] which seems to demand more than one person's full-time work, to get it done in the time. There is such a *huge* mass of literature to look at, in various languages and all ages; I don't seem able to get past the fringes.

It was very nice seeing Miss Browne[76] again—she is as nice as ever. It is good to find that we weren't mistaken in our adolescent passion. It is nice to meet and talk as equals. I feel she has such an interesting mind that one could talk easily for hours. She is now 70; and I somehow felt a little sad in some ways—at least, she said she wouldn't mind dying. I so much should that I am always sorry when people feel that. I think she would like to live alone; she has a great love of solitude and freedom, and does live with a sister. She was just off for 3 weeks by herself on the Yorkshire moors, which she obviously felt would be a great rest;

---

[75] *The Minor Pleasures of Life.*

[76] Bertha L. Browne (1863–1963), who taught History at Oxford High School when R.M. was there.

not having to say (as she put it) when you are coming in, or where you've been, or whom you met, or anything else. We agreed that living alone is a wonderful thing—if one likes it. But we also agreed that there are very many who would hate it.

No, I don't see the *Church of England Newspaper.* Do you take it in? I don't feel *very* strongly about Intercommunion, but will join a society for it if you do. The whole thing is, of course, ludicrous; but I don't actually understand it, it all seems too trivial to be visible, almost, with all the important things to be done for people. I suppose Rome should lead the way—but won't, of course …

12 o'clock striking, I must dash out with this. Very much love. Pepys says Deal[77] was a very mean little place in 1661.

Your loving E.R.M.

7, Luxborough House, Northumberland St, W.1
9 December, [1934]

Dearest Jeanie,

… The League of Nations Union do publish a lot of rather useless stuff, I think. Still, I am sure one ought to support them. I have been sending 'messages' etc. to say I approve of the Referendum;[78] I really can't see what harm it can do, and I do think it is good for us to be made to think.

No, people don't at all agree about the answers. Quite a lot of people don't see any point in abolishing private arms

---

[77] Jean Macaulay was then working as a District Nurse at Deal.

[78] The Peace Ballot organized by the League of Nations Union and other societies.

manufacture, and don't think it more dangerous than to have it in government hands. What we all *are* agreed on, of course, is in wanting peace; the rest is just a question of ways of obtaining it, and thousands of people say this is so much a matter for experts that it is a pity the public should even think about it. I can never see this point of view, and think the more we think and say about it the better. But the government says it may hamper them in their dealings with foreign governments, if the people of England have stated what they think about such things. It is all very difficult.

'Justice' is, of course, a fine slogan. But, in such an unjust world, a dangerous one. I mean, how are we to bring it about, except by force, and force is the thing to avoid. What is the good, e.g., of the League of Nations Union shouting for justice for German Jews, Socialists, and Democrats, or for Italian Democrats, or Russian bourgeoisie, or for Hungarians in Jugo-Slavia (though this they are doing) when it can't enforce it? Of course the League itself is working half its time on all these European things, oppressed minorities, etc., but the drawback is that no one seems to care twopence about the oppressed of other nations except us, except when they are of their own political party. So we get called busy-bodies: as, indeed, we are, and always have been. We annoyed Europe dreadfully in the 17th century by sending deputations abroad to investigate continental cruelties and we are still at it. I *think* it's a good thing, on the whole, though it makes us unpopular.

I am sending you the Christmas number of *The Spectator*, with a series of articles on the English character in it. I wrote on 'Have we improved?'[79] Of course we have. You might see if you agree

---

[79] See *The Spectator*, 23 November, 1934.

(p. 792). If you have any time, read the others too …

Very much love …

E.R.M.

7, *Luxborough House, Northumberland St, W.1*
23 January, [1935]

Dearest Jeanie,

… Will writes that he is sorry to disappoint Uncle Regi,[80] but that the chances of his marrying are negligible, whatever accrued to his bank account by doing so. He says that if he had been told this 20 years ago, he might have done something about it, though probably not, but that now it is n.b.g. Still, all this might be upset if he should meet the right woman, and I'm sure the knowledge that he would be able to support a family comfortably would put him in a better mood towards her …

Are you interested in the making of English Saints? I enclose an article I wrote for *The Spectator* on it,[81] hoping the Archbishop of Canterbury might read it and act on it. I don't see why the saints should all be left to the R.C.'s. They say no-one else knows where the dead are, whether in heaven or not, and you mustn't saint a man who is elsewhere. More[82] and Fisher[83] are good ones, but are only sainted, of course, because they were

---

[80] R.M.'s godfather, R. H. Macaulay.

[81] See *The Spectator*, 18 January, 1935. This was one of R.M.'s articles headed 'Marginal Comments' which she had been contributing to *The Spectator* since the beginning of the year.

[82] Sir Thomas More (1478–1535), Lord Chancellor of England, canonized in 1935.

[83] John Fisher (d. 1535), Bp of Rochester, canonized in 1936.

executed by Henry VIII for not acknowledging him head of the Church. I think some of Bloody Mary's martyrs should be sainted too …

Very much love. *E.R.M.*

7, Luxborough House, Northumberland St, W.1
17 February, [1935]

Dearest Jeanie,

… I am sorry I disappointed you about the saints. Perhaps I dislike that particular kind of sanctimoniousness too much to be fair to it. It always makes me think of Suor Commanina, at the Convent School,[84] turning up her eyes like a Madonna, or, worse, turning them down in the street when a man passed, saying to us *'Abasso gli occhi!'*[85] But even to that one should be fair, of course; and I dare say a sympathetic (and amusing) picture might be made of it; only a 600-word article about another person (Sir T. More) gives little time.[86] To-day, I have been writing about the King of Abyssinia[87]—again, far too shortly, as I've been reading masses of stuff lately about both him and his country (some lovely 16th century travels there written by a Portuguese missionary,[88] and other things) and a shameless Italian publication about how fertile the country is, and how it *'fa piangere il*

---

[84] The school at Varazze to which R.M. went as a child.

[85] 'Look down!'

[86] R.M. means her 'Marginal Comments' article of 18 January.

[87] See 'Marginal Comments', *The Spectator, 22* February, 1935.

[88] Jeronimo Lobo (1593–1678).

cuore[89] to think how it is being wasted by not being cultivated by Italians. They are determined to get hold of it, I'm afraid. Of course I haven't touched on that, only on the king, and legends of his country & history, and about his coronation 4 years ago. Really, I should like Italy to get the country, if they could without fighting, but of course they can't. And, as someone lately pointed out, it is several centuries since Italians won a battle. They ran away every time in the last war. A British Tommy from the Italian front told some one I know that 'the French used to shoot them in the back'—rather annoyed that he wasn't allowed to do the same, apparently. Anyhow, out of all I'd been reading about Abyssinia I had to pick 600 words only, so it was very poor.

I don't agree about human nature being the most delightful thing we know. I think many things are more so. Think of a lovely mountain side, smelling of lemons and silver with olives, and the sea below. Or a coral lagoon, with coloured fishes swimming in it. I won't mention poetry, because you will say it is by human beings …

Very much love.

E.R.M.

15 September, [1935]

Dearest Jeanie,

… I am sending you an article by Inge on our animal brethren,[90] to help you in your relations with them. I will also

---

[89] 'Wrings the heart'.

[90] 'Our Poor Relations' Intelligence', *Evening Standard*, 11 September, 1935.

send the *New Statesman* presently, which has a nice article by Y.Y.[91] on how much the nations value each other's good opinion,[92] and an article which interested me on contraception.[93]

Aren't you relieved about France coming down on the League side?[94] It seems to have had no effect so far on Mussolini, who announces that Italy is strong enough to fight the whole world, but it is a comfort to have France with us about it, instead of having to make a fuss alone. Only I expect we shall between us force some arrangement on Abyssinia which she doesn't want. Mussolini seems to get madder & madder; I hear that when Eden tried to talk to him at Rome in the summer, it was quite impossible; he would only shout and thump the table and froth at the mouth, just like Goring. Dictatorship has a terrible effect on the human reason.

Will suggests that everyone should draw lots, and the shortest would have to shoot the Duce. I quite agree. It would be a noble death for the assassin. I *do* wish some one would; I don't believe anything else can now stop this business. Do you think I ought to go out and have a try, as I feel so strongly about it? I don't feel it would disgrace the family name, but rather honour it. I should have done that which was righteous in the sight of the Lord, also of the nations. I should probably be made an Abyssinian saint. Tyrannicides used to have statues erected to them in old days …

I think [H.G.] Wells is right about the moral character of the brain being affected by a flaw. One has to judge morality and

[91] Robert Lynd.

[92] 'Good Opinion', *New Statesman*, 14 September, 1935.

[93] 'Sex and Aesthetics', by Harry Roberts.

[94] A statement of France's attitude towards the Italo-Abyssinian dispute had been made by M. Laval on 13 September.

immorality from the outside standpoint, and if a person has a brain that doesn't see that stealing is wrong, and steals, he would be called immoral by others, I suppose (unless he was definitely imbecile). Still, I don't remember the passage, and might not agree with it if I read it. Wells is very interesting to talk to about his family—he is fond of them, but they annoy him, he says, by their narrowness, and by 'the accent of their minds'. He is a most loveable person, somehow, in spite of his faults; and very friendly and kind to me always, which I always feel rather odd, we are so different …

I had a beautiful day yesterday, driving to Surrey and walking for 3 hours over Leith Hill—very wild and beautiful. I went to see Stane Street,[95] the bit of Roman Road they've been clearing on Leith Hill common. They've cleared the brambles and trees away from about 100 yards of it, and come on Roman cobbles and flints that paved it; they are laying turf over it. It seems to have run for miles, right across that part of Surrey; a queer feeling it gives one, standing on it. I don't wonder Mussolini gets maddened by his Roman heritage and wants to conquer the world …

[No signature]

7, Luxborough House, Northumberland St, W.1
6 October, [1935]

Dearest Jeanie,

Thank you for yours of Sept. 25th. Since then, the world has

---

[95] The Roman road from Chichester to London.

been turned upside down by this wicked man ('the Duce, he goes too far', the Italian fruiterer at the corner of East Street says)[96] … I see on the placards that Adowa has fallen; it was bound to, of course. It is all too ghastly. The one bright spot is the almost universal (outside Italy) feeling that it is a very wicked war. In England only Garvin in *The Observer* and the *Daily Mail* think otherwise. But I am dreadfully afraid, now that France has refused to take part in any but the mildest and most useless sanctions, that the League can do nothing to stop it. And that idiot Garvin going on 'Do be cautious, or Italy will leave the League'— as if a country behaving like that was any use in the League. I went to Mass at the Italian Church in Hatton Garden[97] this morning, to see if the sermon mentioned the war. It didn't, but was on the text 'Do to one another as you would be done by', and was about how Christians should love each other, and especially Catholics; there was no hint that Christians were failing in this just now. I suppose he didn't want to annoy his congregation of patriotic Italians.

Did you hear Inge the other evening on the Dangers of being Human? I didn't, but read it later in *The Listener,* and thought it very good.[98] To-night I shall hear Robert Lynd on Belfast[99]— only I don't believe he will be audible, he has a very low, gentle, murmuring Irish voice …

I have changed my car … my new car is another Morris, only a year old, and with very little use before I had it; it is rather smaller than the other (10 h.p.) and handier, and goes much

---

[96] Italy had invaded Abyssinia on 3 October.

[97] St Peter's, Clerkenwell Rd.

[98] See *The Listener, 2* October, 1935.

[99] 'Belfast Revisited', see *The Listener,* 16 October.

more quietly (I mean, makes less noise). I like it very much. Having a new car should have been one of my Pleasures.[100] The temptation is to drive about all day and do no work. I went to Richmond Park yesterday, it was lovely, all yellowing, and the deer very tame …

Very much love.

E.R.M.

Do you see *The Listener? How* rude Chesterton is in his letters to his critics![101] Almost incredible.

6 November, [1935][102]

… I'm glad our foolish broadcast[103] came over well. I was rather alarmed on Sunday at being rung up by … the *Express*, asking me if I would 'like to mike a stitement' about my mention of various advertised products, which the B.B.C. has a rule against mentioning (which I quite forgot when speaking). I said the Debate was unrehearsed, and that I had made whatever jokes came into my head. They obviously thought I had taken bribes from Kruschen and Lux. They said they were going to 'feature' it, but fortunately they didn't—perhaps I persuaded

---

[100] In *Personal Pleasures* (1935).

[101] G. K. Chesterton was replying to Dr G. G. Coulton and H. Binns in connection with his June broadcast on 'The Liberty that Matters' (in a B.B.C. series on Freedom). See *The Listener,* 2 October, 1935.

[102] Postcard.

[103] 'An Unrehearsed Debate: That Women are bored with Emancipation', broadcast on 2 November, 1935. The proposer was E. Arnot Robertson; the opposer, R.M.

them it was too silly … anyhow I was much relieved …

Much love,
E.R.M.

7, Luxborough House, Northumberland St, W.1
10 November, [1935]

Dearest Jeanie,

… My reason for voting for the Labour candidate in Marylebone is to increase the opposition to the Conservative candidate,[104] who is a safe winner … It is very bad for any member to have a safe seat. So I am urging my fellow Marylebonians to vote for Dr Elizabeth Jacobs, the Labour candidate, on these grounds. They are all Conservatives, but quite see my point, and agree with me that a few more votes against our member would do him no harm, but stir him up. I agree with you that I don't want Labour in at present. For one thing, I don't like any of their leaders much. And their policy of nationalizing the Banks would send down our world credit, and make trade recovery harder. I am all for Socialism later, but not yet. Though really, what all the parties promise us is so much the same that it doesn't seem to matter who gets in. Of course the National Government is safe to win as a matter of fact … (I am voting for A. P. Herbert for Oxford.)[105]

Their cry of armament increase is very cunning, as working men hope it will mean employment for them, and they are far

---

[104] Capt. A. S. Cunningham-Reid.

[105] A. P. Herbert was standing as Independent candidate for Oxford University.

more in number than the taxable classes, who know it will mean higher taxation. Baldwin is very shrewd, I think.

I feel Abyssinia is abandoned to her fate. Sanctions will do no good at this date, and the Italian army seems to be strolling unopposed over the land (fortunately). If there is no more bloodshed than this, it won't be too bad a war. I suppose Italy will be allowed to settle there in peace. It is all very, very wicked, but I hope the climate won't suit them and they will get tired of it soon …

Very much love,

E.R.M.

7, Luxborough House, Northumberland St, W.1
15 December, [1935]

Dearest Jeanie,

… Everyone is delighted that Hoare has broken his nose skating, and we all hope it hurts.[106] I should like to be in the House of Commons for the Thursday debate, and see him face his angry foes. There is nothing he can say which can make it sound better. Even if he and Baldwin tell us that they were frightened of Mussolini bombing Malta unless they bribed him off with half Abyssinia, it will sound very poor and cowardly. *The Times* says the only way we can recover our lost prestige in the eyes of the world is to repudiate the suggestions at once, and apologise for having made them. I expect Hoare will have to resign. I hear that

---

[106] After the announcement of the Hoare-Laval Pact, Sir Samuel Hoare went to Switzerland for a skating holiday, and on I December had a slight accident and broke his nose.

M.P.'s have never had so many angry letters from their constitu-
ents. I wonder if they have to answer them all. I suppose so, if
they want to get in again next time. This must make them very
much annoyed with Baldwin and the Government, and is enough
to make them vote against the Government on the Vote of
Censure. I've not written to my member, as I thought he was
probably getting enough without me, and I had no time, and
would have also found it difficult to think how to put it.

I notice that disapproval vibrated in the voice of Mr [Stuart]
Hibberd when he gave the news to-night; the B.B.C. voices are
not at all impartial.

I don't quite agree with you about 'how can babies die better'
etc. When killed by gas or bombs, their death is a sin on someone's part, and it is better they should die without malicious
intent. If gas is ever dropped here, I shall feel it a bad way of
dying …

Very much love,
Your loving *E.R.M.*

*7, Luxborough House, Northumberland St, W.1
18 December, [1935]*

Dearest Jeanie,

… You got me wrong on death. To be gassed for peace would
be a good death for *me* (though not for babies, who don't care
about peace) but a bad action on the part of the gassers, so not
on the whole a good human performance, any more than mar-
tyrdoms were …

I don't believe Hoare did (or does) feel like Judas. I believe he
thought he had done quite right, though now we have all told

55

him, it must have dawned on him that he hasn't. I should like to have heard what passed between him and Baldwin and the rest of the Cabinet before he resigned to-night. I wonder if Baldwin will pretend to-morrow that he disapproved all along. *The Times* prophesied only this morning that he and Hoare would justify the Proposals. But now is Hoare's chance for the speech of repentance that you want—only he won't make it. Baldwin, I suppose, can't, without resigning himself.

We really have done very well, making ourselves felt like this. I feel very proud. They know now that we are their masters, and that what we say goes, so long as we have the chief newspapers to speak for us. I hear that M.P.'s got thousands of letters, and felt they had to answer them. I heard of a very good man, who said to some one I know that he wishes he had died before all this happened, he was so ashamed. I don't wish I had, do you? I am enjoying it …

I quite agree with you about Lord de Clifford's trial. A disgusting exhibition, and *so* expensive.[107] And what did his Counsel mean by saying that driving on the wrong side of the road was no proof of negligence? It seems to me one of the most negligent things a motorist can do.[108] Haste for post.

Very much love,
E.R.M.

---

[107] The ancient ceremony of 'trial by peers' was enacted in the House of Lords on 12 December, 1935, when Lord de Clifford was tried for manslaughter caused by reckless driving, and acquitted.

[108] Lord de Clifford had stated that he went over to his offside to avoid an oncoming car. Sir Henry Curtis-Bennett submitted that there was no evidence of negligence: 'Lord de Clifford had taken what seemed to be the only course …'

3 June, [1936}

Dearest Jeanie,

Thank you so much for your letter. I *had* to meet my black Emperor,[109] so asked Canon S.[110] if he could give me another date, and he offered next Wed: 10th. As he kindly put it 'Sheppard is always here, Haile only once,' so I see him at 5.0 next Wed:, which gives us a week more to think of further things to say to him. I must say them quickly, as I think his time is as full as a dentist's, he has to look in his book, and puts down names for every hour of the day. So I must get down to the agenda quickly: first, Peace; then Stewardship;[111] then Any Other Business, so send any along that you think useful. Shall I leave him the Church Assembly Report? I expect you want it back, and he probably has one.

I shan't ask him about Danger, as I can think of that for myself. There are any number of dangerous sports. Some, of course, are only accessible to the well-to-do, such as flying, ski-ing, mountaineering, polo, punting, exploring wild lands, shooting lions, speed-racing, etc. All these are largely done by both young men and young women who can afford it (young women of the well-off classes enjoy danger as much as their brothers, I think, though not, for some reason, in the poorer classes. This seems to me a real class difference). Of course poor people can't do most of these things; but they can climb anything handy, sometimes ride

---

[109] The Emperor of Ethiopia, Haile Selassie, had just arrived in England.

[110] Canon H. R. L. ('Dick') Sheppard.

[111] Jean Macaulay had started a society called the League of Stewards, 'to encourage the spirit of stewardship', and she and R. M. hoped to win Canon Sheppard's support for it.

motor-bicycles very dangerously; or even pedal-cycles can be made dangerous by any rider who likes to; or walk in the streets; tease bulls and savage cows and horses; swim far out to sea; sail in storms; all kinds of things.

I remember getting lots of thrills by walking along high walls, climbing to the tops of difficult trees, etc. when young. I don't myself believe that liking for danger as such does play much part in causing wars. You should see *Things to Come*,[112] in which special mention is made of the dangerous and exciting sports they had after war was banished.

I quite agree with you about controversy. I said that, in the comments I sent the B.B.C. on their Peace Week programme that they sent me a memorandum on. I'm not quite sure it was a great success last time we had foreigners here for the purpose, as the Nazi Jewish persecutions made the Englishmen too cross, and besides, the Nazi, instead of standing up for them and discussing them, only said there were none, which made the discussion absurd. Which is, I'm afraid, what Mr Thomas would say to Lloyd's about his Budget disclosures,[113] and the non-stop driver to his victim. One must have frank admission, of course, before a discussion can begin. One might stage one this week between the Negus and Signor Grandi[114] or some other Italian. Only Haile can't talk English, I think. He had a black interpreter at Waterloo, who translated to him the address he was given, and translated to the givers his thanks to the English for their sympathy. He had a great reception from the public to-day, though only met

---

[112] R.M. means the film *The Shape of Things to Come*.

[113] An enquiry into a leakage of Budget secrets (involving J. H. Thomas, Secretary of State for the Colonies) was then in progress.

[114] Then Italian Ambassador in London.

by an inferior Foreign Office official, which I thought a shame. The King went to Devonshire for the day.[115] Eden should have come to Waterloo, I think, and one of the Princes. I am afraid the Government has decided to snub and keep him under, to please Mussolini. Nearly all the papers (not *News Chronicle* and *Herald)* are ignoring him now, and accepting 'Italian East Africa' as a fact. The Council meeting[116] on 16th will be most awkward. Haile says he will be there, and won't leave England and Geneva until something is done about it! He is in for a long stay, I fear, poor man. I think it is a horrid shame, the way governments all behave. Cummings[117] says we are preparing for an Anglo-Italian pact, and I expect he is right. Though I can't see what good any pact with Mussolini can do, as he doesn't keep them …

I will write to you after my Sheppard interview (of which I really ought to take notes, I feel) and tell you what he says. I have a crowded day—a literary prizegiving in the afternoon,[118] then dash off to St Paul's by 5, then dash back to a Liberal reception, home & dress, then to the Opera. Everything has got crowded onto that afternoon. The evening before, Margaret comes up and goes to Scotland by night train. I'm so glad I don't.

Very much love,

E.R.M.

---

[115] On 3 June, 1936 King Edward VII$_1$ visited the Duchy of Cornwall estates in Devonshire and Cornwall.

[116] The forthcoming meeting of the Council of the League of Nations.

[117] A. J. Cummings, political editor of the *News Chronicle*.

[118] The presentation of the Femina-Vie Heureuse and Heinemann prizes by Max Beerbohm.

11 June, [1936]

Dearest Jeanie,

... I think you had better become a full member of the Brotherhood[119] ... But find out more about it first. You could ask Sheppard ... He is certainly a most friendly and interested person, and extremely easy to talk to. We didn't really nearly finish about Pacifism, as he talked so much about other things, and told me so many stories. I was there an hour, and alone, but must go again sometime, he says, and finish discussing Peace. He quite sees the dilemma, and is torn in both directions himself, but always, he says, comes back to the view that Christ would say we mustn't attack and kill one another. This doesn't dispose, as he knows, of the bully who is attacking and killing the weaker power, and what line we are to take with him; but there seems to be something called non-violent resistance (see Aldous Huxley, enclosed) which they think would work. When you meet him you can go on discussing it. I think I never met a clergyman so genuinely and pleasantly interested in people and their affairs. I had to try not to waste time answering his questions about when and how I worked, my sisters, where I went for my holidays, did I go to church much (No, was the answer to that), were you Church, what kind of nursing did you do, etc. etc. I don't wonder people find him sympathetic and nice ...

I was amused by his view of Kenneth Mozley which is also mine (they live next door, being both Canons of St Paul's). He thinks K. has 'a medieval mind', and lives 600 years too late. He

---

[119] R.M. means the Brotherhood Movement, a pacifist organization which celebrated its Diamond Jubilee in May 1936. Canon Sheppard was then national President.

has seen him address a service for working and other men, all in the mood for some live religious teaching, and give them a doctrinal address on the Atonement etc. They looked entirely blank and uninterested, of course. It really is dreadful how the clergy go on. Canon S. thinks it is bad for them to become bishops and archbishops, and that both Canterbury[120] and York[121] have become conventionalized and timid. However, he still has hope for the Church. I told him I had too, despite its curious and disappointing history.

I'm sorry you think Cecil wrong. I think his letter is very useful, so do most pro-Leaguers.[122] If the public manage to make enough fuss now, we *may* save the League still; if not, people seem to think it will just collapse into being an instrument for doing nothing, and the Covenant will lapse. *The Times* has gone most disappointing; I was shocked at that leader on Cecil, so were many people.[123] I was told by Sir Walter Lay ton (one of the directors of the *News Chronicle)* that the *Times* Editor[124] has changed his views and is going antiLeague and antisanction, owing to the influence of [Lord] Lothian and the Astors on him. He spends week-ends with the *Observer* Astors at Cliveden, and is

---

[120] Abp Cosmo Lang.

[121] Abp William Temple.

[122] Lord Cecil of Chelwood, President of the League of Nations Union, had written on 27 May to the Secretaries of all branches of the Union, urging them to encourage members to write to M.P.s, the Prime Minister, and the Foreign Secretary, insisting on full support for the League.

[123] A leader in *The Times* on 8 June commented that 'the branches of the League of Nations Union would render better service to their own cause if, like Mr Eden, they would frankly recognize the admitted defects of the League and Covenant'.

[124] Geoffrey Dawson (1874–1944).

influenced by them, as well as by the *Times* Astors. Canon Sheppard is much disappointed with him, so is every one of our way of thinking. The Italian Press, on the other hand, says that *The Times* 'has at last, though late, turned to realism'. Realism always means something bad, I notice. I am very sorry, as it was the only non-Opposition paper that took a right line, and it has so much influence. I hope the phase may pass, but it is a bad moment for it. Did you see Cecil's letter yesterday?[125] I enclose it in case you didn't. I think it is good.

Margaret and I had a nice evening on Tuesday. First we went to the Negus's garden party,[126] for which I had an invitation. We didn't talk to him, but saw him. Then we saw *The Littlest Rebel*, a very nice American-Civil-War film, with Shirley Temple. You should see it.

Just off to the House of Commons, for which I have been given a ticket, and I hope to hear Thomas & Butt on their iniquities.[127]

Very much love.

E.R.M.

I enclose a rather nice cartoon of Dick Sheppard and Lansbury, by Low, which well puts the dilemma.[128] He quite agreed with it.

---

[125] A letter from Lord Cecil of Chelwood to *The Times* on 'The League and Italy'.

[126] A garden party in honour of the Emperor of Ethiopia.

[127] On the day R.M. wrote this J. H. Thomas and Sir Alfred Butt resigned from Parliament, as a result of the Budget leakage enquiry.

[128] The cartoon shows Sheppard, George Lansbury, and 'Anti-War Youth' astride a horse which has stopped short at a signpost pointing to '100 per cent Pacifism', and, in the opposite direction to 'Organization of Law and

17 June, [1936]

Dearest Jeanie,

… I'm glad you had a nice letter from Canon Sheppard … I think he may be really keen on the Stewards, it is quite in his own line of thought, I gathered. It will be fine if he takes it up. You would like him very much, he is so friendly and enthusiastic and has such a live idea of Christianity. It is wonderful how he has won the respect of his intellectual superiors, such as Aldous Huxley and Gerald Heard….

The Government has obviously quite decided to abandon sanctions. Eden will say so on Thursday, I expect. Lord Cecil was very bitter about it, speaking yesterday at a lunch given to the Negus. He says the new French Government would be willing (he thinks) to go on with them if we were.[129] Vernon Bartlett is, I am sure, correct in prophesying the end of them. The weak point in keeping them on is that they are such poor ones that they make no real difference to Italy, and are only slightly inconvenient; they certainly wouldn't ever 'bleed her white'. They would really only be a gesture. The only one which would have been good was oil. I don't feel I know *what* we ought to do now. The Abyssinians are anxious, of course, for help, and say it is not too late, and that at least we can try and prevent millions of

---

Order'. It is captioned 'Sorry boys, I can't go both ways at once'. See *Evening Standard*, 8 June, 1936.

[129] Lord Cecil of Chelwood, speaking at a Foyle's Literary Luncheon on 15 June, at which the Emperor of Ethiopia was a guest, said he had been told that 'to suggest that we ought even now to carry out our obligations would be Midsummer madness'. He had just come back from France, where, he said, there were 'many mad people'.

Italian immigrants turning the natives off their land to starve, which they say will happen, and they are probably right, as the colonists will all be given land, and all the cultivable land belongs already to Ethiopian peasants. I doubt if the Emperor has much hope now of getting back. I am told he is getting very bitter… There is a strong popular sympathy with Haile. People line up and cheer wherever he is known to be going. I think they feel they are trying to make up for the rudeness of the government to him. I feel ashamed when I think of him myself. The Cabinet are now longing for him to go away, he is so embarrassing. Baldwin hasn't seen him, either, and Eden only for 20 minutes. Meanwhile, the King goes to Ascot and all about, and has a good time.

Later. I heard the *Times* correspondent who was in Addis Ababa just now, giving an account of things. He is very interesting. He said the Eritrean troops were the only good soldiers with the Italians. He thinks Abyssinia will be made very uncomfortable for the Italians, for many years. If only we could keep them from trying to colonise it!…

Did you see A. P. Herbert's little verse[130] in to-day's *Times?* It is bad verse, but may have a popular appeal, I hope. I enclose Gilbert Murray on the hopes for the League. He is still hopeful, I see.

Very much love.

E.R.M.

---

[130] 'Not Enough', a satirical comment on a Rome report that 'the lifting of Sanctions will not be enough … only a reversal of the League verdict that Italy was the aggressor in Abyssinia would really meet the case'.

7, Luxborough House, Northumberland St, W.1
10 August, [1936]

Dearest Jeanie,

... I was sorry you missed Dick Sheppard on the wireless. We thought him excellent; quite the best wireless sermon I have ever heard, very stirring and keen. I wish more sermons were like that. He really did make goodness sound like an urgent and desperately important job to be tackled; his idea was that we should all tackle it for 24 hours, on Monday, just to try it. I wonder how many people did! And what were the results. Perhaps huge gifts of money to useful things; perhaps businesses ruined through a day of honesty, or quarrels made up, or crimes confessed. We shall never know. He said that if we most of us cared twopence about the wretched conditions so many of our fellow-creatures lived in, they could be ended. When the sermon is published in the *St Martin's Magazine* next month, I will get it and send it you. It was a great change from the usual conventional maunderings of the clergy....

Your loving E.R.M.

I am asked to sign a petition for voluntary euthanasia. Is this right? No hurry; send a p.c. sometime, yes or no.

1939–1941

In the autumn of 1936 Jean went to South Africa as a missionary nurse, accompanied by her friend Nancy Willetts. Early in 1939, however, Jeans health gave way and they returned to England. By the summer she had taken a District Nursing appointment at Romford, Essex.

None of Rose's letters to Jean written during this period have survived; the correspondence now begins again during the week before Britain declared war on Germany. By this time Rose had already volunteered—with 'Elk', her beloved Morris car—as an emergency driver for the London Auxiliary Ambulance Service.

Flat 7, 8, Luxborough St,[1] *W.1*
28 August, [1939]

… This suspense is very trying.[2] 6 o'clock News just over, and

---

[1] *R. M.* had not moved, but Northumberland St had been re-named.

[2] Sir Neville Henderson, British Ambassador in Berlin, had flown to London on 26 August, bringing a statement from Hitler emphasizing his demands

Henderson just flown back to Hitler with reply—I suppose he'll fly back to-morrow with Hitler's. How long can they keep it up? The longer the better. But I can't feel much hope. Meanwhile, we are all blacking out, stuffing up cracks, laying in sand, etc. I think this is a good thing, as it gives people something they feel useful to do, and may actually diminish effects of raids, and therefore lessen fear and prevent collapse of nerves in crowded districts, and prevent a bad raid being a knock-out blow. Of course the front will be *far* worse, but there's nothing people in general can do about that, unfortunately. My ambulance shifts will be every night 10 p.m.–7 a.m. for a week, then day shifts for the next week. But, as I am only part-time, I shall suggest that I go home to bed at 3, not 7, when there's no raid on, so that I can get some sleep and be fit for writing next day. The first 24 hours I am to spend evacuating patients in Elk[3] from St George-in-the-East, [the hospital] down by London Docks. The hospitals are very short of cars for this. The idea is to clear out beds for raid casualties. I expect the patients will be very cross & disgusted. I hope they'll all know where they live, and that I shall be able to find their homes easily. I'm so glad you have found a nice flat—sorry it's ground floor, as it's not so good against burglars, and you'll have to bolt the windows when out. I feel we are living in a very bad dream, and still hope to wake before too late. But I fear Hitler daren't recede now from his claims, he would be afraid of losing face…. Yes, I will carry my *carte de visite* about with me always.

Perfect weather: how we are wasting it. What a shame to carry all those 40 English and Americans who wanted to land at

---

on Poland. The statement had not been made public.

[3] This nickname was derived from the registration number of R.M.'s car: ELX 299.

Southampton to Germany !⁴ If war breaks, they'll be interned there and may never get home at all. I'm sure steamers have no right to do that to fare-payers....

Very much love.

E.R.M.

Flat 7, 8, Luxborough St, W.1
6 September, [1939]

Dearest Jeanie,

It was so nice meeting together to-day, in spite of the miserable circs.⁵ Perhaps hell too will be broken by such little gatherings from time to time. I've just had two young Air Raid Wardens in, very polite, to say I had a window that 'might be better masked'; we went round the flat to locate it, and found it was the glass panel over a bedroom door, which I have now drawn the curtains across. What a life!... I hope your wireless arrived, in time for you to hear the 9 o'clock news, and Harold Nicolson after it; he was very good, comparing 1914 with now. As he says truly, there was much more excitement then, and less sad realisation of all it means. He said he didn't think, and he hoped not, that much anti-German feeling will rise this time, spy mania, alien-hunting, etc, as it is not 'the Germans' that we are against, but the Nazi Government, which we know many Germans hate themselves. He says *all* his German friends do. I don't meet anti-German

---

⁴ The German liner *Europa*, due to call at Southampton (from New York) on 28 August, had proceeded direct to Bremerhaven with about 40 passengers for Southampton still on board.

⁵ Britain had been at war since 3 September.

feeling, certainly. I'm afraid there may be some anti-us feeling among Germans, as it has been so worked up; but I hope all our great civility to their merchant ships will soothe them—or will they only think us smug? Or, more likely, they will be told we have sunk them without warning and saved none of the crew, as we did the *Athenia*[6].... What an intense longing for peace everyone (except perhaps the Czechs, who want their independence back) must feel, with all ... [the] minor hardships as well as the great hardship of war. The evacuated mothers are many of them complaining bitterly about country life—no gas or electricity often, coal fires, hard beds, too few shops, etc.—and their hosts and hostesses of course resent this. Some of them will probably return to London and face the bombs, I expect.

> Very much love:
> Your loving *E.R.M.*

Flat 7, 8, Luxborough St, W.1
14 September, [1939]

Dearest Jeanie,

... I enclose *K.H.*[7] His 'reasons for being at war' are sound, if one admits the legitimacy of general war at all.[8] I don't. If Nazism

---

[6] German sources had suggested that the British liner *Athenia*, which was torpedoed on 3 September, had been attacked on orders from the British Admiralty, so as to provide material for anti-German propaganda.

[7] The *K.H. News-Letter Service*; a weekly news-letter by Commander Stephen King-Hall.

[8] Cdr King-Hall gave his reasons as follows: 'We are at war because France and Great Britain and the Dominions ... stand in the world for an interpretation of life which is sometimes called democratic. This ... insists on the

really can't be defeated except by war, I say, let it win (for a time) in spite of all its horrors & cruelties. It is less irrevocable than war. The war is pitiful in its side effects, quite apart from the fighting etc. Any number of small businesses and workmen are ruined by it already, and men being sacked all round because their employers are reducing staff. A very nice young garage hand at my garage said to me to-day 'I suppose I shall be sacked soon, even if I'm not called up. It doesn't seem as if these people' (governments, he meant) 'can be human, not to be able to think of some way to settle things except by ruining every one's lives.' I find that the less people know about public affairs and read the papers and understand world politics, the more they feel that—naturally. It is the informed ones who feel 'anything to stop Hitlerism'. I don't know about the Quakers, but I think they would say, if you *have* promised to commit an awful crime, you must announce at once that you aren't going to—of course with *very* abject apologies for having promised and misled a small nation....

I like letters which don't refer to the war. I got a nice one yesterday, from an Oxford don, asking me for the date of a manuscript poem, and telling me what work he is doing, editing Bishop Corbet's poems.[9] The more people who can be thus detached the better, I'm sure.

Very much love …

Your loving *E.R.M.*

---

value of the individual … includes racial and religious tolerance … freedom of discussion in the written and spoken word.'

[9] Hugh Trevor-Roper, who with J. A. W. Bennett was working on a new edition of Richard Corbet's poems (published 1955), had written to R.M. questioning the date 1612 which she had given for the poem 'Great Tom' in her anthology *The Minor Pleasures of Life* (1934).

I ride a bicycle now a lot.

Sunday [18 September, 1939][10]

I hope to come on Wed: afternoon—by road, as we have a week's respite before petrol rations. It was a great sight last Friday night to see the cars queuing up for miles round each garage to fill up before midnight. Lots of them were also filling containers, which was illegal as well as selfish. And then after all it was put off....

Germany is now obviously about to use gas on the Poles. And Russia invading their eastern frontier.[11] They must be very nearly finished. Then the Great Temptation[12] will be offered us by H., we shall refuse to yield to it, and then our turn will begin.

Love,
E.R.M.

Wednesday [21 September, 1939][13]

I got back all right, tho' lost way 2 or 3 times. Am now listening to Greenwood explaining why we are at war.[14] ... Best news

---

[10] *Postcard.*

[11] On 16 September the Commander of the German troops before Warsaw had issued a 12-hour ultimatum to the capital, and on the next day Russian troops crossed the eastern frontier of Poland along its whole length.

[12] 'Peace with Ignominy', see below, p. 91.

[13] *Postcard.*

[14] Arthur Greenwood, M.P., was making a broadcast speech to members of the Labour movement in Britain and the Empire.

was Czech revolt—they are being ruthlessly suppressed, but must be making themselves troublesome, and it may spread. Already it is in Slovakia as well as Bohemia, and is joined in by a lot of German residents there. Greenwood is telling us we are fighting against the 'arbitrament of force'. Seems an odd way of doing it, using the methods we are fighting against. Also, he says, to restore Poland. What a hope! I feel *anything* may happen, and have decided, I think, for the present to store Elk at Liss[15] and be a part-time ambulance driver without a car. I called at the Ambulance Station on way home. They want more full-time drivers—but I don't think I shall be one: we discussed the war. A man (gent:) said he'd rather be shot through the head than 'cave in' now. A woman (wife of doctor just going to front with R.A.M.C.) said she'd rather cave in for ever than risk her husband being killed. Another woman thought much as we do that this war would settle nothing, and that we shall have war after war, whether we lose or win….

Very much love.

È.R.M.

28 September, [1939]

Dearest Jeanie,

… It was so nice seeing you yesterday. In the evening I dined with the Nicholsons[16] (Dorothy Brooke that was) and met Sir William Beveridge, now Master of University College, Oxford.

---

[15] At Margaret Macaulay's house (she had moved to Liss, Hants, from Petersfield).

[16] Sir Walter and Lady Nicholson.

He was very depressed about the war, but thought it necessary, to get 'a decent international order' and prevent weak countries being continually attacked and smashed like this. I said, was the war at all sure to lead to this result, even if we won; he thought it would, and that a world federation *must* follow. I don't see that it need, myself, or any evidence that this war won't be just another one in the long series. He says nearly all the undergraduates are either getting commissions or looking forward to soon, and all inspired by idealistic hopes of 'smashing Hitlerism' and getting international decency. He said he finds *no* military spirit among them, or anything but distaste for war as such. But it is the ancient idea that you can drive out evil from the world by a war against it. He says they face dying, and don't seem to think about killing, which is, I suppose, the normal reaction of the young and inexperienced. It is all tragic and pathetic, and must be the same in Germany, only young Germans don't think they are fighting evil, or fighting for international decency, but fighting for Germany— a lower motive, but quite as strong. I feel sadder when I have been seeing all these informed & intelligent people, because they are quite sure we shall have the war, and that it will be pretty awful. They think we shall win it in the end, but after how long and after what waste of life! Sir W.B. said I couldn't really hate war as much as he does, because I want to stop this one, and he feels sure that would only lead to others, and he wants to stop the others by having this. Who hates war most is unimportant: I think we all hate it. But I feel more and more strongly that, if we really have this one, the whole world will be thrown back for years. How *can* our rulers take it on themselves, all this killing? I suppose they too think it will stop other wars and protect the world from Hitler methods in future. I see no hope now but in a German revolution, and I don't think we shall get it in time.

The Budget is alarming— *what* waste of money is going on![17] We shall be a ruined country in about a month, at this rate. The big surtax payers will be left with only 3/- in every pound. How cross Uncle R. would have been!... And 7/6 is bad enough for us smaller incomes. Half the London shops are closing or closed, and their staffs sacked. And all this government-paid A.R.P. work etc. is taking men out of industry, and ruining the industries, and paying the men out of public money. The world seems to have gone quite crazy....

Very much love.

E.R.M.

Monday [3 October, 1939][18]

I think things move, and Peace with Ignominy is gaining in the country. Push on with the good work. I don't like all these stores of food and men[19] arriving in France, it will look so silly bringing them back. But we might pretend it is for manœuvres. However, we must just make up our minds to look silly, of course. We have already run through a fortune over it. It is an interesting cleavage among people of goodwill. Virginia Woolf tells me the editor of the *New Statesman* [20] has gone over to Peace, and will come out with it in next number. She is for Peace, Leonard (her husband) for the war. The Communists and the Fascists both for Peace, to

---

[17] Sir John Simon's 'War Budget' demanded economies in Government departments.

[18] Postcard.

[19] The British Expeditionary Force.

[20] Kingsley Martin.

please Russia and the Nazis. The Church for War. And the Universities, and the House of Commons, and the Judges, Barristers, Clubmen, journalists (Vernon Bartlett, King-Hall, etc.) and nearly the whole press. My Mrs Browne[21] for Peace, on any terms. The war party are sure Hitler will make war on us in a year or so if we let him get stronger now. The Communist *Daily Worker* is very funny just now, it makes out the Nazi attack on Poland as a Polish invasion of Germany and Russia, and Poland's being crushed by Gemany as a kind of spontaneous disintegration, a falling to pieces from internal weakness, from which Russia has delivered her and 'established Peace in Europe'. What with these and the Mosley party, any one might be disgusted with the idea of peace on their terms. Just heard Ebor.[22] Smug. His idea of our unanimity shows what limited circles he moves in. He should meet 'Ubby.[23] And his Conference should come now, not after the war.[24]

> Much love.
> *E.R.M.*

5 October, [1939]

Dearest Jeanie,

    … What can be the mysterious 'contingency' which may arise

---

[21] R.M.'s charwoman.

[22] Abp Temple had given a broadcast address on 'The Spirit and Aim of Britain in the War'.

[23] Mrs Browne's husband.

[24] He had advocated a 'true Congress of Nations' to decide the terms of Peace 'when the fighting stops'.

(B.B.C. announcement) and cause us to have to fill in our addresses on our identity cards? How they love mysteries! I can't see what harm it could do to have them filled in now, and alter them if we moved. I think they are just childish. Latest news I get of peace-situation in War Cabinet is that they are 3 for peace-with-ignominy to 6 against. The 3 are Halifax, Simon, and Hoare. This is what Lord Ponsonby[25] reports. He adds that Chamberlain is the most implacable of the lot, feeling that H. has personally affronted and betrayed him. Lord P. says there are 16 peers for p.w.i. (this phrase is mine, not his, by the way. I know that is the peace I want—

I mean, I think it's the only kind we shall be offered). The worst point about it would be not the ignominy, nor the triumph and scorn of our foes, but its probable shortness. He might turn on us when stronger, as this article suggests,[26] and attack us. Anyhow, this is what they all think would happen. But time is on our side.

I am following with interest the Clackmannan election, where Andrew Stewart is a stop-the-war candidate. The results will be very informing.[27]

I'm glad you have a telephone now. I rang, but you were with that expectant mother. I hope her expectations are now fulfilled.

A sensible talk from some woman about evacuees the other day, I thought. She advised householders to learn to put up with a little dirt, and evacuees to learn to put up with a little soap & water. Very sound. Country cottages can never have been thought so clean before, I should think! It seems they are shocked at

---

[25] Lord Ponsonby of Shulbrede (1871–1946).

[26] It has not been possible to identify this article.

[27] In the Clackmannan by-election in October 1939 Arthur Woodburn (Labour) gained a majority of 14,000 over Andrew Stewart (Pacifist).

insects and dirty habits in a way that shows they never heard of them before.

> Very much love.
>
> *E.R.M.*

I am fighting for the establishment of a supreme authority in Europe whose laws and judgments shall be accepted by all European nations.

Flat 7, 8, Luxborough St, W.1
9 October, [1939]

Dearest Jeanie,

 … I do agree about demanding a conference [of Nations] at once.[28] The column to-day on p. 7 of the *News Chronicle* ('War Diary') says what I feel about it, don't you think so?[29] I enclose some other cuttings, to illustrate to 'Ubby and others what the various views on our war (or peace) aims are (but you'll never have time to read them). The best statement is H. N. Brailsford's.[30] This is the view held by the majority of the (educated)

---

[28] This had been urged by D. Lloyd George, see below p. 94.

[29] In 'Our Turn Now' *(News Chronicle* 'War Diary', 9 October) Hitler's terms, in his recent Reichstag Speech, were described as 'utterly unacceptable'.

[30] In the *New Statesman* ('Our Way with Neutrals', 16 September), H. N. Brailsford wrote: 'In positive terms our war aim is not merely self-preservation but the maintenance of the values that constitute Western civilization—humanity and intellectual freedom foremost among them. By diluting our ranks with powers that know nothing of these values, we might compromise that supreme objective.'

people I meet. So, also, are the views expressed by the Dominions, and by the article from *The Times*. What they boil down to is that we will call the war off if (a) Hitler is prepared to evacuate Poland and Czecho-Slovakia at once (including removing his Gestapo from the latter) and make their restoration & independence a subject for negotiation at the conference (so far he has expressly excluded this); (b) ... H. retires, and leaves us another government to deal with, which hasn't broken all its pledges. It is obviously absurd to be signing treaties and guarantees with a man who has shown that his promise means nothing to him but a trap to betray those who have also signed it. He guaranteed the independence of Austria, Czecho-Slovakia, and Poland, each separately, before marching into them and taking them, so naturally the other nations near him, including France and us, feel it is useless to deal with him again. He seems to be absolutely without scruples in this respect; in fact, he has said in *Mein Kampf* that treaties aren't to be observed when the good of the nation demands their breaking—it would be like trying to bind an eel.

Anyhow, *all* nations, belligerent and neutral (except Italy & Hungary & Russia) feel that he makes lasting peace impossible (that America feels this is very important, as America might, if he were gone, take the lead in negotiations). So it seems to me that our first condition should be his abdication. If he *really* wanted to avoid a general war, and not merely to consolidate his gains while he prepares to spring again, he would resign now. Any patriotic leader would. It would at once end the whole business. But of course he won't, and of course he won't give up his conquests; he would rather have a war against us and France, though he is afraid of this, than give up the prestige and the material gains he has got, and hopes to get, out of them. He says that 'Central Europe should be an indivisible block', under the Reich. That is what the rest of Europe is ready to fight against. As Brailsford says, it means slavery to all peoples who come under its rule.

I do understand these aims and this point of view, quite well. My own is, like yours, that they aren't worth a general war, and that an *immediate* conference should be called. It even might achieve some of the aims; in any case, it would gain time, and would, as Lloyd George said, force H. to state his terms clearly before the world—to 'talk *to* us, not *at* us'—and be judged by the world in conclave. Then, L.G. says, if we couldn't agree, the war. That is where I should part company with him; but he is doing excellent work in urging the conference, and is receiving thousands of letters supporting him. I *do* hope it happens.

The Church is, as usual, behaving deplorably. It should be throwing all its weight on the side of calling off hostilities while we negotiate; instead, its spokesmen seem to be nearly all encouraging us to 'endure the trial of war, and trust that God will defend the right'. Canon Morris, chairman of the Peace Pledge Union[31], is giving up his orders in disgust, which I think is a mistake; all clergy should stay in, and try and give the Church a less bad name. I am going to a small gathering to-night where Canon Raven (another pacifist) is speaking; he is v.g.—a very able Cambridge Master of a College.[32] I shall be interested to hear his views. But mostly the clergy are deplorable. Better, however, than the R.C. ones. I went in for 10 minutes yesterday to the R.C. church near here,[33] where there was a sermon going on. It was all about how the Supreme Being had created various orders of

---

[31] A pacifist organization formed in 1935, under the leadership of George Lansbury and Canon Sheppard, 'to express the positive side of pacifism'.

[32] Christ's College.

[33] The Church of Our Lady of the Rosary in Marylebone Road.

Angels, good and bad. I *cannot* think why we have endured all these centuries all this lifeless nonsense. I thought as I sat there, what if the congregation all rose up and mobbed the preacher, and beat him up, and the women scratched his face and the men kicked him, saying 'We want something to the purpose, not angels & devils; give us bread not stones.' Why don't they? Or (at least) occasionally protest? (In all the Churches, I mean.)

I can't sympathise with Hitler, by the way. His origins don't at all excuse his extreme brutality and treachery. The kink in his brain does more, of course. But he is so *horribly* cruel. It is the quality that is hardest to get over in any one, I suppose. There is only one thing left for him to do—go. I think we should say this much more plainly than we do—though we do say we can't treat with him.

By the way, the cutting 'Keep it dark' is for your opinion on whether halibut liver oil (full of Vit. A.) really helps one to see in the dark better. If so, I must take it. (It's not an advertisement, the article.)

Very much love....

E.R.M.

12 October, [1939]

Dearest Jeanie,

... Just heard Chamberlain.[34] Obviously war will proceed, as the conditions seem to be that German troops must leave Poland and Czechoslovakia and that Hitler must make us believe his word. First condition he won't fulfil, second he can't, so that

---

[34] On 12 October Neville Chamberlain rejected Hitler's peace proposals.

seems to be that, and I think we are for it.

No acknowledgment to our telegrams will be made, I fear![35]

I've just read the debate on B.B.C. in Hansard—the papers give very little of it. I liked best the M.P.[36] who said, let them give the best music etc. at stated times each day, and keep the whole thing from being vulgarized to suit the vulgarest tastes, which is what happens now. Others said it should be *more* vulgar—i.e. more Variety, and the news and talks more 'bright & brotherly', which sounds like an Oxford Group meeting. The fact is we *can't* get on without 2 programmes; it's like setting us all down to read the same books.[37] My experience of our taxi-drivers at the Ambulance Station is that they like it on, but don't listen; they play cards all through the News, however important it is, and talk loudly through it too, which prevents other people hearing. It just doesn't seem to strike them to listen. I wonder how common that is. The vulgarity at present is dreadful, as one M.P.[38] said, crooners and jazz and silly facetiousness. However, there is the News. I don't complain, as some do, that this is 'colourless'. Noel-Baker complained of our lack of propaganda and explanation of what we are fighting for. He would like the Trades Unions told what the Nazis do to trades unions everywhere, the religious told about the Church treatment, every one told about the cruelty in the

---

[35] R.M. and Jean Macaulay had persuaded some of their friends to join them in signing telegrams to Neville Chamberlain, as a last-minute effort to stop the war.

[36] H. G. Strauss, M.P.

[37] There was only one programme at this time, allegedly because of the danger of giving navigational aid to enemy aircraft.

[38] A. MacLaren, M.P.

camps, and the spying, and about how the Poles are being treated.

When 'Ubby asks what the war is about, he would be told all this, and that (I suppose) we aim at stopping it, or at preventing it spreading. I don't know. It might only make all the 'Ubbies angry and full of hate—but perhaps this is the idea. It seems the neutral countries complain that they get only German propaganda. What a bore all this propaganda idea is. A new bore, too. In old-time wars, no one seemed to bother about it much; but I suppose they couldn't get it about, anyhow....

Very much love.

E.R.M.

Flat 7, 8, Luxborough St, W.1
Thursday [after 19 October, 1939]

Dearest Jeanie,

I am sending with King-Hall (who gets increasingly naval & military) a rather interesting analysis of Hitler by a psychoanalyst doctor, who is a professor of psychology at Oxford.[39] I don't know if he has met H. A psycho-analyst who analysed H. would have a very exciting and alarming time. I think H. is probably too mad to be cured by it now, and would only be made worse, perhaps he would burst.

---

[39] A letter from Dr William Brown on 'The Make-up of Hitler 'was published in *The Times* on 19 October. He identified Hitler's main tendencies as follows: (1) an hysterical tendency, (2) a paranoid tendency, (3) a growing megalomania, and (4) a compulsive tendency towards more and more 'bloodless victories'.

I have been thinking the situation over, and it does seem an appalling indictment of our civilization and intelligence that we can't remove from the scenes into a Home for the mentally unsound a man obviously so mad as he is now getting. Shutting him up, on the published diagnosis of an international commission of alienists, would blow up and show up the whole Nazi business, I think (which murdering him might not do), and we could have peace at once. Instead of even *trying* to get down to this, we think to solve the question by massacring the innocent men of all the countries, who have nothing to do with any of it. Really I suppose strait waistcoats for all the governments are indicated, but we can't hope for that. But one for H. is imperative, and I think I shall start a League for it.

I was amused by the remark in the News to-night that, now 'The Link'[40] had been dissolved, its work was being carried on by 'the British Council for the Christian Settlement of Europe', whose activities were being carefully watched by the Government....

Very much love.

E.R.M.

There is a gap in the surviving letters between mid-October 1939 and June 1940. By that time Rose's somewhat complaisant attitude towards Nazi aggression had changed into the frame of mind in which, amid bombing and the threat of invasion, she was to write to Jean, 'The great thing here is to embattle everyone's MIND.*'*

---

[40] An Anglo-German organization, accused of being an instrument of Nazi propaganda, which was closed down in September 1939.

6 June, [1940]

Dearest Jeanie,

Here are various oddments … I hope you'll like the book,[41] when you get any time to read it. I'm afraid it's rather a lot of Spanish politics, which interest me but perhaps not you. But it also has people in it. It comes out on 17th, probably timed for the big bombing of London.

I hear the most pessimistic prophecies from those who are best informed, but they can only be guesses, of course. I am sorry that so many of my friends are on the Nazi black-list, either as Left-Wing, anti-Nazi journalists, writers, publishers, public speakers, or what not. [David] Low is, for one, I hear. And, of course, the Jews, such as Victor Gollancz and Leonard Woolf, and Philip Guedalla, who are anti-Nazi also. Some people have schemes for taking the identity cards from corpses after raids and assuming new hames, but I fear the Gestapo will be up to that.

I hear hundreds of walkers, cyclists and motorists are now lost in the countryside, all sign-posts and names of villages taken down,[42] and the public advised to give no information to enquirers, which seems cruel. I feel there should be some shibboleth. Mind you stop *at once* if a man with a gun tells you to, as they now have leave to shoot those who don't, and a lot of untrained men are wandering about with rifles looking for parachuters, who are often dressed as nurses. So do be careful. Dear me, what a fantastic world we have come to inhabit! Phillips Oppenheim, it seems.[43]

---

[41] *And No Mans Wit*, R.M.'s latest novel.

[42] In case of airborne invasion.

[43] The novels of E. Phillips Oppenheim (1866–1946) dealt mainly with adventure and political intrigue.

Marvellous weather. Did you hear the bombing in the eastern counties last night again? Portsmouth too seems to be getting it….

Very much love.

E.R.M.

University Women's Club, 2, Audley Square, W.1
14 June, [1940]

Dearest Jeanie,

Many thanks for your cards. I only read the first one after my clergyman[44] had gone, as he came too early, and your card came just as he did. But I know he would say (and think) that the Church does teach universal love, though it doesn't practise it successfully, of course. Still, it would have been interesting to discuss it with him. Also clerical knowledge of psychology. At least—would it? He … has a habit of uttering slightly unanswerable clichés which aren't true—e.g. 'Beauty is the *only* truth, isn't it'—this in the course of suggesting that novelists should concentrate wholly on 'showing God' to their readers. I expect, not being one, he can't understand that novelists do much better when they write of some aspect of life as they see and know it, to the best of their ability, and aren't thinking about God and beauty, but about the human beings they are representing. One can't really argue about that. I think his is the professional point of view. He thinks I have 'an immense power for good', and should 'use it for God'. I have been often told that, but never by

---

[44] It has not been possible to identify him.

people who write, and know how novelists write their stuff best. He is vexed about the Churches pulling so little weight; but he himself, I gather, has quite a little clientele (largely of shop assistants) who come to his services and who consult him. I think he is probably eager to help people, but perhaps something of a humbug unconsciously…. However, he is really keen in his job, which is a great thing.

I have just been at the French Red Cross (25, Belgrave Square, s.w.i) and have probably got a job as an ambulance driver, to go fairly soon if it comes off. No private cars can now get over. This would be driving ambulances for the French army at the front— interesting, quite, and I hope it comes off…. I would rather, actually, drive an ambulance than work among refugees, as I have had more experience of it. I must now improve my mechanical knowledge, so as to be able to cope with all repairs if necessary. I will let you know any more I hear. I shall store my car again. If I *should* (improbably) get bumped off in the mêlée, I leave it to you. But that is most unlikely, I dare say I should be more likely to perish here. I shall slightly regret having to leave London if we are to be invaded, as who knows what will happen to people, or to my flat? I must have some one to look after it and keep my books & things from the Germans. Perhaps I had better lend it to some one who will take care of it and keep Mrs Browne on….

Much love….

E.R.M.

I'm so glad you like the book.[45]

---

[45] *And No Mans Wit.*

Dearest Jeanie,

King-Hall writes in much more chastened mood than usual, though angry at having been so misled all this time. I am afraid he is only too often misled, like the rest of us. But his proposals for the future seem good—though I don't like his estimate of a 5-years war. News still goes on of great dissensions in France. Reynaud is said by one paper to be under arrest, but this may not be true. Anyhow, old Pétain and his gang are said to be the worst possible leaders for the situation, being right-wing, clericalist, and slightly pro-Fascist, so more inclined to come to terms with Hitler than the bulk of the nation would be. The most heart-rending stories one hears, I think, are of the Gestapo let loose in Paris and elsewhere to arrest those refugees and internees who have fled from them before. I am afraid there is great bitterness against us in France, for not having sent them more troops and armaments in all these months. What *were* we thinking of, going on slacking as we did? We have let them down terribly—they us too, of course, by not fighting better and always letting the enemy through to get behind us, but that was much less bad than our long apathy and indifference and slackness. They say Churchill's union proposal[46] was rejected by the French Cabinet by 13 votes to 10, and not mentioned on the French wireless or press at all. They thought we were after their colonies, it seems. What tragedies alliances lead to!...

---

[46] The British Government's offer of an act of Union between Britain and France, which had been announced on 16 June.

The Cambridgeshire town in which those houses were wrecked on Tuesday night was Cambridge, by the way. I hope to have details of it from Dorothea[47] sometime soon. I am dining with the Ogilvies to-night, and shall hope to make a few suggestions about programmes.[48] They are very nice people, both of them.

Very much love, it was *so* nice seeing you.

E.R.M.

Collins says my book is going well, in spite of the War. I expect it scores from so few novels coming out just now; so has fewer competitors.

Thursday [25 June, 1940][49]

… What a *good* idea about Canada—I do hope you will go.[50] Will could meet you at the place of landing, I suppose there wouldn't be time for you to go to Alberta. I know they want nurses to take the children.

What a nuisance if Romford visits are really stopped…. I suppose they are afraid of spies. It *is* a bore if it goes on. In fact, I think you had better move to another district if possible, as we mustn't be parted for the duration—may be 20 years. But I'll do

---

[47] Dorothea Conybeare, R.M.'s first cousin.

[48] F. W. Ogilvie (later Sir Frederick Ogilvie) was then Director-General of the B.B.C.

[49] *Postcard*.

[50] Jean Macaulay had volunteered to take parties of evacuee children to Canada.

my best, with my identity card and a lot of urgent business to transact.

Did you have warbles last night?[51] We did—and woken up again later by the All Clear, so feel very jaded to-day. I haven't yet heard where the bombs fell or what they did, except that a bull was killed, a good riddance. They are now bombing the South-West too. Harold Nicolson says the Gov: are much afraid of public morale being shaken by bombing, so that they clamour for capitulation. I met him and Mr Ogilvie and H. G. Wells at dinner last night. Poor Mr O. is told he *must* be lower brow in talks for the simple, and higher brow for the educated, etc., and has a very rough time altogether. I told H.N. how good his talks were; he has been rather hurt by the attack in the House of Commons.[52] I am improving my bandaging to-day, also stretcher-bearing, but this isn't good for my back just now, and I hope to leave it to others in real life.

Love till to-morrow.

E.R.M.

[After 29 June, 1940]

Dearest Jeanie,

I am sending *Picture Post*, which came out late this week. Tom Wintringham is going on in it about Arming the People.[53] It is

---

[51] This was the first air-raid warning in London since September 1939.

[52] Harold Nicolson was then Parliamentary Secretary to the Ministry of Information. In a House of Commons debate on 28 May his broadcasting style had been rudely criticised.

[53] 'Arm the Citizens', *Picture Post*, 29 June, 1940.

thought to be a great way of keeping us determined not to sur-render—that, and promising us a better England. And we really *should* do something more about rubbing it in day & night what an awful England it would be under the Nazis. I hear that it is very common to hear people say it would be as good as it is now, so why not let them come quietly instead of bombing us first? If that spirit grows, we are done. It was very strong in France, apparently. There was an interesting article in *The Star* last night about the state of affairs which had led up to the French col-lapse—I do hope we shall avoid it. A mixture of Right Wing, very anti-left & slightly (therefore) pro-Nazi politicians, more afraid of social revolution than of Hitler; of Communism; and of sheer defeatist apathy. The great thing here is to embattle everyone's *mind*. There is a terrible lot of bitterness and anger in the B.E.F. By the way, I've not yet seen the Savings Committee (I hope to to-day) but *all* intelligent people tell me it would be absurd to sell investments now—it is simply annihilating money (about half one's capital) which otherwise would be used for use-ful purposes, when things improve. Better than that, hand one's investments over bodily to the State. The National Savings Com-mittee are asking not for investments but for loose money *not* invested.[54] I will let you know when I have talked to the N.S.C.

Very much love....

E.R.M.

---

[54] On 18 June the Chancellor of the Exchequer (Sir Kingsley Wood) had made an appeal to 'patriotic citizens in a position to do so' to lend money to the nation without interest till the war was over. On 21 June he reported a 'magnificent' response.

Friday [19 July, 1940]

Dearest Jeanie,

Here is King-Hall. You will notice (I hope) that you are becoming quite alone among right-minded people in your views on the alien question.[55] …

To-night I have to read aloud for 4 minutes at 11.55 at the B.B.C., in the 'And so to bed' series. They get a different person each night (well known, or moderately so) to read anything they like. I shall read two poems of a somnolent nature, which I shall recommend for saying to oneself after the light is out, to send oneself to sleep. You won't hear me, you will be, I hope, long ago asleep.

What *is* all this fuss about not repeating things 'Haw Haw'[56] is supposed to have said?[57] I thought the man last night very tiresome and silly about it. I can't see what harm it can possibly do, to believe that Germany hears things quickly about us. I wish they would explain. They seem to me to get fixed ideas about things, and not really know any reason against them.

I am waiting eagerly for the peace-kite,[58] aren't you. If it seems

---

[55] Jean Macaulay was then in favour of interning all aliens, whereas in Parliament, letters to the press, etc., it was being argued that there should be a 'sifting process' and that 'friendly aliens' should not be subject to internment.

[56] 'Lord Haw Haw', i.e. William Joyce, broadcaster of German propaganda (executed for treason in 1946).

[57] A Ministry of Information campaign for a 'Silent Column composed of men and women who are resolved to say nothing that can help the enemy' had been launched on 11 July.

[58] It was being rumoured in Rome that a last-minute 'conference of belligerents' might be called to try to avert direct conflict with Britain.

a good one, who knows but that we may encourage it?

Much love.

E.R.M.

24 July, 1940

Dearest Jeanie,

Many *very* happy returns of to-morrow. (How many will any of us have?) I shall be coming at about 4 or 4.30 for a short time, so can also give my good wishes in person. It has been a very fortunate year for me, I haven't seen so much of you for a long time, and it seems almost too good to last. These almost weekly chats are a tremendous pleasure in my life.

I do hope you will get through the next week without breaking down, and that August will be a proper holiday for all of us.... How *thankful* I am that you aren't going to spend it with sea-sick evacuees on the ocean!... Did you like Halifax?[59] I thought him v. poor, he sounded so tired and spiritless. It reads better than it sounded, he read it so badly. Some one said afterwards that he feels self-conscious about talking about religion. If so, he shouldn't do it, but should leave it to the Bishops. I think too he should have replied to Hitler much more circumstantially, it would look better before the wor'd.

I'm so glad we have got the Government down about the Silence Column and Rumour-mongers, and that the sentences

---

[59] In a broadcast speech on 22 July Lord Halifax, as Foreign Secretary, replied to Hitler's summons to 'capitulate to his will'. He defined the freedom for which Britain was fighting, and denounced 'the challenge of anti-Christ'.

will be remitted or revised.[60] It really does make one feel we have a democracy. The Aliens too are going to be revised.

They have started the idea at my Ambulance [Station] of putting down a list of people who would be willing to be telephoned for to come at once during raids. I found I was on it, so had to agree, though not altogether in favour of it. The Commandant had decided that I wouldn't mind, I don't know on what grounds, and I didn't like to undeceive her. But as it takes me about ½ hour to get there (counting getting the car out of the garage) I think the raid might be over before I was there.

What do you think of the new budget? Very much love for the year. It will be, as Aunt Frances[61] always said, a very *strange* year, whatever else it proves. It will anyhow be nice to meet to-morrow.

Your very loving twin,[62]

E.R.M.

[Postmark: Petersfield, Hants][63]
Friday [23 August, 1940]

… I wish you were here, to help pick blackberries. I found a splendid blackberry patch, and Margaret and I went there, tricycling and bicycling yesterday and picked 2 lbs for jam; which Ethel[64] is making to-day, in time for me [to] take away my pot on

---

[60] It was announced in Parliament on 23 July that the 'Silent Column' movement was being abandoned, and that sentences imposed for 'loose or defeatist talk' would be reviewed.

[61] Frances Conybeare (*née* Cropper, 1847–1933).

[62] See above p. 50n.

[63] Postcard.

[64] Margaret Macaulay's cook-general at Liss. See above p. 88n.

Monday…. The jam smells lovely this morning….

De Gaulle was v.g. last night.[65] So was a French speaker explaining to French R.C.'s that R.C.'s needn't be pro-surrender, and explaining away the Vatican utterances. Baudouin[66] says this morning that what Churchill calls humiliating apathy and submission is really Christian meditation which accompanies re-generation. This re-generation idea that the R.C. French are trying to spread is dreadful, as it seems to mean submission, and withdrawal from political thought, and concentrating on agriculture and breeding children. We are having a lull here for the last few days. Our windows shook at the Calais guns last night—we didn't know what it was. Was Deal hit, and was Dover? They don't say….

I liked De Gaulle's contemptuous comments on the new French ministers: *'Le Ministre de la Guerre—*quelle *guerre?'* No wonder they have condemned him to death….

> Much love.
> *E.R.M.*

Wood End, Liss, Hants.
Friday [6 September, 1940]

Dearest Jeanie,

It is *so* lovely here, I wish you were here. Incredibly perfect hot weather. I hope to walk all afternoon & evening over hills and woods. Rather a bomby night, but nothing quite near, I think.

---

[65] General de Gaulle had made a world broadcast as leader of the Army of all Free Frenchmen.

[66] Paul Baudouin, Secretary of State for Foreign Affairs in the Vichy Government.

You probably had much noisier ones. The night before last, I watched the battle over East London, from Paddington Street—most beautiful, with the search-lights, and parachute flares, and the fiery balls from our guns which are said to be tracer bullets, and the sky lit up with gun-flashes, like sheet-lightning, and a wonderful background of stars. The guns were faint, I think about Stratford. I'm so sorry you had such a noisy night, Nancy[67] said it was awful. Do you use wax ear-balls? I think this is important. One can't sleep through bombs, but it does deaden them. Ours last night woke me, and I couldn't sleep again till about 6.0, but otherwise [they] weren't disturbing like guns, and didn't go on long. I'm sure it can't be good for either of you, it makes one headachey & tired. Was any damage done in Romford again?

Civilian raid deaths in August 1,075—about 35 a day—not too bad....

Sunday is National Prayer-Day. What will the Church pray for, or about? I hope they won't be too smug and crusadey, but no doubt they will.

I am finding *Behind God's Back*[68] interesting, especially about the relations in South Africa between British and Boers. How irritating they must both be to each other!

Very much love. Tell Nancy to be 'grim and gay' about the raids, as Churchill says. I suppose gay when oneself and friends aren't hit, grim when they are. I feel rather grim than gay when kept awake at night and finding the Post Office etc. shut by day. I hope the warning system will be revised, it wastes a lot of time now.

E.R.M.

---

[67] Nancy Willetts, the friend with whom Jean Macaulay lived at Romford.
[68] Negley Farson, *Behind God's Back* (1940).

On Wednesday next I am going to a Lunch to hear Harold Nicolson speak on 'The present prospect', so may be rather later than last time coming to you.

Sunday [probably 8 September, 1940]

Dearest Jeanie,

… I was lucky to get home by the train I did, as I hear that the Waterloo services were damaged and suspended by bombs quite soon after, and I might have sat in a train for hours. I hear little by little of the various bomb-damages in London—Hoxton again was badly hit, so were streets in Kensington and round Paddington. What a mercy Aunt Mary[69] is away! Her house is in the thick of it, and she would have gone raving mad …

I see we mustn't say much about raids in letters to Canada, or where they did damage—this is a pity, we must make a code with Will. However, he will hear about last night on the wireless and in the papers. I hear some letters have been returned by the Censor for saying too much. How lucky there is no censorship of English letters to England. Someone from Hoxton told me the dead were lying in the streets there among the ruins like on a battlefield. And thousands everywhere homeless. What a horrible business it all is.

I am seeing Middleton Murry to-morrow, a pacifist who says stop the war; I shall get out of him his alternative to war or surrender, if he has one. But he is too snakey to be pinned down, I think. I wish I knew how much there was in that American article

---

[69] Mary Macaulay (1867–1953).

on invasion. I am a disbeliever in invasion myself.[70] Much love. Take what care of yourself you can in the circs. I have just been told on the telephone that Regent's Park is 'black with crashed enemy planes'. I must go and look, but fear they will be like the ones round Liss—a milkman's dream.

Your loving
E.R.M.

Flat 7, 8, Luxborough St, W.1
Wednesday evening [11 September, 1940]

Dearest Jeanie,

... I hope you aren't having as noisy a night as we are. It began just as I got home, and has got worse ever since. I never heard such a deafening & continuous pounding. It sounds, of course, in Luxborough St and Paddington St, but they are apt to sound closer than they are. The house rocks—but I read to-day that houses can rock a lot without harm. I went down for a bit and cheered up Mrs Gresty[71], and advised her to spend the nights in a shelter for the present. I do hope both that you aren't getting it badly too, and that you won't have to go out to-night after those wretchedly ill-timed babies. I hope they all get christened Siren and Air-Raid, to punish them.

Thank you both *so* much for the 3 eggs. If I had known there were 3 I wouldn't have taken them all, you can have none left, but it is wonderful to see 3 eggs together, almost a miracle; *one* is remarkable. I daren't cook one yet, as it is better not to turn the

---

[70] During the first two weeks of September, 1940, German invasion barges were massing at the Channel ports.

[71] The caretaker at 8 Luxborough Street.

gas on while bombs are about, I believe, but later in the night, if these pests should recede, I shall. I think they are revenging themselves to-night for the Reichstag and Potsdam,[72] which perhaps we should never have touched, it is like throwing stones into a hornets' nest—oh dear, this is *too* much I must get my wax balls. I enclose a box of these, I find them a great help (pick the fluff off first). I am expecting my ceiling to collapse, and the furniture from the flat above to come through on to me…. How fantastic life has become. I wonder if London will soon lie in ruins, like Warsaw and Rotterdam. I hear planes hurtling down, I think—I wonder where. It will be interesting to know to-morrow. I rather wish I was ambulancing to-night.

Thursday. After all most of the noise last night was our naval guns, rushing about on lorries and roaring continuously. I hope they'll go on, though it quite prevents sleep. Margaret has just rung up to know how we both are getting on. Letters take a long time.

Very much love.

E.R.M.

… Oh dear, the night attack has just begun.

Monday [23 September, 1940][73]

Thank you so much for your card—almost a miracle, for it left Romford early this morning and reached me this afternoon. I meant to write before this and thank you for the lovely night on

---

[72] R.A.F. targets on the night of 10 September.

[73] Postcard.

Friday. I missed some big smashes close here, which must have made a great noise. They did last night too. I am getting a bury-ing-phobia, result of having seen so many houses and blocks of flats reduced to piles of ruins from which the people can't be extracted in time to live, and feel I would rather sleep in the street, but know I mustn't do this. However, to-night is one of my ambulance nights, when I sit in a nice dug-out (when not out driving).... I know a pacifist who makes it his war work to go round the tubes spraying the shelterers with disinfectant in the night—very brave....

I think faith in tables is important.[74] I think I shall put my mat-tress under one sometimes. There is a ruined block of flats near here where the bath is hanging upright over the street; I keep thinking, suppose one was having a bath when the bomb fell, what a scene it would be! I hardly dare undress. I feel like an R.C. nun about it....

Much love.

R.

Thursday [26 September, 1940]

Dearest Jeanie,

I had a great stroke of luck to-day. I went to Selfridge's again (really about something else) and they told me they had just unearthed 3 more Lilo mattresses from their bombed dept., so I got one. This is really lucky, as they told me yesterday they saw very little prospect of getting any more, and anyhow not for sev-eral weeks.... Mrs Gresty thought it a good idea for me to sleep

---

[74] As protection in air-raids.

in the passage under the stairs on bad nights, so I will try it to-morrow night.

Last night here was less bad than the one before, I think, but a lot of fire-bombs & fires (also, I gather, in Berlin). From one head-line in a newspaper I thought Quisling had been dropped on us as a bomb; it read 'Quisling dropped'.[75] It would be marvellous if he was, one night....

I have been offered another Home from Home, by the Gollanczs, in Berkshire, any week-end I like, or any other time. People are *very* kind. But I much prefer Romford, of course; tho' I would like to see the G.'s sometime, he knows all there is to know and a bit more, so I might spend some Sunday there. But as to burialphobia, I don't think I shall have it under the stairs; in fact, it is already wearing off, and may have been a passing dis-ease, induced by seeing too many ruins.

The German press says it will now 'hack us to mincemeat', and that Churchill is a fiend in human shape—but he has been that for ages, of course, and they should think of a new thing....

Your loving E.R.M.

... I enclose *Christian News Letter.*[76] Now he is off on dancing.[77]

---

[75] Owing to the intense dislike for Quisling in Norway he had been excluded from the Cabinet in the new regime.

[76] The weekly *Christian News Letter*, first published in October 1939 (by Dr J. H. Oldham) for the Council on the Christian Faith and the Common Life.

[77] The issue of 25 September, 1940 included an extract from a letter from an air-raid warden who had found that gardening and also country dancing were helpful in 'forging new social bonds'.

Saturday [28 September, 1940]

Dearest Jeanie,

Thank you *so* much for sending me that lovely cape. I shall certainly wear it, and it will be most comforting below the stairs, but I shall count it yours, and return it you later, as you may easily have need of it in bed if ill.... [The] Lilo ... is v.g.; I pump it up by mouth, as there are no pumps that fit it, the Lilo pumps having long ago been sold out. I took it to the ambulance station on Thursday night, blew it up, and put it ready for use on the floor, but after all we had a v. busy night, and I went out with an ambulance from 10 till 4 a.m., so never used it. Bombing was v. bad all round that night; I attended an incident in Camden Town—two fallen houses, a great pile of ruins, with all the inhabitants buried deep. The demolition men worked & hacked away very skilfully and patiently, and we all encouraged the people inside, telling them they would be out in a short time, but of course they weren't. There was a mother and a crying baby, who were rescued at 10.0 next morning after I had gone. I drove to hospital another mother, who had left two small children under the ruins. I told her they would be out very soon—but they never were, they were killed. The demolition men are splendid—we passed milk down to the baby, and water for the others, and the men kept saying to them 'It'll be all right, dear. Don't you worry'. They are very nice and matey. I like their way of calling every one (including the ambulance women) 'mate'. So polite, too. One of them was using some language about the bombs that whistled round, when his companion saw me just behind and said 'Look out, lady here', and he said 'Sorry, Miss, excuse my language'. I assured him I felt the same way myself. They are, of course, so used to the job (every night) that they can throw it off when they are relieved, and think about other things—I suppose it is all in the night's work to them. Perhaps it will be to me sometime, but I am still an amateur at it and it rather gets one down. One wonders all the time how many people are at the moment alive under some ruin, and how much they are suffering in body and mind. But it doesn't do to think much in these days, or to start wondering what 'There were a few casualties' covers. Last night I was at home, and took the Lilo down below stairs, and slept a lot, right through the All Clear. There is much less noise there than upstairs. I was very warm in my sleeping-bag on the Lilo. I do hope you too got some sleep. Was it bad round you yesterday? Planes seem to have crashed down all about South England in the afternoon raid. And South-East bombing this morning. We saw a flight of bombers passing over here yesterday afternoon, but nothing dropped near here till night. Yes, Dakar has set us back badly. De Gaulle obviously misjudged.[78] The Senegalese will be badly affected by it....

> Very much love.
>
> *R.*

Thursday [3 October, 1940]

Dearest Jeanie,

I got a bus at once, and rode to Aldgate in 45 minutes. A very ugly ride, of course— *how* dismal East London is! Very few ruins to be seen; I imagine they are more by the Docks. You see many more on the drive through the City, on the 25 bus—these are

---

[78] General de Gaulle, leading a Free French force, and supported by a British naval squadron, had tried unsuccessfully to establish a foothold at Dakar.

really impressive, far more so than the East End, though so much less is said about them, perhaps because they are more damaging to our business life. It makes slow going, as there are so many diversions because of craters. I haven't had so good a view of them before. I was home by 11.0.

Thank you so much for the night, in your perfectly-appointed house, where the visitor's life runs on oiled wheels and the visitor is a pampered drone lying on a soft warm couch and waking to news and breakfast, and everything found but beer, as one used to say to servants. It makes a very light spot in the week, particularly of course seeing you, as I am not only out for comfort and physical pleasures. The *Christian News Letter* is getting much too physical, I consider; this cult of digging and of physical training is more medical than Christian. I shall drop it if it goes on like this much longer.

It looks like being misty again to-night, and we hope for another quiet night. I shall be at the ambulance, where some people get bored by a quiet night and having nothing to do but sit and wait for calls. And if one could be called out to incidents of smash, fire and flood without casualties, as I was the other night, it would be very nice, of course.

Very much love, & to Nancy.

E.R.M.

Wednesday night, 9.45 p.m.
[between 9 October and 27 November, 1940]

Dearest Jeanie,

I had a most odd journey home from Liverpool Street. The

Central London tube was so crammed with thousands of shelterers that I couldn't get near the platform at all, so pushed my way out again, with some difficulty, and took the Metropolitan as far as Moorgate Street, where I had to change for King's Cross. At King's Cross, where I got out, I found a raid had begun and the station was locked so that I couldn't get out, so I had to take a train on the Northern line and get out at Euston, from which I got a lift in a taxi half way home and walked the rest, among bombs and guns and flashes that lit my way. When I got here I found Luxbro' House deserted except for a policeman guarding the door, and a note from Mrs Gresty the caretaker for me, to say they had been advised to evacuate, because of the bomb nearby. So I am here alone for the night, hoping that if the bomb goes off it won't break my windows, which I have opened top & bottom. I have been sitting on the stairs by the street door for a time, talking to the policeman and giving him a drink of sherry, which I always keep in the flat for people who drop in. He says he is 'scared blue' very often, and so are all the police, firemen, wardens etc. I think he was glad to stand in the doorway and not outside in the street, as the bombs have been falling very near. There are obviously some more fires somewhere. As Mrs Gresty and the others below are away, I half think of taking a mattress down below the stairs and staying there till the fury abates a little. It probably makes no difference, but one feels more comfortable there, and that, as we agreed, is the main thing. The policeman says they are certainly attacking this district rather hard just now—perhaps for the B.B.C., or the Telephone Exchange, or the line of stations between Euston and Paddington.

It was a pathetic sight to see the shelter crowds in the Tube, dossing down so uncomfortably for the night, sitting leaning against a wall, sometimes with a baby in a suit-case (open, of course). I suppose it is the warmth that brings them there instead of to the shelters. The policeman said he thought there was danger of people's nerves giving way badly, if this goes on much longer. That would be a great disaster, and could make things very difficult.

I expect you have the same horrid zoomers over head that I have (or others like them); sometimes he shuts his engine off before he drops his bombs; the policeman says that is caddish, and perhaps it is, but it is difficult to discriminate in this business, so much of it seems pretty caddish—or rather barbarian, that is an apter word. I do hope you will get some sleep to-night. How appropriate that Xmas card of mine is just now—the one about the scare-fires, I mean, and the watchmen....

Thursday [afternoon, after lunching out]. Another night over: Luxborough still stands. But London is more and more a devastated area, and bicycling to Soho to lunch, diverted at every street by ruins, craters, and ropes, took an incredible time. I must get back now to see how the bomb is getting on. We had a lot of close ones in the night: some more in the High Street, Manchester Square, the Wallace Collection, and other streets near, including nice little Paradise Street by the public gardens opposite me. I think I shall pack some books etc. in a case, it might keep them safer in case of a cataclysm; a few pictures too. Goring says London will be razed to the ground like Warsaw & Rotterdam before they've done; but Warsaw and Rotterdam hadn't got our A.A. or Spitfires.... Very much love. It *was* nice seeing you.

Your loving *E.R.M.*

Half the big Oxford St shops are now bombed. What will Aunt Mary do?

Flat 7, 8, Luxborough St, W.1
24 November, [1940]

Dearest Jeanie,

… Gilbert Murray says *all* the machinery for political and economic federation after the war is in the League. I lunched with him on Thursday; he was very nice, and had his private sugar in a lozenge box, for our apple tart….

I have just listened to Jos. Wedgwood[79] on wireless—what nonsense he talked! People aren't a bit frightened when the warble goes by day. They know it probably means nothing, and they certainly don't have to restrain themselves with an effort from panicking (I wonder if he does himself). And plenty of people don't mind showing fear in raids by night, and plenty of people didn't like to show fear [in the] last war—everything he said was untrue. I always think him silly, rather. I have hired a wireless, and may buy it in the end, if mine doesn't return, which of course it won't. So now I can hear the news to-night … and Handel's *Concerto Grosso* at 10. I don't care what any one says about not buying things, a wireless I will have. And I am hoping for the insurance money, which I think I shall probably get, as I think I am insured against larceny (i.e. entering & robbing without having to break in).

I am glad to see there are so many complaints in *The Times*,

---

[79] 'Colonel' J. C. Wedgwood, later Baron Wedgwood of Barlaston (1872–1943).

The Spectator, and elsewhere about the vulgar tone of the [B.B.C.] News bulletins, sneering & taunting & triumphing over the enemy. I think they have improved the last day or two, and perhaps will be cured altogether soon. They are worst about the Italians, I think. I *am* sorry for the poor little Italian soldiers, having to scamper so fast and so far—not that they aren't used to it. But to be chased by those fierce Greeks with kilts and knives—I should run like a hare. And then to be jeered at and despised, and cursed by Mussolini. He has sacked 60 officers and more, but that won't help him.

I am reading an account of the Belgian rout in the *Sunday Express*, by the American Ambassador then in Belgium.[80] He gives a fearful picture of the rout of the French army; they really do seem to have behaved like Italians rather, poor things. Combined with the refugee mob, it must have been a frightful affair....

V. much love.

E.R.M.

Flat 7, 8, Luxborough St, W.1[81]
Wednesday, [11 December, 1940]

... Thank you for wire. I was so glad to hear, as they told me many Romford lines were out of use, including yours, and not why. I do hope your bomb will go off soon and not blow up 254,[82] and that you have got out of it the things you most want

---

[80] John W. Cudahy.

[81] Postcard.

[82] 254 Collier Row Lane, Romford, Jean Macaulay's flat.

(including wireless, but I fear this is impossible!). Sunday night here was the worst I have known, I think. Fires & bombs all round; the Poor Institution[83] again was hit, and blazed for hours—so did a lot of buildings near. They dropped two land-mines on 2 blocks of flats in [Marylebone] High Street which not only demolished the blocks (15 killed and many more buried, still) but blew out every shop in the street (including the ones where I do my household shopping; it is very sad, I know all the people there well). The street looked extraordinary next day—chemists' shops perfuming the air with smashed bottles, wine-shops running over, groceries, clothes, furniture, everything, tossed in heaps among the piles of glass. Luxborough House (at least 200 yards away) lost more windows *(not* mine, thank goodness) and part of the wall between my sitting-room and spare bedroom came down (it was cracked before, by the last bomb). They are building it up again now. I'm glad it wasn't my bedroom wall. These land-mines are devastating; these were right round the corner of the street, and not really very close, but the noise and shock were like an earthquake. I thought the whole building was down, and ran downstairs to see. Luxborough and Paddington Streets looked like a scene out of *Things to Come*, all fires, and the Engines so busy they could scarcely get round London. These incendiary explosives are new, and harmless if they fall in a street, as many [of them] die, but much more apt to set buildings on fire than the other incendiaries are. I expect Romford was much the same as us. I rang up next day, but couldn't get on. Since then, quiet has reigned: what next??? Telephone if

---

[83] An Institution of the L.C.C. Public Assistance Department which was almost next door to Luxborough House.

you get a chance and let me know how you are, and about the bomb. I won't come till I hear.

Love.

R.

4 January, [1941]

Dearest Jeanie,

… I see a poem of mine on 'New Year 1918'[84] is quoted in *The Investor's Journal,* an odd place for it rather, but I suppose even financiers like a little verse sometimes….

I go to-morrow afternoon to rehearse my American broadcast, and deliver it 4 a.m. Monday. I wonder if Will will happen to be listening; I know he often does listen to the English broadcasts—talks. He won't know it's to be by me this time until just beforehand. Perhaps I ought to be allowed to say 'Hullo, Will, how are you? I'm fine', as the Canadian and Australian soldiers sometimes do when on the air….

My talk to America is about 'Consolations of the War'. I am mentioning ruin-seeing, the beauty of the black nights and the moonlit ones, the romantic scenes during raids (fire lighting the sky, etc.) increased companionableness, shelter life, the pleasure of waking up still alive each day. The foreigners among us, and the sympathy of Americans. Some one just home from New York told me that Americans didn't like us to be so pompous and grand about the war, so I've tried not to be. People too often are, with all this 'Christian civilization'

---

[84] See R.M.'s *Three Days* (1919).

business and self-praise. I've tried to sound humble, and not once said 'we can take it'.

V. much love.

... *E.R.M.*

During the six months after this letter was written two shattering sorrows came to Rose. Her sister Margaret died in March 1941, and soon afterwards her Luxborough Street flat was destroyed by bombing. She herself escaped—she was away at the time—but the shock of losing all her books, papers, and belongings was cataclysmic and enduring.

After this she found a flat in Hinde Street, off Manchester Square (where she lived for the next seventeen years—until her death). By July 1941 she was beginning to build up a home again, despite all the hindrances of wartime.

20, Hinde House, Hinde St, W.1
24 July, [1941]

Dearest Jeanie,

Many very happy returns of to-morrow—much happier than this one can be. I do hope that by the next one we shall all be happier. It is a *great* thing that you have got through this year without a breakdown, and can now retire on your pension any time you like. I hope you will, directly the work grows too much.... I return your ration book, with very many thanks, having taken 3 coupons and bought a waterproof, so I now don't care if it rains. Remember I owe you 3 coupons.

I have heard from Will to-day. He offers me a typewriter for a birthday present, but unfortunately no typewriters can now be got, and he isn't allowed to send me one. He says he has been trying to figure out how old I am, but it doesn't make sense. Our ages have long ceased to make sense to me, I just accept them. It will be rather grand to be 3-score years, I must say....

Did you see about the D.K.S. order that the Danes are wearing, *Den Kolde Skulder?*[85] I hope it won't catch on in private life; it's the kind of thing children might like in their quarrels.

I enclose two snippets about Wodehouse.[86] It is odd that Duff Cooper should be so vulgar. He could so easily have got the job done by a respectable speaker and not antagonised people. I believe he really simply doesn't know what is vulgar and offensive and what isn't. The *Evening Standard* (the other cutting) doesn't care.[87] It probably likes it.

Very much love for the year....

Your loving E.R.M.

---

[85] 'The Cold Shoulder'. Many Danes were wearing a small badge with the letters D.K.S., to express their feelings about the occupying Germans.

[86] On 17 July, 1941, after P. G. Wodehouse had been released from internment in Germany, and it had been announced that he would give a weekly broadcast from Germany to the U.S., the B.B.C. broadcast a sneering attack on him by 'Cassandra' of the *Daily Mirror.* This broadcast aroused violent criticism on grounds of its bad taste. Four days later Duff Cooper, who was responsible for the broadcast, was succeeded as Minister of Information by Brendan Bracken.

[87] In 'The Londoner's Diary' *(see Evening Standard of 22 July, 1941)* there had been a paragraph in defence of the broadcast: 'I prefer Cassandra to P. G. Wodehouse as a broadcaster, Cassandra is vigorous and vulgar, like the late William Cobbett. He speaks, as he writes, at the top of his voice, and he hates humbug and the enemies of his country.'

1944–1947

The years between 1941 and 1944 (from which no letters survive) were years of continuing strain and intermittent illness for Rose. Early in 1942, and again later during the war, she suffered from a gastric ulcer; heart trouble also prostrated her more than once. These illnesses involved several periods in hospital and times of convalescence with Jean at Romford. Between-whiles, however, she visited Portugal (in the Spring of 1943) in connection with her book 'They Went to Portugal', immersed herself in further researches for it at home, and also enjoyed her usual busy life in London.

Friday [probably 25 February, 1944]

Dearest Jeanie,

I send the 2 Hansards (no hurry about them). The bombing debates were interesting.[1] I thought the reply speeches (to Lord

---

[1] On 9 February, 1944 the House of Lords debated Bombing Policy (with special reference to the 'area bombing' of German towns) and on 16 February the Preservation of Historical and Art Treasures. The latter

117

Lang) of Lords Latham, Trenchard, and Winster in the debate on Feb: 16th *most* unfair. I wonder what it is about any plea for greater humanity or civilized care in war that makes so many people see red. I have heard the most passionate references to 'those old bishops' in shops; one woman said it was lovely to think of the way we 'gave Berlin a doing' on Tuesday night; and she'd like to 'throw old Chichester on top of the bonfire'.[2] It is nonsense of Lord Latham to say 'there is no gloating or exultation' among the English; he can't listen much; Lord Lang is quite right about that.[3]

I see Monte Cassino monastery, which was, before we destroyed it, 'last rebuilt in 12th century', has now become 'a set of 19th century buildings painted inside with German frescoes'.[4] …

I had such a nice letter from Aunt Mary, who listened to my broadcast[5]; so did Sara,[6] and the builder who is doing something

---

debate was chiefly concerned with the dangers to art treasures in Italy, in the light of the recent bombing of the Benedictine Abbey at Monte Cassino.

[2] The Bp of Chichester (Rt Rev. G. K. A. Bell) had challenged the Government's policy on bombing enemy towns, and demanded a respect for the distinction between military and non-military objectives.

[3] Lord Lang of Lambeth had said: 'It is one thing to accept the destruction of military objectives as a regrettable military necessity; it is quite another thing to exult in it, to gloat over it. If it be true that such a mood … of exultation is becoming prevalent among large sections of the people, it must involve a very lamentable lapse in their moral outlook.'

[4] The Abbey at Monte Cassino had been heavily bombarded on 15 February; its destruction by bombing took place a month later.

[5] Probably 'Scrounging and Stealing', an 'unfinished discussion on whether "knocking off" is different from stealing', which was broadcast on 17 February, 1944.

[6] Mary Macaulay's Irish maid.

to the house. The builder thought my opponent had been 'carping', I gather; 'but Miss Rose got the better of him'. I don't know if they knew how carefully prepared and scripted it was; I was pleased to hear that some listeners thought it spontaneous, which is the effect it is desired to produce, of course.

It is snowing; I expect worse with you. I am so sorry you have to bicycle about, and glad I don't. I shall now go by bus to the British Museum. I am being continually frustrated by evacuation of the MSS room there, which has MSS necessary for my subjects, so that I have to leave them wretchedly incomplete & shallow….

V. much love.
E.R.M.

'They Went to Portugal' was published in 1946, and in the following summer Rose embarked on new researches, in Spain as well as Portugal, this time in preparation for her travel book, 'Fabled Shore'.

Hotel Lloret, Barcelona
17 July, [1947]

Dearest Twin (or nearly),

If I post this to-morrow, it may be in time for your birthday…. It took 4 days from the frontier to here, dawdling and stopping at what I wanted to see. The coast is very beautiful, bathing superb, some of the roads atrocious, and v. hard on my tyres, which are causing me some anxiety. One has gone to pieces altogether, and now I have only one spare. The drive along the zig-zag mountain road above the sea yesterday, between San Felíu de Guixols and Tossa, was magnificent—rather like the steepest and windingest parts of the road above the Italian coast, but higher & steeper &

more zig-zag. Fortunately there are very few cars, and I only met, in that 30 miles, one mule-cart and two civil guards who inspected my papers. The Spanish government is very nervy, obviously, about attack. There are some coast places near the frontier where British may not sleep, but only pass through; the French, of course, mayn't go near them at all.[7] I am quite out of touch with the news; the radio doesn't get England, and one has to pick up French stations as one can. The French papers give some news (particularly about the royal engagement[8] and the Conference[9]) but the Spanish give practically none, and make little of the Conference, which is quite natural, as they were insulted.[10] To-morrow is a fiesta all over Spain, everything closed for the 18th, which is the anniversary of Franco's rising, of blessed memory. So there will be great demonstrations and shoutings—but it seems there always are, night & day, in Barcelona. It isn't easy to sleep—very hot, and non-stop noise; cars hooting all the time, as they never do in London.

I am seeing beautiful things. A sad number of old churches blown up in the Civil War by the Reds (perhaps annoyed by the church clocks striking all night, perhaps by the notices on the doors about women's clothes in church, which do sound very suggestive and not nice). Or perhaps merely an old Spanish pastime.

---

[7] In February 1946, following a period of mounting tension in French-Spanish relations, the Pyrenees frontier had been closed, and the Spanish frontier garrisons strengthened. The frontier was not fully reopened until February 1948.

[8] The engagement of Princess Elizabeth and Lieut. Philip Mountbatten.

[9] The Conference organized by Britain and France to discuss the Marshall offer of economic aid had opened in Paris on 12 July.

[10] Spain had not been invited to take part.

Yes, you had better argue with Aunt Mary about R.Cism; but not too much, as she respects your judgment. I do hope she'll go over. I shall look forward to your next letter … But how impossible to join a church with such ideas about not going to church in one's ordinary clothes, but covering oneself up so as not to provoke licentious thoughts in gentlemen! They even have to put on stockings, in the seaside places where no one ever wears stockings. And clothes must not reveal the shape of the body. How can this be managed? What a way to bring girls up! If they are insufficiently covered, the notices say, they may be refused communion in the sight of all. And those who come to confession insufficiently covered will be refused absolution….

Very dear love. *What a* lot to talk about when we meet! Love to Nancy.

Your very loving Twin (or nearly)

Rose

Lis Hotel, Lisbon Sunday, *17 August, [1947]*

Dearest Jeanie,

I am still here, waiting to hear from the *Turismo* at Madrid about whether it is any use my going there….

I had a tiresome disaster last night; I was just going out to dinner with Ann Bridge (Lady O'Malley, the last ambassadress, who is staying here) and when I switched on my engine the bonnet broke into flames. In a second the whole of Lisbon was surrounding the car, including half a dozen policemen, who began flinging my bags out onto the street (silly, as the fire was merely in the engine) and shouting at the top of their voices—you never heard such a fuss.

I think I must have been the only person not shouting. We soon put out the flames by throwing earth on them, and meanwhile some foolish person (I think a policeman) had summoned the firemen, who arrived in helmets & hose long after the fire was out. Then they and the police wanted to see all my car documents, my passport, and heaven knows what—such a fuss, just when I was busy seeing what was wrong. It turned out that the transmission tube to the petrol supply had worn out & fused, and nothing could be done but leave Elk in the street, as my garage, to whom I went for a mechanic, refused to send anyone. Meanwhile Lady O'Malley, to whom I had telephoned that I should be late, kindly sent down her car and chauffeur for me to take me to her house. Elk still stands outside the hotel, immovable till I can get a new tube, and I can't tell when that will be. I do trust I am never in a real disaster with the Portuguese—fire, shipwreck, earthquake, etc; their excitement and panic would be most trying. I can't think what they'd do if Lisbon was bombed! The porter of the *Lis* (who talks French) said, hearing me say '*Quelle agitation!*' that he expected in England people took things more calmly. I said they did rather. Life must be very exciting for them, when even a fire in someone's engine causes all that to-do. It was funny to think of London policemen in the same circumstances.

The extreme inefficiency and lack of brains in most Portuguese is put down by scientists to their negro blood; a census of 50 years ago showed 43% of negro descent. It seems that the chromosomes which cause *physical* racial characteristics are recessive in negroes, and give way before white ones, so that their skins whiten and their hair untwists gradually; but the mental chromosomes remain dominant; so, since the great influx from Africa began, in the 15th and 16th centuries, the Portuguese have been backward mentally—discovered and invented nothing, created nothing, and been unable to organise the country intelligently. This is what the intelligent Portuguese themselves say. But they are amiable and cheerful people, & enjoy life, even when very poor. *Nothing* is done by the government for the poor. But this seems a feature of the Latin countries. Foreigners in Portugal organise relief societies; Ann Bridge, when ambassadress, was president of one. What a humiliation, if foreigners in England had to organise relief for our poor! We are sinking fast, but at least we see to the poor still—in fact, more than ever.

I am reading an interesting novel about Russian life during the war, by an American who lived there. It is amusing and informing, though disjointed. Some of it is very like Kravchenko's account.[11] The author likes Russians and knows them well.

Later. A mechanic from the Embassy garage has arrived with a new tube and fitted it in—what a relief! Now I can go to Estoril for lunch with the Marques's[12] as I had planned. It is on the coast, and good bathing, but I rather despise Atlantic bathing after Mediterranean, it is never really warm.

I am busy running round from one office to another to get a visa for entering Spain again and a police permit for leaving Portugal. *What* a fuss the world has become! To think of the old days when one simply took a ticket and crossed frontiers without passports or visas or any fuss except customs. I feel they will never return. The young can't believe they ever were like that; they think we must have had passports and have forgotten....

Parliament seems to be taking extra long holidays, which

---

[11] V. A. Kravchenko, *I Chose Freedom* (1947).

[12] Luis and Susan Marques (*née* Belloc Lowndes).

seems wrong. I see the Lords propose to hold the fort.[13]

Very much love.

E.R.M.

Hotel Internacional, Madrid
25 August, 1947

Dearest Jeanie,

    ... I hustled round this morning from one place to another—*Turismo* for photographs, Consulate, British Institute, shops to replace the essentials in my stolen bag,[14] but of course couldn't get everything done. At 1.0 all Spanish towns shut down, some things opening for a few hours again at 4, some not. I see in old guide books that the Prado picture gallery used some years ago to be open from 10–6 every day; now it shuts at one. I dashed round it from 11–1 yesterday morning, and saw most, but should have liked longer; it is a wonderful collection of course. The same with churches. What has happened to the human race, that it does less & less work every year? You would say that in England it is the present [Labour] government, but I think that doesn't account for the great psychological blight that has descended on the world, though they make bad mistakes. I wonder what Churchill would, do? I noticed when I read his speech that he didn't say. He said 'I would pass the

---

[13] When Parliament adjourned for the summer recess on 13 August (to reassemble on 20 October) the economic crisis which followed the nationalizing of the coal industry was deepening. It was decided that the House of Lords should return more than a month early.

[14] R.M.'s handbag had been stolen from her car.

necessary decrees'.[15] But anyone could say that. Still, no doubt a non-Labour gov: would be more sensible & experienced, and avoid many of the present mistakes. I don't think we *shall* change the government, as the majority think they are getting a better time out of it than they would under another. Apparently the miners think the crisis is all fancy. Their free coal should be stopped, that would wake them up.

I liked the *Observer* 'Portrait of a Spiv'.[16] At last now we shall recognise them when we meet them.

Yes, *I Chose Freedom* is a nightmare indeed.... It must be much the same also in the Soviet-dominated countries, where people are continually seized and arrested for having been seen with a foreigner, particularly British. An awful atmosphere of suspicion & espionage & intrigue. Spain is *much* less bad, but still rather bad; in Barcelona I was shown the police station where prisoners are beaten to make them talk. I hear that the Spanish Blue Legion, who were sent to the Russian front to fight with the German army,[17] came home much disgusted with the Nazis; the Russian soldiers they got on with all right, as they were plain men like themselves, who went with women; the Nazis, they complained, were sexual perverts, many of them, and they were much shocked at this....

I am so sorry Nancy felt Mrs Whitton's death so badly; it must have been a bad shock.[18] Though a great relief to find it wasn't

---

[15] On 16 August Winston Churchill, as leader of the Conservative Party, had made a broadcast on the critical economic situation in Britain.

[16] 'Profile of the Spiv', *The Observer*, 17 August, 1947.

[17] The Spanish 'Blue Division' had fought with the Germans on the Leningrad front, suffering very severe losses in the winter of 1941–2.

[18] Eleanor Whitton, a District Nurse whom Jean Macaulay and Nancy Willetts knew very well, had died suddenly, aged 47.

you. Perhaps always one should be made to expect something worse than the fact, to cause relief. Instead of which, people say 'someone is ill; is very ill; may die; is, in fact, dead'—which is the worst way, perhaps....

Very much love, and love to Nancy.

Your loving *E.R.M.*

Hotel Inglés, Valencia
27 August, [1947]

Dearest Jeanie,

I reached Valencia again to-day, a month exactly after being here before.[19] I had a much too eventful journey to-day—a tyre went, and I had a terrible job changing the wheel, as when I had it jacked up the car moved back, and upset the jack, and crashed down on its side, and I couldn't raise it without help, of course, but a kind Spaniard from a passing *camion* stopped and helped me; it took ages, as my jack-handle broke, and he had to get his own jack, which was too tall, but at last, after an hour's hard labour in a broiling sun, we jacked it up again and changed the wheel. I said, when he lifted the car up by hand, that he was very strong. 'Not very', he answered, 'We don't get enough to eat'; which was very sad and touching. Of course I gave him a large reward. I feel thankful that we all get the same amount in England, unlike here, where the rich get lots and the poor far too little, owing to *all* food being sold at black-market prices and no one stopping it: there is, so far as I know, no honest and good

---

[19] R.M. had stayed at Denia, south of Valencia, on 27 July, at the beginning of her trip.

Senhor Barbosa in Spain,[20] and Franco doesn't raise a finger against it because of the army. Then, just after I had started, my front bumper jerked off, a bolt having broken when the car fell on its side, and I had to tie it up with a strap till I reached Valencia.

My inner tube was hopelessly cut by the wheel-rim, as the tyre suddenly sprang off the wheel, instead of subsiding slowly as when punctured, so I had to abandon it; the garage luckily had another, at a ruinous price (170 pesetas) but I had to take it, of course, as I can't be without a spare wheel. So I didn't get here till late afternoon. It is rather a charming town, full of old houses and lovely things. I am trying to get leave to go inside the Palace of Dos Aguas but it seems no one can. It is quite worth while returning this way, filling up my experiences and seeing the things I missed before. Last night I had a charming night, in a little town in the country 70 or 80 miles from Valencia—a very clean old *fonda*,[21] and a nice Senora, and a huge kind of kitchen with earth floor, into which I brought Elk for the night, and sat and actually heard the B.B.C. while the Senora cooked my supper in an iron pot over a twig fire. I don't know why one can sometimes get the B.B.C. & sometimes not; perhaps, now it is darker in the evenings, I shall be able to oftener. I have just read a Spanish paper's complaints of the B.B.C.'s attacks on Spain, and its saying that the Cadiz explosion was caused by German mines[22]—did they say that?…

Very much love.

E.R.M.

---

[20] In Portugal Senhor Daniel Barbosa, then Minister of Economics under Dr Salazar, was leading a drive to reduce food prices and to combat black markets.

[21] An inn.

[22] Cadiz had been devastated on 18 August when chemicals in the naval shipyards blew up, setting off torpedoes, shells, etc.

1949–1950

Rose finished writing 'Fabled Shore' in 1948 and then, recuperating from the strain of the war years, turned again to a novel. The devastation caused by the bombing still haunted her, however, and Barbary, the heroine of 'The World my Wilderness', the child of a broken marriage, is shown among the bombed ruins of the City of London, as well as among the ruins of human lives.

This book by no means exhausted Rose's obsession with the theme of ruins—their history, their nostalgic evocations, their symbolism, and their beauty. In 1949 she was asked to write 'a short book on the pleasures of looking at ruins', a subject which proved so fascinating that the book eventually took her three years and became the longest she ever wrote. The research for it involved many pilgrimages both at home and abroad, and in the summer of 1949 she went over to Ireland on one of these intriguing quests.

Eccles Hotel, Glengariff, Co. Cork[1]
16 July, [1949]

Got here at 4.0 this afternoon, after a night at Bowen's Court,

---

[1] Postcard.

131

90 miles away.[2] This is a lovely little bay, with little islands scattered about it, and woody shores and rocks—lovely for bathing. Unfortunately the warm spell is over (as elsewhere) and it is cold and wet but they say will improve. Boats for hire; the boatmen say it would be 'unfair' to them to *swim* to the islands. But I expect I shall. It was a lovely drive from Cork, and a nice crossing. Radio not much good here, as my set can't get London, but we can get Dublin, which gives some news, though mostly about Ireland....

Very much love.

E.R.M.

20, Hinde House, Hinde St, W.1
11 July, [1950]

Dearest Jeanie,

... Is it Miss K——who has proposed herself? People shouldn't do it. The only safeguard is not to have a spare room, like me. I suffered terribly when I used to have one. I hope one day to find an equally nice flat with one more room (some in Hinde [House] have) but shall use it as a work-room, and keep the spare bed under my own as I do now, to be *only* used by you. Nearly as tiresome as self-asked visitors are the people who invite you to some meal to meet someone else, and, when you say you can't go, press you as to which day you *can* go—a very low trick. Harold Nicolson told me of a worse one: a writer who asks him to review his book for *The Observer*, and, when he says he is sorry he can't because it

---

[2] R.M. and a friend, Marjorie Grant Cook, had stayed a night with Elizabeth Bowen.

has been sent to another reviewer, writes to the editor and asks him to get it back for H.N. I certainly shouldn't review it after that. But the writing world (like other worlds) is full of low ruses.

You may be right that Frank Swinnerton partly means a pessimistic answer by a lemon.[3] I think what *I* mean is mainly an uncertain answer. Sometimes, of course, an answer may be both.

I'm glad you were interested in re-reading *The World my Wilderness,* and found the people real. Some reviewers found them so unconvincing as to be little more than puppets—but people's points of view about characters in novels are quite incalculable, so all one can do is to convince oneself that they are real and write accordingly. Of course one may quite fail to put them across, and I am always pleased when readers think I have—particularly, of course, you.

Korean news still bad.[4] Dreadful to think of all the American wounded and captured in the enemy's hands.

Did you read Ian Mackay on Russian Discoveries, which included America?[5] As he says, 'they brought it on themselves'.

Very much love.

E.R.M.

---

[3] In reviewing *The World my Wilderness* (*The Spectator,* 12 May, 1950), Frank Swinnerton examined R.M.'s philosophy of life, as seen in her novels. He concluded that 'she has left us with the verdict that the answer to mankind's various ills, follies, disagreements, would appear to be a lemon'.

[4] U.S. troops in Korea were falling back before the southwards drive of the North Korean forces.

[5] See *News Chronicle,* 10 July, 1950.

[Hotel Cappuccini, Amalfi][6]
17 August, [1950]

Spending 2 nights at Amalfi, in this old monastery-hotel, high above the sea, with cells turned into bedrooms, cloisters, magnificent views, water that only occasionally runs; inconvenient but wonderfully beautiful. No monks left, in spite of picture [on this postcard]: Garibaldi turned them out in 1865. They probably used little water. Bathing all along here is perfect. On 15th we went to a procession and fireworks for the Assumption. No one seemed interested in Mary, only in fireworks. Italy seems less devout than in our day....

V. much love.
E.R.M.

PS. Little chapel off the cloisters has a wonderful *presepio.*[7] *Contadini*[8] coming in from the hills with oxen & mules & wine-carts, the first I have seen.

20, Hinde House, Hinde St, W.1
14 September, [1950]

Dearest Jeanie,
    Many thanks for [the] King-Hall [news-letter], and UNESCO on Race,[9] which seems a very ignorant composition. Surely they should know that body & mind are mixed up together, and that

---

6   Postcard.
7   *'Crib'. In the Macaulay family the Crib at Christmas was a cherished tradition.*
8   'Peasants'.
9   A pamphlet entitled, 'UNESCO Statement on Race', issued in July, 1950.

the genes which transmit physical characteristics transmit mental ones too. And what a *dull* theory !¹⁰ One of the most interesting things about the human race is its racial differences. In America, e.g., the differences between the immigrants of different stocks, however long their ancestors have been there, is said to be marked—Irish, Scotch, English, German, Italian, Polish, Jewish, Negro, Mexican, etc, all with different characteristics. And even in G.B., how different the Welsh are from the Anglo-Saxons, & the Scotch, & the Irish, & even the northern and southern English, descended from Danes, Saxons, Jutes, etc. And what a dull affair the world would be without different racial contributions to it! I wonder *why* they think that a Jew by race, though he inherits his nose, hair, and general look, doesn't inherit, say, his musical gifts, or his commercial cleverness, 01 his sense of God. On looking at the list of authors of the statement, however, I see that there are 3 Jews, one Mexican, one Brazilian, one Indian … all races which are self-conscious and fear the contempt of the races they live among, and have been despised and ill-treated in the past. This may account for it. I remember a Jew, Dr Singer,¹¹ during the Nazi persecutions, who was always trying to get me to sign statements about there being no such thing as race. I never did, as it seemed to me nonsense. They mix up racial sameness with 'the social bond between men', as they put it, which exists

---

¹⁰ It was argued that since all men belong to the same species, *Homo Sapiens,* a race may be defined as one of the groups of population constituting the species; also that there is no proof that the groups of mankind differ in their innate mental characteristics.

¹¹ Probably Dr Isidore Singer (1859–1939), editor of the Jewish Encyclopaedia (1901–5) and founder (1922) of the American League of the Brotherhood of Man.

among different races quite easily. It just shows the danger of grinding axes in scientific matters....

What *are* we to do to get out of Korea with dignity? It is too awful. There is a horrible account of it in *Picture Post*.[12] And there seems no reason why it should ever stop. America should never have rushed in like that, dragging us after her. No wonder the soldiers have no idea what they are fighting about.

I am seeing Gilbert Murray next week and must ask him how he feels about it. But of course he is tied up with U.N. and likes them to try out their paces. I say, let Russia take anything, rather than send people to join in these barbarian wars....

Very much love.

E.R.M.

8 October, [1950]

Dearest Jeanie,

Many thanks for your letter. I don't think you are fair to the *Life of Florence Nightingale*.[13] See enclosed review, which gives a good idea of it. I don't think anyone *could* think it 'spiteful'. The author admires her tremendously: of course she doesn't make her perfect, but her faults emerge almost entirely by her own letters, journals, and comments, and aren't emphasised by the author at all. It would be dull if she had been faultless. She had an irritable and unforgiving temper, a good deal of self-pity, intolerance and contempt (especially for those who she thought were not doing all they could for the reforms she wanted, and who said they were

---

[12] 'We follow the Road to Hell', *Picture Post*, *16* September, 1950.

[13] Cecil Woodham-Smith, *Florence Nightingale* (1950).

tired or ill) and much too much anger with (a) her family and relations, (b) women who wanted to be doctors not nurses. She was
temperamental & neurasthenic. But, with it all, she had no *mean*
faults, and was a magnificent person both intellectually and in
hard work and persistence. One would have loved her if one had
been working for her, but less if one gave it up, or (like her aunt)[14]
left her to return to her husband & children, which Florence
thought was a betrayal of affection. She was too stormy to have
been an easy companion; but all her friends loved her. You should
read the book, and see for yourself what it's like…. If it[15] said she
nursed in order to leave home, the reviewer can't have read it. On
the contrary, she 'heard the call' to go and do some work (she
wasn't sure what) when she was 16, but for years after that didn't
go, because she thought her parents needed her.

I have been looking up the history of English hospitals. Apparently the *voluntary* ones in the mid [nineteenth] century were very
well supported—and from 1901 on the King Edward Hospital
Fund was a great gift-raiser. It was those on the rates that were so
unhygienic—the fault, I suppose, of the Councils responsible for
them. What puzzles me is why the doctors who had to work in
such conditions didn't insist on better arrangements, if only for
selfish reasons. Of course hygienic notions were very poor compared with now, but even so it is surprising. I think the 1850's
can't be called *(relatively)* poor in social conscience—it was a time
of great progress in the poor laws, factory laws, laws about children's labour, etc. But of course social conscience has never been
good, in a general way, though now improving.

I had a lovely day at Bath—really warm; I hoped a little Indian

---

[14] Mrs Samuel Smith ('Aunt Mai').

[15] A review mentioned by Jean Macaulay.

summer was starting, but it was only one day, it seems. I went over the Roman baths, and saw the hot spring coming up; what wonderful engineers the Romans were. Apparently there are many more Roman baths under the town, which can't be excavated. The *Northanger Abbey* people who went to the Pump Room knew nothing about them. Then I climbed a hill and saw Sham Castle, a ruined façade built there by a Bath citizen for him to look at from his house, in 1760.[16] Altogether I had a good day, and did a lot of work in the train too.[17]…

I like the new *Sunday Express* serial about the Saucers[18]—much more amusing and interesting than the Abdication. What *can* they be? Do you think they come from Higher Intelligences who are spying on us? Or are they American experiments?

Very much love.

E.R.M.

---

[16] Ralph Allen's Sham Castle, on Bathwick Hill above Bath.

[17] R.M. was then working on *Pleasure of Ruins*.

[18] This was a news article headed 'Is another world watching us?', not a serialisation.

1953–1958

For over two years after late 1950 *there is a gap in the series of surviving letters to Jean. The course of Rose's life is, however, clearly delineated in her correspondence with Father Johnson (Letters to a Friend' and 'Last Letters to a Friend'). Against the secret background of contrition and penitence, and her return to the Anglican Church after a lapse of thirty years, she busied herself with all her usual activities, and in spite of bad health—for six months she suffered from persistent attacks of undulant fever—she toiled on undefeatably at 'Pleasure of Ruins'. Early in 1953, embarking on yet more research for 'Ruins', she made ready for a trip to Cyprus and the Middle East.*

20, Hinde House, Hinde St, W.1 9 March, [1953]

Dearest Jeanie,

Very many thanks for letter and King-Hall. Yes, his account of Cyprus was very nice, so far as it goes, but he only touched on the beauties before going off (as I knew he would) about the political position, and Enosis.[1] Still, of course that is the object of the

---

[1] Union with Greece.

News-Letters—the physical descriptions one can get from books. It is a most enchanting & exciting & wonderful island, which I have always longed to visit. I see his boat went from Athens, hence the islands. Boats from Britain, or Marseilles, or Genoa, go more directly. Though I believe there is one from Venice that goes via the islands. But it means first a train journey then a boat, and it is all much longer and more complicated than air, and, with all the meals, sleepers, etc, is just about as much, or nearly. I am just going to book my seat, May 16th, 9 a.m. ...

Yes, Bp Cockin[2] was quite interesting. But he tends to imply that non-Christians are apt to be scientific. Any number of non-Christians are literary, classical, what is called humanist; I know very many, and I know very few scientists. So long as they are aiming (as he says) at what is good, better leave them to it, and not bother about trying to persuade them that Christianity is true. Much better for Christians to spend their energies converting other Christians ... to decent ideas.

I went to the licensing of Gerard Irvine to his new charge the other night—a mission church near Hounslow.[3] Rather a picturesque ceremony, he knelt before the Bp of Kensington[4] and answered questions about how he was going to try to behave in the new parish. 'Will you use the Book of Common Prayer as authorised, adding nothing to it?' That, however, is qualified by the clause 'except by lawful authority' .... Actually the parish is very extreme in its services, and obviously the congregation (a kind of factory-working new town, grown on to the old parish)

---

[2] The Bp of Bristol (Rt Rev. F. A. Cockin).

[3] The Church of the Holy Angels, Cranford, which serves a London Diocesan Home Mission district.

[4] Rt Rev. Cyril Eastaugh.

likes it, and was very cheerful and friendly. There was a bun-fight after the service, and Gerard made himself popular at once.…We are mourning the death of the [Grosvenor] Chapel Sacristan, an extraordinarily nice woman[5] who was also a church cleaner…. How much she … liked something … once quoted [in a sermon] about there being no dust in heaven.[6] She was a very clean, tidy, conscientious, kind person, and always found and kept safe the oddments I left in church.[7] She has a Requiem Mass tomorrow; and lies in the Chapel to-night, covered with flowers. I hear from Fr Johnson[8] that the new R.C. fasting rules have gone a long way, and they look forward to very full congregations at evening Communion. Will the Anglo-Catholics follow suit soon? I expect so …

Very much love.

E.R.M.

Thursday [19 March, 1953][9]

… I have missed seeing Tito and his bodyguard sweeping thro' London, I expect they went too fast. What with Catholics and Communists, no doubt he does well to go fast.[10] I met Lord Pakenham last night, who always tries to convert me. But he said

---

[5] Mrs Curry.

[6] A saying attributed to Max Jacob (1876–1944), French Catholic poet.

[7] R.M. was by this time a very regular worshipper at the Grosvenor Chapel in South Audley Street.

[8] Rev. J. H. C. Johnson, S.S.J.E., see above p. 22.

[9] *Postcard.*

[10] When Marshal Tito appeared in public during his visit to London in March 1953 he was heavily guarded and evoked few cheers.

he had been delighted to hear that I was now a practising Anglican, which was big of him. I fancy he thinks it is [a] step nearer Rome. He asked me what I did for a central Church authority, did I go by what Canterbury said. I said I didn't need an authority, and that if I was R.C. [I] shouldn't take any notice of what the Pope said. What about the interpretation of Scripture, he said. I said I read Bible commentaries by good scholars, if anything puzzled me, but didn't think it mattered a lot, and what I believe in was the Light that lights every man, trained up by reason, and the Bible after all, and the Church too, were only products of the Light, not its sources. However, he kindly said he still had hopes of my conversion. He is really a very nice, nave man, and seems to take a genuine interest—tho' he ought to know that I am a hopeless proposition. But who knows, I might come back from Cyprus a Greek Orthodox. I am going to Cyprus at the right time; they say next year it may be submerged by the Army, who regard it as an 'outpost'. What a point of view!

Love …

E.R.M.

King George Hotel, Famagusta, Cyprus 17 May, [1953]

Dearest Jeanie,

I got here last night at 8.0, after a very smooth and beautiful journey: I spent last night in Nicosia, and came on here at lunch-time. Nicosia is inland, and is the capital, but quite small. When I went out last night to see it, the hotel manager said 'You will have to be careful, or you may be killed.' I asked why, and he said there were the municipal elections on, and people got very excited and stampeded. (Very different from London ones!)

However, the streets were actually extremely quiet. There is a beautiful Greek medieval cathedral, turned into a mosque by the Turks, like so many Greek churches, when they took Cyprus 300 years ago. They whitewash the inside and take away all ornaments, monuments, and stained glass, and put in vulgar-looking patterned white glass instead. I don't care for mosques inside. The man who drove me to Famagusta to-day said it would be 'boiling' with election excitement. Cypriotes, he said (being one himself) are excitable. There are 2 parties, Communist and Nationalist. He is Nationalist. The Nationalists officially want Enosis (union with Greece), but he says most of them don't really, as without the British occupation they would probably starve. One noticeable thing about the streets of the towns is that there are practically no women. None at all last night in Nicosia. My driver said Cyprus women don't go out alone, and never in the evenings. What would happen to a woman who went for a walk alone, I asked. He said, her father would beat her. Also they never walk out with boyfriends. The British soldiers must miss this. There is a lot of Turkish blood, obviously; the people are much darker than Greeks, and some have a Turkish look. No wonder, after so long an occupation. No doubt they absorbed rather a Turkish view of women, too.

This hotel is right on the beach, and about 2 miles from old Famagusta, the walled town. The walls are splendid, and the citadel, and St Nicholas's Gothic cathedral, a magnificent buttressed 13th century church, now a mosque, with a perky minaret on it. Inside it was white-washed and carpeted, and Moslems were praying aloud in corners—all men, of course, unlike R.C. churches, where they are mostly women. Round the cathedral stand ruined fragments of medieval churches, and some domed Moslem buildings, in a littered desert of thistle and grass and palms. There are a few streets, and a square. Otherwise all is desolation. It was, seven and six and five centuries ago, a very flourishing and rich city, and thick with churches and convents built by the crusaders. But it was devastated and thrown down by the Turks, and later nearly all the buildings were torn up and the stones taken to build Cairo. It seemed haunted by the rich life that went on once, the trading in the harbour, and the bells of all the churches; and now nothing but the sound of the wind in the palm trees and among the grass, and the rustling of the sea....

There is *no* way of getting about Cyprus but on foot, bicycle, or car. No buses—or scarcely any, and the few there are get filled up with goats & hay & hens and now and then a camel. So I am hiring a self-drive car, to explore in, making Famagusta my base this week.

The British are doing their best to make the island hideous with Nissen huts, barracks, etc. What I feel is, what's the sense of making an island a military base if it means making it ugly? Because if it's ugly, why fight to keep it?

V. much love.

E.R.M.

20, Hinde House, Hinde St, W.1
8 September, [1953] (Nativity of B.V.M.)

Dearest Jeanie,

Thank you so much for yours, and for sending de Caussade.[11] What a shocking way to write to a postulant considering

---

[11] J. P. de Caussade, *Ordeals of Souls: A Continuation of His Spiritual Letters* (trans. A. Thorold, 1936).

her vocation! 'I forbid you in the name of God and by all the authority he has given me over you, either to listen to or examine into this subject in any way, and I command you to act about it as if the devil suggested that you should poison all the Religious !'[12] What did he think a postulant was supposed to do, except think over her vocation? I suppose the poor girl never dared to say any more about it, but became an unhappy nun. If that is the way all postulants were dealt with, no wonder many nuns were unhappy....

Did you hear E. M. Forster's nice talk on Indian art, last night and the night before?[13] He is now just off to Portugal for a fortnight, and I hope will give a talk about his impressions of it.

I eat plenty, and always have a good mid-day meal; if at home I cook a bit of meat, and potatoes with it, and have fruit; if out lunching with a friend I also eat well. To-day I shall eat *very* well, as I am lunching at the expensive Dorchester, in company with some other writers, with a rich American publisher, who should feed us richly....

Very much love.

E.R.M.

After 'Pleasure of Ruins' was published, at the end of 1953, Rose turned her thoughts towards her next trip abroad. Both Yugoslavia and Russia attracted her, but neither of these ideas came off. Eventually she made plans for the expedition to Turkey which was to inspire 'The Towers of Trebizond', and meanwhile her busy round in London continued as usual.

---

[12] See Letter IV, 'To a Postulant' (Mme de Lesen).

[13] 'Another Art', a broadcast talk reviewing Prof. Benjamin Rowland's *Art and Architecture of India*.

Holy Innocents [28 December, 1953]
(I hear the Spanish call it All
Fools' Day, instead of April 1st)

Dearest Jeanie,

… Christmas already seems a long way back, how nice it was, talking, eating delicious food, and sitting with the lit Crib hearing the carols, so very peaceful and elevated and nice. I got home in good time for my dinner in Hampstead, where I collected some more comparisons, such as 'as cool as a cucumber' and had more plum pudding, and next day went out to lunch and more p.p. again, & turkey & mince pies, so I have done well. Now back to normal, though many shops & public offices are still shut; we have decided on 4 days Christmas holiday each year….

I was told that there are plenty of 1928 Prayer Books about in the shops. A Prebendary told me that they all have the 1662 book printed with it; also that they still have [the prayer for] George V, as they mayn't move with the times. I'll remember to bring mine on Saturday.

I hope you have had a comparatively quiet time since Boxing Day. I am now very anxious that you shouldn't get worn out so that you retired and went to S. Africa,[14] I should feel so lost that I should probably go and do mission work in Tonga, and convert them to the C. of E. so that they needn't keep Sunday so hard. I might even convert Salote.[15] I suppose you wouldn't care to come too? You nurse and I preach, and both of us eat sucking-pigs and yams with our fingers; which Nancy would cook for us. The

---

[14] Jean Macaulay had long been attracted by the idea of living permanently in South Africa.

[15] Queen Salote of Tonga, a Wesleyan Methodist.

perfect life, think it over seriously…. I got home laden with your presents—butter, shortbread, tea. You and Nancy are like good fairies. I shall like to hear what kind of Xmas your catechumen had.[16] I'm sure if anyone can convert her you will.

Very much love.

E.R.M.

20, Hinde House, Hinde St, W.1
19 January, [1954]

Dearest Jeanie,

Thank you so much for returning the Prayer Book, which you ought to have kept till Saturday. What I am looking out for is the 'Alternative Order', as printed in the large missal[17] that we use at the [Grosvenor] Chapel, with all the collects, prayers, introits, proper to each day; there is a small edition of this, but now out of print. I have it on order from Mow-brays in case it gets about again. At St Stephen's [Gloucester Road], where I went on Sunday, the Order is rather different, and threw me out. It is a beautiful church and a beautifully sung service. I am told … that in all those very extreme churches, a lot of 'Roman patter' goes on among the priests under the shelter of the singing of the introits etc., but I didn't hear that. I hoped that T. S. Eliot, a churchwarden there, woul dtake the bag round, but he didn't … I feel that my spiritual home (outside the Chapel) is only among

---

[16] Doris B——, whose parents Jean Macaulay had nursed, was receiving teaching from her about the Christian Faith.

[17] *The Altar Missal*, edited by a Priest of the S.S.J.E. (Mowbray 1936), some-times known as the 'Cowley Missal'.

the Cambridge Platonists, whom I am re-reading now, or some of them.[18] Their words shine among the tiresome theological discussions and pronouncements of their age, full of reasonableness and morality: 'The pith and kernel of the Gospel consists in Christ inwardly formed in our hearts. Nothing is truly ours but what lives in our spirits. Salvation itself cannot save us so long as it is only without us.'[19]

By the way, they would think the good agnostic in a more hopeful state of grace than the bad Christian: 'He that endeavours … to comply with that truth in his life which his conscience is convinced of, is nearer the Christian, though he never heard of Christ, than he that believes all the articles of the Christian faith and plainly denyeth Christ in his life.'[20] This kind of talk got them into trouble with both Protestants & Roman Catholics as heretics and 'Bible-scorners', so did their praise of pre-Christian good men (except Jews, who were allowed goodness because in Scripture).

No, of course committing a sin is *far* worse than desiring it. But when people keep saying that we are more cruel than our ancestors because of bombing, there seems a fallacy in it, considering the appalling tortures they too perpetrated, both in war and peace; I mean, they did what they could, and I think were *more* cruel. I wonder if the atom-bombing *has* made us more cruel. Some people, perhaps; but in others there was a great horror of a revulsion from it, after Hiroshima when its human effects were

---

[18] R.M. was probably reading *The Cambridge Platonists: a Study* by F. J. Powicke (1926).

[19] A free rendering of one of Powicke's quotations from Ralph Cudworth (1617–88).

[20] One of the quotations from the *Discourses* of Benjamin Whichcote (1609–83) included in Powicke's *The Cambridge Platonists*.

described. I think if I had ever been for it (of course I wasn't) it would have changed my mind. I think I agree with you about our various moral improvements and declines, on the whole. I wonder if John Betjeman will.[21] He is against something he calls 'progress'; I am never sure if this means moral, intellectual, economic, scientific, artistic, political, juridical, hygienic, or what. Whatever it is, he doesn't believe in it—but one can never bring him down to exact facts, he is apt to set up bogies and tilt against them.

I thought 'Beg to differ' last night was good.[22] I was glad Celia Johnson struck a more educated note when … [someone] said that wives, when their husbands were away, always 'wondered what they were up to', and she said 'That's just a music-hall point of view, surely.' She has a good influence on the team, I think; so have Joyce Grenfell and John Betjeman. Gilbert Harding is a very tiresome man, I can't think why the B.B.C. use him so much.

I hope you haven't been blown off your bicycle again. No big gales, but a tiresome wind; no frost, but chilly. I think people must come out to 8.15 church in order to cure their colds & coughs by prayer. They would cure them much quicker in bed, and not pass them on. But I must try and not become like mother about colds.[23]

Very much love.

E.R.M.

---

[21] Plans were being made for a broadcast discussion between R.M. and John Betjeman on 'Changes in Morals'.

[22] 'We Beg to Differ', a broadcast discussion on various topics between Kay Hammond, Joyce Grenfell, Celia Johnson, John Clements, Gilbert Harding and John Betjeman.

[23] Grace Macaulay was always very nervous about colds. In church when others coughed or sneezed she sniffed ostentatiously at a eucalyptus-soaked handkerchief, to the great embarrassment of her family.

I think I shall keep a Nicest-Thing-Each-Day diary too. To-day, visiting Yugo–Slav Tourist office and seeing lovely maps and photographs of Yugo–Slavia. Or, getting a nice letter from an old clergyman containing some ruin-poems he had written, not good but enthusiastic. He says he read *The Lee Shore* in his first curacy, and has liked it ever since. *All* Ms poetry sent me is bad always....

Sunday [14 February,] 1954

Dearest Jeanie,

... Yes, I heard the two elderly ladies on the Welfare State.[24] I used to know them both slightly. They didn't differ enough, I thought. How *good* that kind of person of our generation is apt to be! So high-minded and high principled. I have known, and fortunately still know, so many of them. They have a lot of inner light, and comparatively seldom commit the sin against the Holy Ghost. Their distinguishing mark, I think, is a sense of social responsibility and care for other people's welfare, and gentle womanliness....

I enclose an article on B.B.C. religion, which I think is too critical. I don't agree that it is a dilution of the tenets of the various Christian sects; though it is probably better to teach the things they agree about than to talk about Election and Papal Infallibility, both very minority tenets, and both pretty silly. (Which is the sillier, would you say? I think about the same!)....

---

[24] 'Talking of the Welfare State', a broadcast conversation between Violet Markham and Dame Rachel Crowdy-Thornhill.

Do you know what 'the feminine role' is? I am accused of rejecting it, by a correspondent (a psychologist) who disagrees with me that men tend to be cleverer than women. She perceives evidence of this rejection in my novels. How does one reject it, I wonder? And what *is* it? Except being a wife & mother (as the masculine role is that of husband & father) I don't know what it is. And she doesn't seem to mean that....

My holiday plan is in the soup, as regards the Yugo-Slav villa: my publishers (Weidenfeld & Nicolson) have offered to pay my expenses somewhere, if I write about it. I think of Russia, but fear it won't be possible. Of course really my next book should be a novel, for Collins. Mark Bonham Carter (of Collins) says that W. & N. are behaving like Satan, tempting me with the kingdoms of the earth to leave the path of duty.... Meanwhile I am writing poetry, which I like to do sometimes. What a self-pleasing life I lead, while other people bicycle to sick people in the cold!...

> Very much love.
> *E.R.M.*

20, Hinde House, Hinde St, W.1 g
March, [1954]

Dearest Jeanie,

    … No thank you, no more butter till after Easter (if then).

    Faith, hope, and belief. I think (as I said) that hope is the first stage; hoping, against all probability, that what you would like to believe is true, even though almost knowing it can't be. Faith next; the affair still improbable, but worth accepting as a working hypothesis. Last, belief: really thinking a thing is true—it only (in my experience) comes by fits and starts, and doesn't cover the whole ground, at best. Perhaps I shall never exactly *'believe'* in God, and shall always have to stick in the faith stage. Hope, of course, goes with all the stages.

She[25] won't stop being a catechumen until baptism; if, indeed, she qualifies for one now—but I think she does, as she is under instruction. She is still in the *audientes* stage, and is allowed to attend church services. You might take her to see a baptism, also get her to read the baptismal service (in 1928 [Prayer Book] version). If she gives in her name for baptism, she will enter the *competentes* class. 'To catechumens in this class, the great articles of the creed, the nature of the Sacraments, and the penitential discipline of the church, were explained, as in the Catechetical Lectures of Cyril of Jerusalem,[26] with dogmatic precision.' You won't have time for this, so you should pass her on to a clergyman. This stage lasts 40 days, and 'special examinations and enquiries into character were made at intervals during the period. It was a time for fasting, watching, and prayer…. Those who passed through the ordeal were known as the *perfectiores,* or *electi.'* If the catechumen lapses during the period into *idolatry or other grievous sin,* he is thrown back and has to go through a penitential discipline, varying, according to the nature of the offence, from a few months to 3 or 5 years. But they may still have baptism on their death-bed, as it is necessary to salvation. But if *through their own neglect* they die without baptism, they are buried without honour and not prayed for by the Church. You had better tell her all this, so that if she perseveres in wanting baptism, she will know what she is in for.

_____

[25] Doris B——, see above p. 156n.

[26] St Cyril, Bp of Jerusalem *(c.* 315–386).

I made a mistake in mentioning my burglars[27] to Father Johnson, he has become very nervy and anxious about it. He writes 'you tuck in this horrid experience at the end of your letter, as if it were merely rather annoying, but not what so many of my penitents call "grievous",' and he suggests all kinds of precautions against its recurrence. I usually try to remember not to tell him anything at all disturbing.

I am reading a book called *Myth and Ritual in Christianity*[28]. It says 'The word Myth is not to be used here as meaning untrue or unhistorical. Myth is to be defined as a complex of stories— some, no doubt, fact, and some fantasy—which, for various reasons, human beings regard as demonstrations of the inner meaning of the universe and of life.'…

Very much love. Wet again!

E.R.M.

Stephen Spender thinks no strings are attached to the Soviet offer of fare-payment. It is a literary propaganda stunt, about Tchekhov.[29] But I *might,* out of politeness, have to look at a few tiresome things such as schools, hospitals, maternity homes and factories. It all depends how many. Most of my time *must* be spent in the Crimea & Caucasus, seeing things there. Tchekhov's home was in the Crimea, fortunately.

Rose finally decided to travel in Turkey, and spent about four weeks

---

[27] In February 1954 R.M.'s flat was burgled, see *Last Letters to a Friend* (pp. 147–8).

[28] By A. W. Watts (1953).

[29] R.M. had been considering going to Russia in a party in honour of Tchekhov.

there in the summer of 1954.

Alexandretta
25 June, [1954]

Dearest Jeanie,

It was such a nice surprise to find a letter from you this morning at Antioch, forwarded from Trebizond.... Antioch was interesting, but nothing left of ancient Antioch except the Citadel on a high crag, which I didn't climb to. I saw the early church in a cave, (the earliest Christian church), and went out to Daphne. Antioch has an interesting medieval quarter, which used to be the whole town till a century ago or so; narrow twisting streets of little craftsmen's shops—coppersmiths (wasn't that where the malevolent Alexander lived, or was that Ephesus?),[30] carpenters, jewellers, etc. I spent yesterday with a kind, intelligent, German couple, who talk English; he is an archaeologist, and she rides about the mountains with him bear-hunting. They are, I think, the only people in Antioch who know anything about the antiquities—Turks neither know nor care—so they were very useful. They said the Turks are rather anti-British, because of 1915 and the Dardanelles. But they like Germans, their allies. I spent 2 nights at Antioch. It was very hot.

Did you have time to listen to me and John Betjeman, I wonder?[31] I had a letter about it from an unknown who said he had liked it, and was glad I had protested against J.B.'s view

---

[30] It was Ephesus. See II Timothy 4. 14,15: 'Alexander the coppersmith did me much evil....'

[31] R.M. means their discussion on 'Changes in Morals'.

[that] we were 'living on our spiritual capital'.[32] By the way, have you a Koran? I shall like to see what it says about women in the mosques. The German archaeologist told me the men wouldn't let the women be photographed, because the Koran forbids anyone to be photographed, but men, being strong souls, can disobey without their souls being destroyed by it, whereas women, whose souls are very weak, can't. I wonder if the Koran also says women are 'unclean'. Moslems think they are, but they may have thought of that for themselves.

I have just been talking to a young German couple in this hotel, who are touring Turkey on a motorcycle and writing a book about it. She wears trousers, and is much derided, but says she has learnt to ignore it. I wish all the Turkey guidebooks now in process had appeared in time for me to bring one. Suddenly everyone seems to be writing Turkey books, there having been none for about a century....

I long to see you again & tell & hear everything. It is difficult to imagine it cold and wet, with this enervatingly hot weather here. A young Turk, practising his English on me, told me it rained on 200 days a year in London. I dare say it does, should you say?

Why does the Crockford preface rock the Church, and in which direction?[33] Perhaps only to sleep. To which I must now go

---

[32] Replying to a question from R.M. on the moral effects of present-day irreligiousness, John Betjeman said: 'I think we're living on the spiritual capital of the past, and that it will soon run out ... we can't go on being morally sound if we forget the model of our soundness, and He is, I submit, God become man, Jesus Christ.'

[33] The anonymous author of the Preface to the 1953–54 issue of *Crock-ford's Clerical Directory* had criticised the currently proposed revision of

157

myself. This *is* a lovely place, with lit battleships in the harbour, and crowds of palms all round the shore. I wish 1 dared bathe. I expect the German girl does. Very much love, & don't die of over-work, it's not worth it.

Your loving *E.R.M.*

Istanbul
1 July, [1954}

Dearest Jeanie,

    … I am now here for the week-end, and to-morrow hope to go to Troy, if I can reach it. I don't feel very energetic, but it would be a shame to be so near and not see it, when I shall never be here again. Istanbul is hot, but not so intensely hot as the south. At Smyrna I had a room you wouldn't put a goat in— very small, looking on a well, with a window of another bed-room in each of the four walls, and practically no air. I didn't feel very well, actually. But I got to Ephesus yesterday by train— only 50 miles but three hours each way. A little village, and the ruins of Ephesus 2 kilometres away—marble courts & forum & theatre & gymnasium & columns—it must have been a grand city when the locals shouted 'Great is Diana of the Ephesians' for hours in the theatre when St Paul was there. The great temple of Artemis (one of the 7 wonders of the world) which was destroyed and lost for centuries and only found again in 1869

---

canon law relating to the remarriage of divorced persons in church, and advocated leaving decisions to individual parish priests, who could seek advice if needed.

(after our grandfather[34] was there) was excavated and neatly arranged by British archaeologists last century; but the wretched Turks of course have let it go under a marsh again, and there are now only a few columns showing above a pool of water, and canes growing round them. They have no idea what Ephesus was, or how great the temple. There is the ruined acropolis, with Byzantine and Turkish Castle, and the columns of Justinian's great Basilica of S. John on the hill by it. It was all very desolate and moving, and just what I had read of.

I'm sorry, it was my fault not enclosing the letters on Pacifism.[35] You have got the wrong idea; I never said Pacifism was *simple*, but couldn't understand all this about 'Christian perfectionism' etc, because it does seem to me a question of human decency, not of perfectionism at all and scarcely even of Christianity—except in so far as Christianity confirms and demands human decency. I think Einstein was wrong in persuading Roosevelt to use atom bombs.[36]

I hope you took notes of the Billy Graham discussion; I should

---

[34] Rev. W.J. Conybeare, co-author with Rev. J. S. Howson of *The Life and Epistles of St Paul* (1852).

[35] A correspondence in *The Times* had followed a leading article on 'Christianity and Bombs' (7 June), which supported the views of the Archdeacon of London, Ven. O.H. Gibbs-Smith (that the New Testament lent no countenance to absolute pacifism, that the pacifist had 'the heresy of perfectionism' in a world which had not achieved perfection, and that the infernal machine was not the bomb but the 'unprincipled and unconsecrated human mind').

[36] In a letter to President Roosevelt dated 2 August, 1939, Prof. Einstein recommended that supplies of uranium should be guaranteed and that research in nuclear fission should be speeded up.

like to know what lines they took.[37] They are very different men: MacLeod is better; also, being a Presbyterian would, I imagine, have more sympathy with B.G. than Muggeridge, who is either R.C., Anglican, or (more likely) nothing.

What extraordinary letters people write to people they don't know! I have got a *most* impertinent one from a man who is furious because I said on the [B.B.C.] 'Critics' that I saw no reason why children shouldn't see the X film we were discussing. Apparently I said that I had been allowed to read what books I liked as a child, and they had done me no harm. He said on the contrary, I flattered myself, they had obviously done me *great* harm, if I was willing that innocent children should see X films. I wonder in what mood people write these impertinent letters— I suppose indignation. But it is difficult to imagine such rude impulses being yielded to. I suppose Aunt Mary might. But she wouldn't write so vulgarly, being educated. I don't like getting rude letters; it is like having mud thrown at you. I never answer them, of course.

It is rather restful to be in Istanbul for a few days, though I am again in a room unfit for a goat. I sit in a lounge outside it, where it is much cooler. I hope to get on with my writing here—novel, poetry, articles etc., and, except Troy & seeing a few people, shan't try to do anything much. I do look forward to the cold wet sponge. I had an interesting talk with a German this morning who has lived in Turkey … for 17 years. He thinks Turks on the whole (as I do) the stupidest people in the world, and not really belonging to Europe, which they drifted into over the centuries

---

[37] A discussion on 'Billy Graham and his Greater London Crusade' between Malcolm Muggeridge and Rev. George MacLeod was broadcast on 25 June.

from the eastern plains. He thinks Ataturk has done something to improve them, but even now the taxi-drivers can't find their way about, and the trains can't do more than about 20 miles an hour, and the economy of the country is getting worse and worse. He thinks the women (outside the large westernized towns) will take at least 50 years more to recover from the Koran and cast off their hot muffling clothes. The Prophet was very firm about their not letting men see their faces or hair. Perhaps in the Middle Ages it *would* have been rather rash of women to let Turkish men see much of them. But the men aren't told to behave decently, it is the women who mustn't tempt them. He says the women usually die early of such unhealthy clothes. He asked the Turkish maid why she didn't dress like his wife in hot weather; she said she couldn't, her religion forbade it. An awful life it must be. Besides being hot, they are scorned and unfit to pray.

Very much love.

E.R.M.

20, Hinde House, Hinde St, W.1 4 February, [1955]

Dearest Jeanie,

… I should certainly encourage your catechumen to hope. But if she can also do a little believing, she will pray with more confidence and on a firmer basis. But very likely she can't. Mere hope is rather frail under the stresses of life. But of course everyone must do what they can, and not worry….

I am getting very confident on the bicycle.[38] As my porter says,

---

[38] Since R.M.'s car had been stolen and damaged, on 19 January, she had been getting about London by bicycle.

it will keep my weight down. No mishaps so far. At least, not to me, though a bus banged into the back of a car which stopped for me while I crossed at the pedestrian crossing. Bus drivers are taken by surprise when cars stop for crossings, it seems to them so odd and wrong. *My* car got banged in that way once. Buses are the rogue elephants of the road, and probably unteachable. I think it is being so powerful, and power corrupts. Now great new roads are being planned, which will speed up traffic dangerously....

The car sounds not *too* badly damaged, and I hope in a few weeks to get it back.

A lot of talk about abolishing war going about. I wish they'd think of a way!

Very much love.

E.R.M.

20, Hinde House, Hinde St, W.1
20 February, [1955]

Dearest Jeanie,

I hope you still survive, and aren't having an awful time walking about in the snow and ice. I find this much more tiring than bicycling, & less safe. Today cars and pedestrians were glissading all about the roads, while my rubber tyres gripped the icy surface firmly, and I only glissaded when I jumped off or walked. The snow lay deep when I first went out, coated with ice; later they had thawed some of the streets with salt, though not the pavements. I went to early Mass at the Chapel and the later one to S. Paul's,[39]

---

[39] At this time R.M. was in the habit of worshipping both at Grosvenor Chapel and at St Paul's, Knightsbridge.

where Fr Henderson[40] preached a really splendid beginning-of-Lent sermon, the best of its kind I have heard, I think. I am glad he is so near me, so that I can get there even without the car....

I have a Shrove Tuesday party here; after that, says Fr Henderson, parties should be laid aside for Lent. Also smoking, drinking, eating nice things, idling, self-indulgence, spending money except when necessary—he made it sound like a hard campaign; and, he added, if we don't behave better by the end of it, it will all have been wasted effort. I'm sure bicycling instead of driving is very Lenten. And certainly your bicycling about in the snow is. I wish your colleagues would take Lent to heart, & be content to be a little put upon.

I saw a ridiculous film yesterday instead of coming to you, a Japanese film about Samurai,[41] detestable creatures, gibbering and yelling and fighting.... I thought *Sailor Beware*[42] good, which we saw for the 'Critics' for next week.

Very much love.

E.R.M.

20, Hinde House, Hinde St, W.1
22 February, [1955]

Dearest Jeanie,

I had better hurry and give my [definition of] minimum Christianity before I finish your letter; I've not read yours yet. I haven't much time for mine, as I am fighting against time this morning. But

---

[40] Rev. E. B. Henderson, Vicar of St Paul's, Knightsbridge.

[41] Akira Kurosawa's *Seven Samurai*.

[42] A comedy by Philip King and Falkland Cary.

I think I should call a person a Christian if he believes in God, (I call it 'believe', but you can translate it into 'hope', as we probably mean the same—I mean 'believe enough to pray to') and in something that may be called Christ's 'divinity', i.e. that he was connected with God in some way we are not, that he survives in spirit, and can be communicated with. I *think* this is what distinguishes a Christian from (say) a Unitarian. A non-Christian may make his communion and get good from it, of course, though it can't well mean quite as much to him as to someone who thinks there was (and is) something special about Christ and his relationship both to God and to human beings. Of course one may say none of it is 'belief, but only 'hope', but that is just a question of words and names. It has nothing to do with behaviour, as non-Christians can be as good, and Christians as bad, as anyone else. Now I will look at yours. I have. Of course the two great commandments were pre-Christian, as Christ himself said, so I don't think that can be a definition. I'm not sure what 'love incarnate' means, it is too vague, and doesn't imply any special relationship of Christ to God, which I think is one of the ingredients. I feel my definition is more exact. Yours would almost cover Jews, who accept the two great commandments in the Old Testament and believe (some of them) that Christ was full of love though not divine.

I have just heard that my car will be *3 weeks* more, as they haven't yet started on the repairs. I am furious, and not full of love at all. But my bicycle is a great comfort, it is very safe in snow and ice, but so much colder and slower than a car, of course. All right for Lent. I don't call Lent self-denials 'penances' but training in self-control and hardness, as Fr Henderson said, which is useful at any age....

Very much love.

E.R.M.

20, Hinde House, Hinde St, W.1
15 March [1955]

Dearest Jeanie,

… I am nearly all right now. No temperature, in fact too little. For some time I thought I was normal and didn't know why I felt queer, but, knocking the therm, down further, found I was between 95 and 96. It sometimes now reaches normal, but is variable, and I go on feeling rather tired. No doubt, as you suggest, I am radio-activized: perhaps we all are. If so, it's not too bad, and perhaps it *wont* be the end of civilization. All the same, I'm glad Richard Acland has made his gesture.[43] I wish he had put it rather differently; if I were him I would have said that it very likely wouldn't bring peace or non-aggression at all, why should it, but in any case we mustn't commit so dreadful a cruelty. I think I would rather we were wiped out or ruled by Communists than do it; but then I am old. I complained of the same thing in the pacifists of the war and before the war; they would go on saying that non-fighting would make Hitler not fight too, as he would be so touched, instead of simply that fighting was a barbarity not to be committed in any case, which is a strong position. Did you hear that Cardinal Griffin said that, in case of a just war, it would be all right to drop atom bombs on the 'unjust and violent aggressor'?[44] Really he ought to be deprived of his

---

[43] Sir Richard Acland had resigned his seat as Labour member for Gravesend in protest against the Labour Party's acceptance of hydrogen-bomb manufacture in Britain.

[44] Cardinal Griffin (1899–1956) preaching in Westminster Cathedral on 13 March said, 'the problem … rests upon whether this bomb can ever be brought sufficiently under control that, given a just war, it can be directed

job for imbecility. I don't know if he thinks the bomb can pick out the Kremlin and have no further effects, or that *all* the people of a hostile country are unjust and violent enough to deserve radio-activization or mutilation and death. Yet no one protests against his speech in public. What a world of humbug it is! I had an interesting talk yesterday with a young Jew, whom I met travelling in Palestine etc. in '53. We made friends there, and went to several places in Israel together. His father is a London barrister, and he is down lately from Cambridge, and writing on art. He isn't himself a believing Jew, but knows about it of course. He thinks Christianity most extraordinary; he was taught it at Rugby. He thinks the main difference between it and Judaism is that Christians seem to look back to Christ's life and death, as the mainspring and centre of their faith, while Jews look forward to the gradual coming of God's kingdom on earth. He doesn't see why Christians speak of being 'redeemed by Christ' and the world being so also, when obviously it isn't redeemed at all. He can't understand what Christians think Christ did for them, beyond teaching. Like most non-Christians, he accepts as Christianity a theological system which is still taught, both in pulpits and in schools, but which most thoughtful and educated people have laid aside as primitive. It was complained of in a book I was reading by an old Etonian.[45] Religion must be very badly taught in schools, I imagine. He was at Eton over 50 years ago; it may be better now; but this boy was at Rugby only a few years back. He thought it odd that I, for instance, should put my own interpretation on things, quite different from the orthodox one; he thought

---

only against unjust and violent aggressors. The answer to this must lie with those who have access to the necessary scientific knowledge.'

[45] Sir Lawrence Jones, *A Victorian Boyhood* (1955).

that Christianity should be either accepted, or discarded, not stretched and lopped to fit different minds & periods. Perhaps it is a pity so much got written down about it, to crystallise it, and that it is never revised. Meanwhile we must just take what we can and as we can, and leave the rest.

No, we don't mention Billy Graham in any church I attend. I believe we think he mustn't be discouraged, as he is on the side of the angels, but that it is a pity he doesn't mention the sacraments, and takes this sudden & emotional view of conversion….

I only heard a bit of Dr Matthews on Psychical research.[46]I don't see the football poolers listening to him….

'Any Questions' panel must of course know as much about conscience as we do; what is the matter is that they dislike giving serious answers to any but political questions. I think this is a great pity. I wonder if 'Any Answers' will put them right.[47] There might be letters from women who choose the dull job of living at home with invalid parents, and married people who decide to stay with their boring spouses instead of going after a more amusing one whom they love, and people who choose dull jobs because they feel they must support someone, besides from every one whose conscience tells them to write dull letters and clean the house instead of doing something more interesting and agreeable.

---

[46] 'The Churches and Psychical Research', a broadcast talk by the Dean of St Paul's, given on 9 March.

[47] In 'Any Questions?', a weekly feature in the B.B.C.'s Light Programme, 'questions of the moment' put by members of the audience are discussed by a panel of well known personalities. 'Any Answers?', a 'radio correspondence column', deals with letters from listeners to the previous week's 'Any Questions?'.

I enclose some cuttings to amuse you. The letters are about whether reporters ought to pester surgeons while they operate on Siamese twins; it seems they climbed up the walls to get a view and take photographs.[48] I am glad medical opinion is so much against them. The other cutting is about how Stephen Spender walked out.[49] Do you think it was rude? A reporter asked me after lunch why he had gone, and I said I supposed he had an appointment, as I am always purposely dull to reporters. But it seems he got on to Stephen afterwards and was rewarded. He was angry at Dylan Thomas, a friend of his, and lately dead, being read aloud for ridicule. Of course Lord Samuel should have talked about Betjeman's poetry, not the poetry he disliked. But he is over 80, and should be listened to patiently, at least at someone else's lunch party at which one is an honoured guest, as S.S. was....

Very much love.

E.R.M.

p.s. The great news is that my Car returns to me on Thursday! I can scarcely believe it—and feel it will have a collision en route

---

[48] The question of the relationship between the Press and hospital authorities was raised in February 1955 when an operation to separate confined twins was performed 'secretly', in order to avoid the sort of 'persecution' that had occurred when the Boko conjoined twins were separated at Hammersmith Hospital. On that occasion reporters and photographers forced their way into the hospital and waylaid doctors and staff, and some took photographs through windows.

[49] At a luncheon on 11 March the William Foyle Poetry Prize was awarded to John Betjeman for his book of poems, *A Few Late Chrysanthemums,* and Lord Samuel was one of the speakers. When he ridiculed the poetry of Dylan Thomas, Stephen Spender got up and left.

from Peterboro' or something.

Dearest Jeanie,

… My young Jew was surprised at the way I 'trimmed and shaped' theological doctrine, as written down in the creeds and the Prayer Book, to my own taste and needs. He thought a religion should be either accepted wholesale, as defined by its formulas, or discarded, as he has discarded Judaism. Though he admitted that most of his educated Jewish friends who hadn't discarded it only accepted it with reservations. I told him that it seemed to me nonsense about wholesale acceptance, which wasn't either necessary or usual, anyhow among Anglicans. There is no idea of his becoming a Christian, though I suppose any one might. But he seems quite happy as an agnostic.

Perhaps one day I will write that book, if I live long enough.[50] I have an intuition that I shall die in three years, i.e. in 1958, so must bustle about and do a lot of things in the time. When do *you* expect to push off? My own death is very credible to me now, tho' it usedn't to be. I must go before you, as it will be my turn first; also, I couldn't go on without Saturdays at Romford….

I thought the 'Critics' rather dull, as most of the subjects were dullish. If I had been there, I would have said that a good programme about modern Sheffield would be impossible, it is such

---

[50] Jean Macaulay does not recall what 'that book' refers to. She often used to say to R.M., 'You ought to write a book about that'.

a dreadful place, and the only possible programme would have been about it as it was once, when it was a market town set among the hills; that might have been interesting; I like towns (as they were once) recalled. No interest to be got out of steel etc., or cutlery. But it is beautiful country, only now ruined by these awful towns. I suppose a country can't be both commercially prosperous and remain beautiful, it has to choose. Just as it has to choose between cheap living, I mean low prices, such as we once had, and high wages for those who work. We have quite rightly chosen the last, so nothing will ever be cheap again. A flower shop once told me that flowers will never be cheap again because the growers now have to pay such high wages to their people. The same with books, rents, fares, everything. Luxborough House, now replaced by a new block of flats, is now asking £400 a year for flats of two rooms, kitch. & bathroom; I paid £200 for four rooms, and much better ones.

I don't approve of the new *Highway Code*, which seems to me to be aimed at letting cars drive faster. It advises users of Zebra crossings to wait for gaps in the traffic before crossing. One might wait 10 minutes for that; besides, if there is a gap in the traffic a zebra is needless, one can cross without it. I am sorry about this, as the traffic is already very bad about zebras, and this will encourage them. Also drivers are advised to switch their headlights on in badly lit streets. This makes a most dangerous dazzle and causes accidents, but of course lets the driver go faster. I think the code has a strong pro-motorist bias, whereas I regard vehicles as dangerous creatures which badly need curbing. Not a word I think (however) about pedestrians and traffic lights, which *did* need saying …

Very much love.

E.R.M.

Dearest Jeanie,

… Why is anyone shocked that God should know we aren't all equally good? I don't understand it. If he thought we were, I suppose he must see no difference between one kind of behaviour and another, in the same person at different times, which would be very discouraging. But there seem no limits to folly in thoughts about God.

I liked Fr Huddleston's article in the *News Chronicle*.[51] I'm glad he goes on hammering away at it; it may in the end have an effect, specially if the Commissioner reports to his government how shocked we all are by them here.[52] There wasn't nearly enough of that kind of outspokenness here in the thirties when Hitler was ill-treating the Jews, and the anti-Nazi Germans say that if there had been more of it we could probably have stopped it without a war. I wish the U.N. would condemn our behaviour re Cyprus; it might in the end persuade us to hand it over and let the Cypriotes determine their own fate.[53] I am not sure there shouldn't be some outspokenness about the Turks' treatment of women. I have just read a book by a young Turk about life in the country districts there, giving a very bad account of it. If they

---

[51] 'It is time we shunned South Africa' (*News Chronicle, 27 June,* 1955).

[52] Fr Huddleston quoted the South African High Commissioner in London (G. P. Jooste) as saying that 'hostile criticism *does* hurt', and commented that this was a very healthy sign, for it meant that 'at last one South African is beginning to feel … a little bit cold shouldered by civilized people'.

[53] At this time political relations in Cyprus were exacerbated by an intensification of the Eoka terrorist campaign.

have to go out with their husbands on some business, such as seeing a doctor, they have to walk several yards behind him with their shawls over their mouths, and not pass any men, or overtake any, and if they are heard to speak the husbands can beat them, and they can't even speak to the doctor, who has to be told what is the matter by the husband or son, and they may only nod or shake their heads. Tho' the law doesn't allow him to kill them, public and religious opinion does, and it is continually done with impunity. The little girls are still often married when quite small, & often ruined in health and nerves by it, as the husbands don't wait till they are older to live with them. This too is against the law, but the law doesn't seem to run much outside the large cities. We seem to need another crusade! They behave better in New Guinea, about which old Canon Benson here [at St Paul's, Knightsbridge] has just written a book[54] & has handed the MS to me to read ...

I have a poem about Trebizond in *The Times Lit. Sup.*[55]; do you see it?...

Fr Derry[56] was very pleased with the success of his appeal last Sunday week in his sermon that the congregation at Sunday early Mass should make the responses, which before that no one but me did, so far as I could hear. This Sunday there was quite a noise, and in his sermon at noon he thanked us. I told him he had better tell us to do something else now and we might do it. He might even beg us to be good, which he doesn't do enough, though his sermons are quite interesting. I wonder if I have the

---

[54] James Benson, *Prisoner's Base and Home Again: The Story of a Missionary P.O.W.* (1957).

[55] 'Dirge for Trebizond', see *The Times Literary Supplement*, 24 June, 1955.

[56] Rev. W. R. Derry, Curate-in-charge at Grosvenor Chapel.

courage to suggest this sometime. I like him very much, and he has a sense of humour.

How brave Mary Stocks is! One week she says she doesn't like cooking, another that she doesn't like watching games. I thought the clapping after this remark was very slight, and showed shock.[57]

Very much love.

E.R.M.

20, Hinde House, Hinde St, W.1
18 October, [1955]

Dearest Jeanie,

… I didn't hear the 'Critics', but shall this afternoon, and will notice what they said about the book[58]. I don't expect it is like my style; very few people judge rightly about styles; as someone once said in reviewing me, foolish people sometimes compare me in style to Jane Austen, to whom I am completely unlike in way of writing. I shall be interested to hear what this book is.

The inn which wants a plaque with my name (I don't know if it yet has it) is a tiny inn[59] on the shore at a tiny place called Puerto de Llansá, the first place I stopped at on my Spanish tour, which I describe in *Fabled Shore*. They are very proud of me, and keep a copy of my book and point out the bit about

---

[57] Mary Stocks was a member of the 'Any Questions?' panel on 24 June.

[58] March Cost's novel *By the Angel, Islington* (1955), which was discussed by the B.B.C. 'Critics' on 16 October. The programme was repeated on 18 October.

[59] The Miramar, see R.M.'s *Fabled Shore*, Chap I.

themselves to visitors, saying I sent them the book, but this is a pleasant fancy. They were charming people. I dare say Llansá is now a bustling resort, instead of a very small fishing village on the shore.

I enclose a piece from *The Times* about the C. of E. in South Africa. It seems that the schism and separatism come from that side, not from the Church of the Province.[60] They obviously regard the latter as not protestant enough for them; it was going very far to refuse the Bishop leave to confirm.[61] As they seem not to recognise the Bishops I suppose they do their own ordinations, as the Non-Jurors used to in the 18th cent. It would be interesting to read a history of their career, written from inside. They must be very narrowly protestant and probably are in communion with the Dutch Calvinist church, as well as in sympathy with the South African government policy.

I think you got Lady Pakenham wrong. Surely she said[62] you must leave by trains at the odd hours because this would show you *had* planned beforehand when to leave, whereas if you give a round number it looks as if you had just got bored and decided to go. It would *never* do to be natural, surely. If natural, one might easily say on Saturday evening, 'I am off first thing after breakfast tomorrow', before the week-end had really got going; or, if it

---

[60] The Church of England in South Africa, which developed from an evangelical minority, has always remained strictly apart from the Church of the Province of South Africa (formed by Bp Gray in 1870).

[61] In a letter to *The Times* (11 October, 1955) Rt Rev. A. B. L. Karney, former Bp of Johannesburg, reported that on one occasion, hearing that one of the so-called Church of England churches had some candidates for confirmation, he offered to confirm them, but the offer was rejected.

[62] In the 'Any Questions?' programme on 14 October.

was a cocktail party, 'I am bored, I must go now, I don't see any one I know here.' Naturalness in life must be heavily curbed….

V. much love.

E.R.M.

I have now heard the 'Critics'.[63] The book was *By the Angel, Islington,* by March Cost. John Connell said its style was like no contemporary novelist 'except possibly Miss Rose Macaulay'. Freda Bruce Lockhart said it was less like me than Stella Benson. As I've not read the book (being, like Ivor Brown, 'allergic to angels') I can't tell which was right.

8 January, 1956

Dearest Jeanie,

… I went to church this morning tho' not early. I have a slight inhibition from communicating at mid-day Mass, which is odd, as I don't at all mind a 10.30 one, though this is equally after breakfast; also, I know our vicar[64] has no objection, not being at all spikey. I suppose it must be early habit; but it is much the same to me whether I do or don't, so I don't mind. I think we are very lucky in this vicar, whom I like more and more, he is so genial & unshy & friendly; he took me yesterday after Evensong to the basement room he has to live in till the vicarage is rebuilt and gave me a drink, before I drove him to a hospital near me to see

---

[63] Freda Bruce Lockhart, Philip Hope-Wallace, Tom Hopkinson, John Connell, Eric Newton.

[64] Rev. D. B. Harris, who had become Vicar of St Paul's, Knightsbridge in September 1955.

a sick churchwarden. He is amusing company.... I keep meaning to ask him why he doesn't use women as servers, since men are so scarce. I did suggest this in a letter to Fr Johnson. He writes, 'As to your suggestion concerning servers of both sexes— *no;* it would not do at all; arrangements as to who should serve whom would be dangerously assimilated *[sic]* to the filling up of a dance programme, and for the priest it would, more often than not, be utterly distracting, worse than anything that can happen now, whether the she-server were nice or nasty. "We have this treasure in earthen vessels." Think of all these modern business offices. Do you think that sex appeal has become a negligible distraction, *or ever could,* in this world?' This seems to me to be an exaggerated view, but casts an interesting light on one of the reasons, perhaps the main reason, why women aren't allowed in the sanctuary during Mass. Perhaps the natural unfitness of women to take part in anything holy, combined with the natural egotism of men in wanting to keep it to themselves, were only secondary reasons, rationalising the main reason, which was this sexual disturbance set up in men by the proximity of a female. Apparently the primitive Church did try it, but it was soon stopped. Of course the difficulty might be got round by a rule that women servers must be elderly, like college bed-makers in Oxford & Cambridge; perhaps no one under 60, or perhaps 55. This would lessen the number of women applicants for the job. I think one difference between men's and women's sex feelings is that attraction towards the priest may easily make a woman feel more religious, while attraction towards a woman almost certainly makes the priest feel less so. Probably because male sex attraction has a far more physical basis, and more physical reactions, than with women, with whom it may be almost purely emotional and unbodily. I shall ask Fr Harris sometime what his view of employing women would be. His answer might be that it is against church tradition.

I send two cards I had overlooked, in case they are any use for children. I like the one with wolf and sheep in dangerous contiguity …

Very much love.

E.R.M.

20, Hinde House, Hinde St, W.1
20 January, [1956]

Dearest Jeanie,

… I went to the opening meeting of Union Week, where we were addressed by a R.C., an Anglican, and a Methodist.[65] All were good, but none got down to the point, which is what are the obstacles in each case, and how, if possible, surmount them. I felt the R.C. should have said about the Pope and about Anglican invalid Orders, and the Anglican should have said about episcopacy and how [to] get round it, and the Methodist about the Methodist objections. Instead of which, each spoke about their own Church, and quite well, but this wasn't the point of the meeting. Of course the ideal thing would have been if they had all said, 'We are divided by many points of difference of belief, but we should ignore them all and allow intercommunion.' All they said was, 'We must pray this week that the question of unity may be solved, in whatever way God wills.' I wanted to get up and say, '*I* know what God wills', but didn't like to. Last night I

---

[65] A meeting initiated by the Council for the Week of Prayer for Christian Unity, an Anglican body, was held in London on 20 January.

went to Westminster Cathedral where there is a course about it.[66] Last night the preacher dealt with the Orthodox Church, but this seemed pointless, as they already have intercommunion with them.[67] Tonight it will be the Anglican Church, which would be much more interesting to hear, but I can't go. The last one is very ambitious—'The Conversion of the whole world'.

I am reading Milman's *Latin Christianity from 4th Century* [68] again; that is, I don't think I ever read it all through at once before, only in parts. It is a wonderful and interesting story, and throws a lot of light on human nature, which has been more extraordinary in its dealings with religion than almost anything. I have just got to the beginnings of the cult of the Virgin. I see some Italian has written a history of this lately,[69] reviewed in the *Church Times*, which I should like to read. Obviously it was an inevitable cult. It has now reached a peak that can scarcely be heightened. The next doctrine the Pope is meditating is on her position as perpetual and essential mediatrix.[70] I was talking at the French Embassy the other day to a Dominican I know (Welsh, and very intelligent); I remarked that the Churches had, I thought, all gone very wrong about war; I thought he looked wistful, and wondered if he was wishing *he* could say that the

---

[66] During the week ending 25 January (Feast of the Conversion of St Paul) special services with sermons were held at Westminster Cathedral.

[67] The Roman Catholic and Orthodox Churches are not, in fact, in communion, though in an emergency the Sacrament can be adminstered by a priest of one Church to a communicant of the other.

[68] H. H. Milman, History of *Latin Christianity* (6 vols., 1854–5).

[69] Giovanni Miegge, *The Virgin Mary: The Roman Catholic Marian Doctrine* (trans. W. Smith, 1955).

[70] The possibility that a doctrine of Mary Mediatrix of all graces would be defined became remote after the death of Pope Pius XII in 1958.

Church had gone wrong about anything. It is a great advantage to be able to.

Two of my [nurse] friend's [trainees] … have just become district nurses instead of joining hospitals as most do. They are loving it; one thing they like is the kind way they are regarded by the public in general, not only their patients. When they run into taxis on their bicycles, or get in their way, the driver, after beginning as usual to swear at them and call them bad names, such as bitches, cows, etc., suddenly sees they are nurses and at once changes his tone, saying,'All right, ducks, no harm done; didn't see you were a nurse.' They say it is the same everywhere, in shops, queues, buses. They treat Sisters in the same way, I think. It is wonderful that their uniform can soothe even a taxi-driver's rude and savage breast. I expect you find the same. But these nurses are in London, a much less polite place than Romford….

[No signature]

20, Hinde House, Hinde St, W.1
21 March, [1956]

Dearest Jeanie,

… My godchild[71] (who is getting confirmed tomorrow) is acting Mr Bennet in *Pride and Prejudice* on Friday, and wants me to go and see it, so I said I would if she can get me a ticket. She will tell me tomorrow. I don't know how well she will act Mr Bennet, but I must see her if I can….

Gerard Irvine, who sees a lot of people who have been converted by 'accepting Christ', was explaining to me the other day

---

[71] Mary Anne O'Donovan.

what they believe. They believe that, by Christ's death, his righteousness is 'imputed' to them by God, so that their sins are covered by it, even when they sin again; once they are accepted, they are saved. This does seem to suit many temperaments; it leads to much more emphasis being put on Christ's death than his life, and very little on the Holy Spirit and the inner light. Of course as regards right living, all good religions sincerely held incline to this, according to the character of the holder; it would be difficult in Christianity to say that more right living is achieved by one kind than another. But it is certain that, for right living, each individual had better try to find the kind of beliefs that suit his own mind; if he tries to hold those unsuited to him he will make little of them. If I tried to hold the evangelical 'imputation' views, they wouldn't get me anywhere, and if a natural evangelical tried to pin his hopes and faith on the sacraments without much stressing the atonement, it would worry him. Luckily there is something for every one.

I went to a meeting of the Guild of St Raphael[72] this evening in St Paul's [Knightsbridge].... It wasn't interesting unfortunately, as there was no healing, but only a list of the 'cases' read out and how they were getting on, and they might have been any ordinary invalids, and as I didn't know any of them, I couldn't feel much interest. It would have been better to say what had been done for them by prayer, and how often, and when. I shan't join the Guild.

I think you misunderstood Gilbert Murray on pity. He really doesn't attack it, or attribute to it the worst passions of mankind, though he says it has often led to revolutions etc.... Certainly pity

---

[72] An Anglican Society for prayer in association with the Church's ministry of healing.

for the downtrodden and oppressed has often in history led to ruthlessness against the oppressors. Even at this moment, those who pity the sufferers from Communist tyranny are wishing to start a movement against the Russian visitors Krushchev and Bulganin,[73] and tyrants have often been murdered by those who are sorry for the tyrannised. So I think there is a lot of truth in it. He is himself one of the most compassionate of men.

I regret the movement for being rude to K. & B. Malcolm Muggeridge who edits *Punch* means to reproduce a cartoon of 1844 when a Czar was here who had brutally put down a rebellion, flogging people to death.[74] People were angry because he [the Czar] was received by the Queen, and they mobbed him at the Docks when he went there.[75] I told him I thought it would be a great mistake, both insulting and unwise. Obviously Georgi [Malenkov] is trying to ingratiate himself with us.[76] There is a rumour that he has been sacked from Russia and won't be

---

[73] After it was announced that the Soviet Prime Minister, Marshal Bulganin, and Mr Krushchev, First Secretary of the Soviet Communist Party, would visit Britain in April 1956, Malcolm Muggeridge led an attempt to stage a protest meeting at the Albert Hall. This meeting was not permitted, but another was held in Manchester on 26 March.

[74] This Leech cartoon 'The Latest Arrival of the Zoological Gardens' was re-published in *Punch* of 18 April 1956.

[75] When Nicholas I of Russia visited England in June 1844 he was not mobbed, but in general was received with enthusiasm. There was, however, a minority attempt to arouse opposition to him. Handbills, calling him 'a much greater tyrant than Nero or Caligula' were distributed, and a protest meeting, attended largely by foreigners, was held in London on 6 June.

[76] Georgi Malenkov, Soviet Minister of Electric Power Stations, had arrived in Britain on 15 March. During his subsequent tour he received a very favourable reception and press.

allowed to return, so will ask for asylum here; but this is probably nonsense.[77] Asiatics, such as Russians, are very mysterious, but oddly naive too. One never knows why they act as they do. Anyhow I'm glad Georgi is making friends with us, and I hope K. & B. will too.

Thursday. Just back from the confirmation, taken by Bishop Wand. He gave a nice address, much better than in 'Lift up your hearts', where he says things that mean nothing to me about propitiation and atonement, but no doubt they mean a lot to many listeners. I met Maisie Fletcher there, seeing a grand-child's confirmation ...

There was a very odd letter from a clergyman in today's *Times* saying that nowhere in the Prayer Book are Bishops said to be a necessary part of the C. of E.[78] I looked it up, and of course in the preface to the Ordination services it says just this. For a clergyman this seems a very odd mistake. I wonder if any one will point it out.[79] He also says that deacons are asked to say they 'unfeignedly believe all the canonical scriptures'. I thought this had been altered to 'Do you believe they were inspired by God?' but apparently this is only in the revised P.B.[80] I believe it is commonly used, but I suppose not always.

---

[77] The expulsion of G. Malenkov from the Central Committee of the Soviet Communist Party did not take place till July 1957.

[78] Rev. M. A. P. Wood, Vicar and Rural Dean of Islington, was writing apropos of relations between Methodists and the Church of England.

[79] No one did.

[80] In the 1928 Prayer Book the reference to the canonical scriptures in the Bishop's question is qualified thus: 'as given of God to convey to us in many parts and in divers manners the revelation of himself which is fulfilled in our Lord Jesus Christ'.

Did you listen to the play about Cranmer?[81] It was quite good. Do you think he would have recanted his recantation if he hadn't heard he was to be burnt after all. He didn't know himself whether he would have had the courage, so I suppose we can't know either.

What do you think is behind Sir Eugene Goossens's behaviour?[82]

When I get time, I shall try and get down to thinking out some theory about God's part in the universe that seems to me a possible hypothesis.

Very much love.

E.R.M.

20, Hinde House, Hinde St, W.1
25 March, 1956

Dearest Jeanie,

Thank you so much for your letter and Fr Waggett.[83] I thought I had a copy, but can't see it about. Have you [another] one, and don't you want this? It is a book I have always liked very much; quite the best I know of its kind....

We are having good addresses from Fr Harris every day [during Holy Week at St Paul's, Knightsbridge] on how to

---

[81] *The Trial of Thomas Cranmer* by Anne Ridler.

[82] On 13 March it had been announced that Sir Eugene Goossens had been temporarily relieved of his duties as conductor of the Sydney Orchestra, and the next day that he had been served with a summons for importing 'prohibited goods', later stated to be obscene films and photographs.

[83] P. N. Waggett's *The Heart of Jesus* (1902), a series of Holy Week addresses.

discover, and want to do God's will…. He suggested three ways of making decisions (all to be used together): consulting one's conscience (which should be kept in the right direction, like the needle of a compass, which, even if it has been deflected from the right direction by sin and misuse and neglect, still shows it is alive by quivering), (2) praying for guidance and reading the Bible, (3) considering the circumstances in which one is placed. Not like the married Anglican priest who, on visiting St Peter's, told his wife he felt that God had called him to celibacy. He had forgotten his circumstances. At least, Fr Harris said he had; possibly, of course, he merely didn't care for them much.

I suppose each person joining the Church or getting ordained must decide what measure of belief in creeds is necessary and honest and possible. Of course no intelligent person would worry about the 'symbols', such as ascending and descending and sitting; 'rose again from the dead' presents rather more difficulty, I suppose. 'Born of the Virgin Mary' is a fact not a symbol, of course; but I don't know if many ordinands let it worry them unduly; I hope not. The real crux is probably the second paragraph of the creed, down to 'came down from heaven'. If they can't take that, they had better not be ordained. I don't know what I should have done if I had been an ordinand. But my principle is that the less trouble they make over it the better, if they feel they would make good priests….

Fr Derry has just rung up to come in to tea this afternoon. I now have to support *2* clergymen with my Easter offerings.[84] How much for each? I can't well consult either about this.

I wish you had time & opportunity for Holy Week services. I

---

[84] Since becoming a regular worshipper at both St Paul's, Knightsbridge and Grosvenor Chapel.

got two palms on Sunday, one from each of my churches, so send you one, in case you got none.

Very much love.

E.R.M.

20, Hinde House, Hinde St, W.1
[probably 21 April, 1956]

Dearest Jeanie,

… I went to the S.P.G. Rally in Albert Hall on Tuesday evening, it was cram full and very impressive. I had been given a seat at the last moment, in a loggia, and could see and hear the platform well. There were a lot of bishops, a huge choir, Fr Huddleston and Fr Raynes[85] etc. Bish. Roberts[86] presided and introduced. Fr H. was excellent, very reasonable and persuasive.[87] I liked Dr Barker,[88] too; do you know him? I think he works among Zulus.

I feel rather sad that poor K. & B. are getting, apparently, such a chilly welcome from Londoners.[89] Hardly anyone is cheering, even when they put a beautiful wreath on the Cenotaph. I'm afraid people have been got at by Ukrainians, Poles, and papists.

---

[85] Rev. Raymond Raynes, C.R., Father Superior of the Community of the Resurrection.

[86] Rt Rev. B. C. Roberts.

[87] In his first major speech since returning from South Africa, Fr Huddleston denounced 'white supremacy'.

[88] Dr Anthony Barker, author of *Giving and Receiving: An Adventure in African Medical Service* (1959).

[89] Since Marshal Bulganin and Mr Krushchev arrived in London on 18 April, they had not been received with any public enthusiasm.

It is a pity, and makes war more not less likely. If they were sent away with friendly feelings, it would warm their hearts. They must feel envious of Malenkov; no one wants to kiss them....

V. much love.

[No signature]

20, Hinde House, Hinde St, W.1
29 May, 1956

Dearest Jeanie,

... I am *so* glad you like my foreword.[90] I was a little doubtful lest it should seem to give too solemn and religious a touch, but after all that is what it is largely about. I shall be most interested to know what you think of the whole novel when you read it; perhaps in your holidays.

Did you see a letter from a Presbyterian passionately rejecting the idea of union with the C. of E.? He said our Prayer Book was far too formal, stiff & cold. But of course union wouldn't mean using one another's forms of worship. Though I suppose for Presbyterians who really can't like our liturgy, it would be n.g. to be allowed to communicate at our services. I don't really know just what 'union' would mean, besides that.

Fr Harris preached a v.g. Ember Day sermon on Sunday, emphasising what the clergy are for, and the great need for more good ones. He said afterwards that at Bedford[91] he regularly deputed lay readers, men & women, to say Evensong when he and his curate couldn't be there. It is pitiful to see

---

[90] 'Dialogues of Mortality' in *The Towers of Trebizond*.
[91] He had been Rector of St Mary's, Bedford (1945–55).

services full of eager women communicants and perhaps a man or two but usually not (on weekdays) and such a shortage of help. It is all rather mysterious and wants analysing by intelligent psychiatrists—I mean the male disturbance at the idea of women as priests or deacons. It can't be the competitive economic reasons that apply in most professions; but it is something very deep-seated.

On Corpus Christi I am driving to Nashdom Priory, near Burnham, to take part in the Priory C.C. procession, or at least to walk behind it. If fine, it will be nice; if wet I shan't go....

Very much love.
E.R.M.

Dear old Miss Browne,[92] who must be about 95 I should think, or more, wrote a very ill-scrawled letter saying she is all-but blind now, but goes to a Blind Library in Guildford and hears books read aloud from records. What a good idea this is.

20, Hinde House, Hinde St, W.1
25 June, 1956

Dearest Jeanie,

... I have a rather full week—Africa meeting in House of Lords tomorrow, meeting at Dominican Priory Saturday, French Book Committee lunch Wednesday, de la Mare memorial service St Paul's Thursday, besides a lot of ordinary engagements. I have heard from [the] Bihar Diocesan publication society about reprinting Eleanor's book, and they are going ahead with it.

[92] See above p. 61n.

Apparently it is one of the best books on bible readings published in Bihar language.[93]

No, I wasn't hurt by my tyre burst. Tubeless tyres don't puncture easily, but, like other tyres, they blow up when cut by sharp kerbs etc. when going fast. I wobbled all over the road before I could stop, but luckily without harm, as there was nothing just behind me. Nothing can be done to prevent it except to try not to hit sharp edges with the side of the tyre....

We had a v.g. [sermon] ... yesterday from Fr Harris, about the shock of realising that one's regular prayers and communions aren't 'making a ha'porth of difference to one's behaviour or one's attitude towards other people'; his plea was that we should make them more effective, and not think them an end in themselves. I think your [ideal] Service would be very thoughtful and helpful, but would take a very long time. It would have to begin about 8.0, & not end till I.O. It would help if people made their notes beforehand, not at the time. I quite agree about the pauses. Even our sins aren't given any time to remember. The Prayer Book needs mother's rows of dots.[94] During the Offertory sentences we should think of what we are meaning to try to offer (apart from money); during the exhortation, of those of our neighbours we might not be in charity with, during the

---

[93] R.M.'s sister Eleanor (1887–1952) had devoted much of her time as a missionary in India to the translation, editing and production of books and magazines, all into Hindi. The book mentioned here is *Din-Ba-Din* ('Day by Day'), a translation of Bible notes.

[94] Grace Macaulay had taught her children to pause, when saying their prayers, so as to remember their sins. When away she left them prayer-cards, with rows of dots meaning 'stop and think'. Jean, a very literal-minded child, took the usual six dots to mean that she had to remember six sins.

thanksgiving of the good works prepared for us to walk in. There might be an annotated P.B. published, with spaces for such details.

I'm afraid you will be terribly disappointed with my novel,[95] if you expect the kind of book John the Baptist might have written. I don't think it is really reformist at all, only full of churchy chat and speculations. Next time I will perhaps write a reformist book, putting in all my plans for a better Church, and send copies to all the Bishops and important clergy. Perhaps it had better be a novel, the central character a vicar, who in the end resigns because his reforms aren't allowed, and becomes a hedge preacher.

I was reading an article the other day about the ancient Jews; how they were so wholly religious, and therefore so ready for new revelations of God, because they cared for no secular arts. Unlike the Greeks, Romans, Chinese, Persians, Etruscans, Indians, Egyptians, of the same periods, they had, apparently, no secular literature, drama, poetry, music, painting, sculpture, architecture, carving, or anything, and concentrated entirely on religion. No philosophy, even, except religious or moral. I wonder if this philistinism about the arts & culture is the best background for strong religious interests. It may be. Certainly the more artistic and cultured popes weren't very religious. I wonder how far religion and secular culture pull opposite ways, as Gregory the Great always maintained. It seems important to combine them. Of course it isn't quite true that the Jews had no secular poetry; there is the Song of Solomon, and may be some more that hasn't been preserved. But on the whole they concentrated on goodness, and on God. They seem to have outgrown this single interest now....

---

[95] *The Towers of Trebizond.*

Now I must write a review, answer 3 letters, and make my will (good works prepared for me).

Very much love.

E.R.M.

20, Hinde House, Hinde St, W.1
10 July, [1956]

Dearest Jeanie,

Here is Canon [Charles] Smyth of Westminster.[96] One sees that it is much more difficult for the unthinking than for the thinking man, who can always think of senses in which he can believe. You are wrong that a clergyman can't have both brains and integrity; I have known many with both. What he mustn't have is too literal a mind, he must be a little subtle. Dorothea writes, by the way, that she thinks bishops usually now ask the deacons the 1928 revised question.[97] I expect tomorrow there will be a lot of letters telling the Brigadier that people do go to church, not only a handful of old people.[98] …

---

[96] A letter from Canon Charles Smyth was published in *The Times* on 10 July in a correspondence on the ordination of deacons. Some correspondents maintained that many deacons were troubled in conscience at having to reply 'I do believe them' to the Bishop's question 'Do you unfeignedly believe all the Canonical Scriptures of the Old and New Testament?' Canon Smyth. pointed out that these words raise no difficulties when interpreted in the light of the Thirty-nine Articles.

[97] See above p. 185*n*.

[98] Brigadier Hanbury Pawle, in a letter to *The Times* (9 July) had stated that 'the congregations of our lovely churches are now reduced to a mere handful of old people'.

Miss Markham was v. sensible on old age.[99] She said the first thing was to face it without dismay. She mentioned the shock she had when, long ago, she was waiting for the lights to change before crossing the road, and some kind person came up and said 'Shall I help you across, ducks?' and the shock it was to a man she knows when he heard some people speaking of him as 'such a nice old gentleman'. But when one has settled down to that, she said how good & interesting life still was, and how many new things to discover all the time.

Subtopia means, I take it, the country round and near a town, which is apt to get built over and spoilt. *Topia* is Greek for place, and *sub* means near (when it doesn't mean under), as in suburb *(urbs*, town). Utopia is a *good* place, from *eu*, well.[100] I suppose Subtopia hasn't been a word long enough to get in a dictionary.

I don't go to all the P.E.N. meetings, but have some tomorrow.[101] My protégée, Sheila Davies, is greatly excited by seeing so many writers, and goes about starry-eyed, thinking it all wonderful. I tell her who they are, and introduce her when there is opportunity, so I hope she will get to know some, which is her great ambition. It is touching to see someone feeling so young about writers.

I have changed the *News Chronicle* for the *Telegraph*, which is a good deal less silly and vulgar. And I have ordered *Reynolds [News]* instead of *Sunday Express*.

---

[99] Violet Markham was then aged 83.

[100] 'Utopia' is derived from the Greek *ou* (not) and *topos* (a place), thus literally meaning an imaginary country.

[101] R.M. was assisting at a London Congress of the International P.E.N.

Wednesday. Only one letter printed today,[102] but many received. They ought to print some from the Universities.

Much love.

E.R.M.

20, Hinde House, Hinde St, W.1
July 15, [1956]
(St Swithin's, & has rained.)

Dearest Jeanie,

... I'm afraid that the 'Believe' correspondence is now over, as *The Times* had a leader about it yesterday, which is enclosed. They say that if any deacon feels the declaration a stumbling-block, it can be removed by proper instruction. It would seem simpler to change the words, but apparently this is difficult. I don't quite know how they ... have the effrontery to say that believing 'means believing that the scriptures contain everything necessary for salvation'; it is a great twisting of plain words, and certainly not what the original composers of the declaration meant. Our 1662 Prayer Book is, I suppose, the only P.B. that has this form[103]; the American one hasn't[104]; I'm not sure about the Scotch, but I

---

[102] On 11 July *The Times* published a letter from Rev. J. A. Ainger of Penrith, affirming that his congregation contained as a rule no elderly people, and included 50 per cent of the younger generation.

[103] The question as phrased in the 1662 Prayer Book was taken over verbatim from the Prayer Book of 1549.

[104] The equivalent question in the Prayer Book of the Protestant Episcopal Church is worded as follows: 'Are you persuaded that the Holy Scriptures contain all Doctrine required as necessary for eternal salvation through faith in Jesus Christ?'

think not.[105] But *thinking* young men can always think themselves out of it, no doubt. Only so many ordinands are *not* thinking young men, and they must either assent to a lie or say 'No'. If I was being ordained and the Bish. asked in what: sense I believed any particular book of the Bible, I should say 'In the same sense that you do, my Lord.' Then he would be in a hole, as he couldn't well say that wasn't enough….

We had a wet day in Cambridge yesterday, but I think the P.E.N. quite enjoyed themselves. We had lunch in Trinity great hall, where the Master kindly presided (Lord Adrian). I sat next him, and enjoyed talking to him. He and Lord Pethick-Lawrence were talking about the Lords debate on the abolition [of capital punishment] bill.[106] Both these Lords had voted for the bill. The Lords can't hold it up indefinitely, so in a year or two it will probably be passed, unless the Commons change their minds about it. After lunch I showed my new P.E.N. recruit[107] Cambridge a little, then went to part of an organ recital in King's Chapel, then she went off with half the company to a place outside Cambridge whose owners had offered us a party. I stayed behind, then about 20 of us had tea with E. M. Forster in his room. He had asked if as many as possible could be foreign delegates, and of these as many as possible dark-skinned. However, he had invited me also, and most of us were white, though I talked to a magnificent Gold Coaster and a charming Lebanese. Then I went to see Dorothea, and the rest of the P.E.N. returned to London by the coach….

———————

[105] In the Prayer Book of the Episcopal Church of Scotland the question is identical to that in the 1662 version.

[106] The House of Lords had rejected the second reading of the Death Penalty (Abolition) Bill by 238 votes to 95.

[107] Sheila Davies.

I shall find this 'believe' correspondence very useful in my Cambridge discussion with C. S. Lewis.[108] I hope some baulked ordinands will still write in and complain, saying what good clergymen they would have made.

I am re-reading Evelyn Underhill's chapter about Psychology and the Spirit.[109] It is v.g.; I mean, exactly what I think myself, about the struggling-up of man from his animal state, with all his animal desires still clinging to him. I like her quotation from St Angela of Foligno's conversation with the Holy Ghost, who said to her 'Thou art my best and sweetest bride, and I love thee better than any one else in the valley of Spoleto'.

Next Sunday at 9.30 a.m. there is a sung Mass broadcast from St Paul's, Knightsbridge, so mind you listen. I shall stay at home & listen. It is a proud moment for St Paul's, and the Vicar is delighted.

Very much love, thank goodness this Congress is over and we can sit back. The Organizing Committee is all but dead. The foreign delegates are, some of them, touchy, and envied one another's parties, places at the Dinner, length of time allowed to speeches, etc. etc. As people go, I think the British—no, the *English*—are on the whole less touchy than most, though touchy enough.

I thought the 'Lift up your hearts' speaker was wrong about the one word in which Euodias probably answered the question 'What is wrong with the Church?' I think she more likely said

---

[108] In October R.M. and C. S. Lewis were to discuss 'Some Difficulties which keep people out of the Christian Church' at the Cambridge house of the Society of St Francis.

[109] In her *Life of the Spirit and the Life of To-day* (1922).

'Syntyche' than 'I am.'[110] I thought last week's speaker very interesting. They are improving....

Very much love.

E.R.M.

20, Hinde House, Hinde St, W.1
24 July, 1956

Darling Twin,

This brings very much love for tomorrow.... I thought the St Paul's service came over beautifully, and I was glad to hear it, for once, from the outside. The music there is excellent, and the choir and choirmaster celebrated. I am very lucky to be able to have it every Sunday; I wish you had too.... Fr Harris was perhaps almost too expository, aimed too much at people who knew little about it, but this may have been useful. He did say that when the bread was broken we offered our selves and lives with it, to be broken in the service of God and of other people; but I should have liked more about the effects on our lives; I have heard him preach well about this, tho' too seldom.... Had I written it for him, it would have been nearly all about this, one could go on for some hours about it of course, but he had only 10 minutes. However, I was glad he set the scene for listeners,

---

[110] Canon Fenton Morley, broadcasting in the 'Lift up your Hearts' programme during the previous week, had taken as his theme the question 'What's wrong with the Church?' Discussing Phil. 4.2 ('I beseech Euodias, and beseech Syntyche, that they be of the same mind in the Lord'), he suggested that St Paul made mention of a private feud between the two women, hoping they would realize that their own attitude was the real answer to the question 'What's wrong with the Church?'

including the incense, which is a good thing to popularize. We now all feel that St Paul's has had a good boost, and, if it wasn't just at the beginning of the holiday months, should hope for a rush of fresh congregation. I wish you could come up some Sunday in your holiday and we could go there together....

I think the meaning of music adds a lot to one's enjoyment of it. Still, the music I enjoy most—Mozart symphonies & concertos, & Beethoven, Haydn, Bach & a few others—has no words and no meaning beyond what one feels as if was in it. And music one doesn't care for isn't really made palatable by a meaning one does care for; in fact, the music matters more than the sense. The most beautiful poetry set to dull music is no use, and much better left in words only....

I think I shall be here most of August. I wrote cancelling my voyage,[111] also told Gervase Mathew, who writes back how healthy it would be for me, but, judging from what I heard from someone who made such a trip last year, it is rather tiring. I hope I am not now past such enterprises, and that it is only this year that I don't feel quite up to it. But let's face it, we are getting old. A nice young woman offered me her seat in a train the other day. I said 'How nice of you. I don't see why I should take your seat, but I agree that I'm much older than you, so thank you very much', and she smiled sweetly and I took it. This seems the friendlier course, I think, even when one isn't tired.

Did you hear 'Lift up your Hearts' this morning? I thought it good, but I never quite liked the idea of those old rotten clouts,[112] they were probably smelly; still, I expect poor Jeremiah didn't

---

[111] R.M. had been planning a holiday cruise in the Aegean.

[112] See Jer. 38. 6–14.

mind, having been so long in that deep dirty hole, which I saw in Jerusalem.

I'm glad you are taking *Reynolds [News]* too. What do you make of the story of the doctor M.P. who was drugged and put in an asylum and certified, till his wife drank the same sherry with hemp in it and went mad too, which showed they had been drugged? He says he is now hunting for the gang who drugged him.[113] It sounded a very odd, mad story…. It surely can't be all that common to be wrongly shut up. I thought they had access to doctors continually, and could be decertified any time they were thought sane. Tho' of course I have read many novels about patients shut up by their enemies for years….

On Friday we will talk about your holiday. Dear me, what should I do without these Fridays, or Saturdays, or whenever the weekly meeting is. How very lucky it is that you are so near; you might be at the other end of England, or in S. Africa or somewhere, and then what *should* I do? As it is, provided you live as long as I do, or even longer, it is all right. All my love for the year. I shall go to Mass for you and St James tomorrow; how right it is that he should be your saint.

Now I must get on with Style in Eng. Religious Lit.[114] I am full of envy & spite, and believe that other people are the same, but not you.

Your loving Twin

---

[113] This account of the experiences of Dr Donald McI. Johnson, M.P. in 1950 was published in *Reynolds News* (15 and 22 July, 1956) when he was campaigning for the reform of the Mental Health Service. For his own account of the events in question see his *Bars and Barricades* (1952).

[114] See 'Religious Writing', an article by R.M. in a special issue of *The Times Literary Supplement* on 'The Frontiers of Literature' (17 August, 1956).

20, Hinde House, Hinde St, W.1
28 August, [1956]

Dearest Jeanie,

... I am glad you are getting on with *The Towers*, and like it.
John Connell told me today that he supposed Laurie to be a man
till the mention of Vere; he thought Vere a male name so that L.
must be female. Actually Vere, like Laurie, can be either. He likes
it, and is reviewing it in the *Evening News* soon. I also met Paul
Dehn in the street, he is on the 'Critics' just now, and says they
want to do the book, not next week, as they are doing the Edinburgh Festival, but probably the week after. We must listen to
that. I expect the two Sunday papers may do it this Sunday, or
possibly not; if so I will bring you *Sunday Times*. The reviews will
be interesting. Some people think it is mainly funny, which I
didn't mean, though no doubt a few jokes got in as I wrote. I am
a little nervous about R.C.s, tho' not really about Moslems. I had
a letter from Stewart Perowne, whom I mention in the Jerusalem
part, as he was there when I was; he is very pleased at being in a
book, and I hope the others I mention will be too; I don't say any
harm of any of them.

An odd thing seems to be happening to me, I am getting
Lower Church. Where will it end? Perhaps in All Souls', Langham Place, sitting under Mr Stott.[115] I am getting annoyed with
all these absurd extreme Anglo-Catholic ways. Not with incense
etc., but with such absurdities as [those which] Kensit mentions,
which are copied straight from Rome, and with the materialistic
view of the sacraments; I am not pleased when the bell goes during consecration. Actually I suppose it isn't Low but Broad that I

---

[115] Rev. John Stott, Rector of All Souls', Langham Place; see below p. 252.

am growing increasingly, though always pretty broad before, but now so broad that all the bowing & holding up trains that goes on at All Saints' [Margaret Street] worries me. It is time I returned to St Paul's and Grosvenor Chapel; All Saints' is too high for me.

Do you mean that 40 bombs over remote seas will make us ill in Britain? It must be stopped at once.

I am rather sorry Archbishop Mathew is abroad in the Aegean just now, when all the hierarchy must be agog to get Westminster and the various jobs that will become empty owing to the general post.[116] He should have been in the Cathedral at the Requiem, with the other bishops etc. Still, he certainly wouldn't get Westminster. I wish he would; it would be splendid for the Church.

Someone writes that my book is very persuasively Anglican. I hope it is. How splendid if it was read by chemists, who took my criticisms of unlabelled Pills to heart! It is a very silly and dangerous practice.

I shall come on Friday. I do feel pleased that you like *The Towers*. I should have been very sad about it if you didn't.

Very much love.

E.R.M.

20, Hinde House, Hinde St, W.1
10 September, [1956]

Dearest Jeanie,

… I am very glad Miss B——liked *Trebizond*, and that it both amused her and increased her sense of sin. What a lot you have

---

[116] After the death of Cardinal Griffin, Abp of Westminster.

done for her to develop and change her attitude towards life. She must be very fond of you.

I do feel glad you like the book; that matters more than any one. One this morning from——, the most enthusiastic I have had, saying it is the most 'improving' book she knows. I had a very nice letter today from the Bp of Tewkesbury,[117] ... I hadn't been sure if he'd like it, but he does. My unre-ligious friends seem to like it too; I have a lot of nice letters from them. I wonder how Gilbert Murray is getting on with it; he was going to read it to cheer himself up. I shall probably call on him when I am in Oxford, and he may tell me. I go on Thursday [to Oxford, and].... on Sunday I go on to Droitwich Spa, to keep Eric Gillett company while he swims in the briny baths; I shall be back on Tuesday. I will write from either Oxford or Droitwich....

Dorothea says she doesn't think she has improved muscularly, tho' she has learned better how to manage to do things.[118] It is very depressing for her. Still, much better than being dead, like Janet Trevelyan & so many others.

I noticed that *Trebizond* isn't going to be done on the 'Critics' next week, I believe because Veronica Wedgwood was going to do it and is off the 'Critics' this week because her father died. Perhaps she will come back the week after. Instead, they are doing *The Red Priest*,[119] which sounds an odd book....

Raymond Mortimer wants me to go on about Laurie in another book, as he liked her idiom of expression. I wonder. It

---

[117] Rt Rev. E. B. Henderson, formerly Vicar of St Paul's, Knightsbridge.

[118] Dorothea Conybeare had been partly paralysed since an accident in 1954.

[119] By P. Wyndham Lewis (1956).

would have to be about something quite different, another set of experiences and encounters, and people and animals. My camel and ape are immensely popular, by the way. It is a great thing to put in something for everyone….

Very much love.

E.R.M.

[Probably 24 September, 1956]

Dearest Jeanie,

… I am still getting some very nice letters about *Trebizond*. I get to feel almost like a priest, with so many people writing to say how much I have helped them in their religion. One writes 'That a person like you etc. should affirm publicly in August 1956 that she believes there is such a thing as sin, and that she is agin it, must hearten many also-rans who had a suspicion all along that this might indeed be so. It will enliven their endeavours to stick to their notion that "what we have to gain is not one battle, but a weary life's campaign", and that it seems, on the whole, better to wear our souls away in a doubtful attempt to see the job in hand through to the finish.'

So many people have alluded to the religious parts as improving that I think they must be, to a certain number of people, and I am very glad of that. I had a letter from Fr Johnson, but he had only got a little way, and wants to write again when he has read it all.[120] I feel he may not wholly like it; his own religion is so unquestioningly devout and single-minded,

---

[120] See *Last Letters to a Friend*, pp. 229–32.

and I don't think he had ever been troubled with doubts. I fear he may think the ape irreverent, and much of Laurie's thoughts & conversation, and other people's. I should be very sorry if he was hurt by any of it, he is so old, and has been so kind to me, and such a constant correspondent for the last 6 years.

Reviews go on coming in; the best *heading* yet was 'Mad camel plays a big part in unusual book', which seems rather to overstate the camel's part.

I hope you have time to enjoy this weather; each day begins with fog, which gradually clears and leaves warm sunshine. The trees in the parks are lovely & golden.

Very much love.

E.R.M.

20, Hinde House, Hinde St, W.1
30 October, [1956]

Dearest Jeanie,

… No, thank you, no flue. Of course if it was from the man I met at dinner last Thursday, I wouldn't start it till this Thursday, so the danger isn't over, but I don't think I shall get it, I have imbibed so much Antistin this last week. No, I certainly shouldn't let you come up, you would catch it; better feel morbid than get flue. Have you got an interesting book to read? This is the best antidote to brooding that I know. Especially a really exciting or interesting novel. If ever you are long without regular work, you must lay in a good supply of these; there are lots of them, as they needn't be new of course. But I hope you will be able to begin work again soon. If not, I can bring you down some books, and you could also begin your Reminiscences. How exciting about the Palace on the 27th![121] I had been meaning to ask you when it was to be. How early in the day, though. You will have to start about 8.0, I suppose, much too early. What a mercy it wasn't arranged for the time you were laid up! It is the chance of a lifetime. Perhaps if you had been ill, I should have been allowed to receive it for you, like posthumous V.C.s.

John Betjeman rang me up this morning to tell me that he had heard from Lady Elizabeth Cavendish, who accompanied Princess Margaret to Africa, that she (Princess M.) was absorbed in *The T. of T.* all the voyage, and kept reading bits of it aloud to her companions…. Later I met Lady E.C. at lunch, and she told me this herself, adding that all the officers on the *Britannia* had a copy with them, and all were absorbed in it: this, I think, must be an over-statement. (I didn't hear that the crew read it.) I feel this is real fame, to be read aloud by royalty. She said she would like to meet me. As a matter of fact, I have met her once, at Mark Bonham Carter's wedding reception. My head will be quite swollen if this goes on. The Cabinet, the Bench of Bishops, Royalty, half Crockford, a number of the Roman hierarchy—why not the Pope before long? Nasser too, I hope, and possibly Krushchev. It might do these last two good. I went to a meeting of Hungarian protest on Sunday,[122] all very eager & noisy. It was got up by Arthur Koestler, to express sympathy. I see that undergraduates are already dashing off to Hungary with medicines for the wounded, and having a grand time. And now Israel invading Egypt. I hear we have a battleship outside Port Said, waiting; I

---

[121] Jean Macaulay was to receive her M.B.E. at a Buckingham Palace investiture.

[122] This was four days after the outbreak of the revolutionary movement against the Communist regime in Hungary.

wish it would go away and not meddle.

I saw a splendid film yesterday, *The Battle of the River Plate*, in Technicolor. Really beautiful, & most life-like. The final self-scuttling of the *Graf Spee* was a splendid sight. So were the battleships and the ocean and Montevideo harbour. Awful killing and wounding by shells, of course, and after the battle would the captain and commanders and other officers have seemed quite so jubilant, with all that agony on board? The German commander, Langsdorff, was made a humane and nice man, who treated all his merchant-sailor captives kindly, as actually he did, fortunately....

I have a letter from Fr Johnson, much vexed with *The Times Lit. Sup.* for saying I had not so far found an answer to my religious problems.[123] He says I *have*, and that I ought to write to the *T.L.S.* and say so.

Very much love for the Saints & Souls. Can you get to church for them?

E.R.M.

20, Hinde House, Hinde St, W.1
Gunpowder Plot [5 November], 1956

Dearest Jeanie,

Thank you *so* much for my first paintbox, which seems to have every needful colour for castle, earth, rocks, sky, sea & trees.[124] The gold for the star and for the streak of dawn in the sky I can

---

[123] See *Last Letters to a Friend*, p. 23.

[124] R.M.'s Christmas card had been printed in black and white, and she was planning to colour it herself.

get in a little pot separately. Thank you so much, I hope it wasn't expensive, let me know when I come. It is hard to find the gold streak in the sky at present. Our Mass this morning at St Paul's was a requiem, praying for those who were being killed in Hungary and those going to be killed soon in Egypt, and praying very sadly for those in authority,[125] that they might behave well and wisely. But, having already behaved so ill and unwisely,[126] is there much hope of change? I understood Gaitskell to mean that the Tories should have a new P.M.[127] But, if Eden resigns, his government would and there would have to be an election. After all, the whole Cabinet was involved in this madness, and not one of them has resigned so far; Nutting wasn't in the Cabinet, of course.[128] The Universities are being useful in protesting; so are the clergy. Canon Collins rang me on Friday night at 10.30 about the protest Christian Action had drafted for the Press; he sent it me later, and I made some suggested alterations, which several people are doing. Of course it won't affect anything, but I think the more Christian protests are made the better. Of course the R.C.s will be too full of Hungary to bother much about Egypt, except for a few individuals, such as Lord Pakenham, Christopher Hollis, and any Liberal or Labour ones. *The Observer* was v.g., and said all we wanted. I think the opposition is so wide & strong that Eden can't go on with it long….

What nonsense [some people do] … talk. It sounds so second

---

[125] i.e. Anthony Eden and his Cabinet.

[126] In deciding on Suez intervention.

[127] Hugh Gaitskell, Leader of the Opposition, had called for Anthony Eden's resignation in a broadcast speech on 4 November.

[128] Anthony Nutting, Minister of State for Foreign Affairs, had resigned on 3 November because of the Government's Suez policy.

hand, the kind of thing the clergy repeat in pulpits, that the one thing God can't forgive is despair. Why should it be? And how ... [is one to] know, anyhow? When one sees the appalling things done all the time, despair seems a very mild offence. I should say God would far rather Eden despaired than attacked Egypt. I hope E. *will* now despair a bit, after all that has been said about him. I rather wish the Labour members wouldn't behave like angry taxi-drivers, all that booing, cat-calling and gesticulating. Still, I suppose most of them are brought up to be expressive when angry, and it adds colour to the scene. I'm glad we get these frequent news bulletins. Each time I hope we shall hear Eden's voice apologising and saying he sees he made a terrible mistake and has ordered the immediate recall of planes & troops, since he sees that people don't mostly like it. But they say that being attacked makes him more obstinate, and the troops seem to be 'getting on very well', as the [*Evening] Standard* puts it.

My Xmas card verses aren't very good, still they are about the picture, and about Christmas.[129] I foresee not sending any of them, if this war develops. Already people are raiding petrol, in case of rationing. A few more oil-pipes cut, and we are for it. Then I shall have to go to weekday Mass next door at the R.C. church, usually, as walking a mile each way so early is too tiring, and

---

[129] On R.M.'s 1956 Christmas card a castle fortress, with one large star above it, was accompanied by this verse:

> *Urbs ad montem*, wearing as a crown
> *Castrum in rupe*, the walls falling down;
> *Portae sine clavibus*, the gates swing wide;
> *Turbae jucundissimae* throng inside
> *In Nativitate Domini*, the dark of Christmas Day,
> And *Oriens, splendor Lucis*, lights their way.

bicycling too chilly. But I can't really believe in a war, can you? I *think* it will be over in a week or two—tho' the disgrace won't.

Very much love.

E.R.M.

20, Hinde House, Hinde St, W.1
[4 December, 1956]

Dearest Jeanie,

… I return this foolish Postal Order, as, if we *are* to begin paying one another for all hospitality received, I owe you far more than this for all my fish dinners at Romford. I won't start discussing whether you really think we should all pay each other for hospitality, as I am sure you don't. If we started that, I should be ruined soon, with all the lunches, dinners, drinks etc. that I go to with people. I don't even repay them in kind, as I seldom give parties myself; I ought to more. I am now just going out to lunch at the Café Royal, then tea at St Paul's Deanery with the Dean,[130] and later dinner at someone's house, so it would, according to you, be an expensive day for me. The only thing I shouldn't pay for is the *Messiah* in St Paul's after tea, which is free. Princess Margaret will also be at tea *& Messiah*. I shall sit far back and leave early, as the *Messiah* is too long.

… [Dorothea] certainly does plenty of thinking about *T. of T.* I don't know where she finds that Laurie and Vere were getting tired of each other; they weren't, actually.

---

[130] Very Rev. W. R. Matthews.

The Doubt man was good last week.[131] Now we have Bp Wand who looks for the Second Coming any minute, which must make life most exciting for him. I expect he hopes for it before his death, which would save him a lot of bother about his will, tidying up etc. I should like this too, but have no hopes for it. It would be so nice all to go out together, as by nuclear bomb only more so. He sounded as if he had no doubts about it. I wonder how many people think this.

I expect Miss B——knows far more than I do about how to take a Greek course, as she has been a teacher. Does she know any Greek yet? I wonder if she has night schools or Polytechnic courses within reach; if not, I suppose she could do it all with books. It seems a very good idea. My Greek is slight, but I should like to improve it if ever I get time. Today we celebrated Clement of Alexandria, with a good lesson on Wisdom, which was his great theme. But of course he's not a classic. It is useful to have the Loeb translations of Homer, Aristotle, Plato, Thucydides, etc., where the Greek is printed down the page parallel with the English, so it is easy to follow.

I enclose the *Times* sermon, good; (stickiness on back is where my pot of gold paint stood on it while I painted my card. I must bring some on Friday to do; I get on very slowly, and shall never do all; many recipients will be Goats, who only get a plain card.)

I may get a cold tonight; tiresome hostess rang up to say they both have bad colds, and did I mind? I said was it flue, because I wouldn't come if so; she said no, only colds; so I shall inhale Antistin before & after & trust in God, who I hope will play up.

---

[131] Rev. Leslie Tizard had spoken on 'Dealing with our Doubts: Finding the cause' in the 'Lift up your Hearts' programme.

Very much love…. People have gone petrol-mad, and there are long queues at every garage, great bitterness, great bribery.

E.R.M .

27 December, [1956]

Dearest Jeanie,

I got home yesterday afternoon in good time, fortified by a delicious cup of soup made by Nancy from genuine chicken. I feel like a man I heard saying in a shop this morning 'Yes, thank you, I had a nice Christmas. Quiet, you know, but plenty to eat. Now I have to spend the week working it off.' I feel like that too, after all your delicious food, especially the Xmas dinner. I've not yet worked that off, tho' I went out this morning to 7.30 Mass at St James's near me, & have since been trying to clear the flat of Xmas litter. R.C. Mass is much less congregational than ours, the people don't even join in the creed, and the priest mutters it; it would be more audible in one of the side chapels, no doubt. But on the whole I feel the Reformation was an improvement, especially now that it has, in this country, righted itself a little and allows of attractive services. Though, if I had to choose between the type of C. of E. in St Paul's, Portman Square, close to me, and an R.C. church, the R.C. would win every time….

I am worried about you, and shall be until I hear that you can stop work. Do let me know when you hear.[132] Nancy is much worried too. She doesn't think you are at all well.

One thing I hope you will never worry about *at all* is money. I,

---

[132] Jean Macaulay insisted on continuing work after her retirement (at the age of 74) until the District Nurse who was to replace her had actually arrived.

as I said, would like, if you will let me, to take over all your current covenants. (Not of course officially, but I would pay you the money.) Will you consider this, and tell me how much they are. Remember I have oodles of money, and they are all things I would wish to subscribe to (presumably). Please let me know how much it would be, when next I come. It is a serious thing to be deprived of one's salary suddenly, having already made commitments.[133] If you got into touch with my brokers ... they would do a lot in the way of improving your finances, selling one thing to buy a better thing, etc. etc. It is worth while ...

Except Alan Pryce-Jones, who spoke up for me, the speakers on novels last night didn't care for mine,[134] they thought it facetious and didn't like religion, sin etc. in novels. Of course some people don't, though so many people do that it was unlucky my getting these. They didn't like 'High Anglicanism', or jokes about it....

[The end of this letter is missing]

20, Hinde House, Hinde St, W.1
26 January, [1957]

Dearest Jeanie,

... I thought the 'Lift up your Hearts' this week rather poor. I hoped he was going to deal with the difficulties and attempts at

---

[133] Jean Macaulay had forfeited her District Nursing pension when she went to do missionary nursing in South Africa in 1936.

[134] Graham Hough, Anthony Quinton, and Alan Pryce-Jones discussed *The Towers of Trebizond* in a broadcast on 'Recent Novels' on 26 December.

reunion, and hopes for the future, not with six men who only started World Councils etc., or did mission work. He didn't even give Temple's views on intercommunion. Year after year they go on fiddling round the subject, never getting anywhere. This evening I may go to the … church with the spiteful remark about South India on the door, as there is a good man preaching, though I wouldn't if I were he. It would be wonderful if he broke out about how unchristian such an attitude is. The vicar couldn't stop him of course.

I have been asked by two bishops to write a play about the Church of the Future, for acting at a congress at Cheltenham in October. Of course I shan't. I get asked to do the oddest things now. I wasn't asked to give my views on Immortality in the *Sunday Times* series, and shouldn't anyhow have done it. I enclose Dorothy Sayers, which is rather interesting.[135]

It was nice to see Mr Carpenter[136] again on Friday evening. He is nearly 80 now, but very little changed. He has retired from being Dean of Exeter, and lives near it and lectures & writes. It was to him that I made my last confession, in 1921 or 2, before giving it up for 30 years. He always had a very nice sense of humour, and tells amusing stories about people.

Rebecca West has sent me her new novel,[137] & I have partly read it. It is very well told and interesting. I must write to her now….

---

[135] A series of articles by well-known people of different beliefs, giving their views on Immortality, began in the *Sunday Times* on 6 January, 1957. The first article, 'The Great Mystery about Heaven and Hell', was by Dorothy Sayers.

[136] Rev. S. C. Carpenter (1877–1959).

[137] *The Fountain Overflows.*

Be careful, it is getting colder.

Very much love.

E.R.M.

20, Hinde House, Hinde St, W.1
3 March, 1957

Dearest Jeanie,

I thought you might like to see the Pope's latest medical pronouncement.[138] Also, the *Times* Saturday sermon, and the account of the wave of R.C. conversions. They are really rather striking. I put them down mainly to a desire for novelty and change, as more exciting than the familiar C. of E. and dissent. Will Britain become a popish country? Much more so than at present, I think. But, in about 50 years, that too will be familiar, and there may be a swing back towards C. of E. People do like a change. And it's much more important to most people to have an interesting religion, with plenty of fuss and doings and pageantry, than one they can really and truly believe with their reasons. Will they get some C. of E. churches back, I wonder. Better give them some than let them stand empty. It will be interesting if it becomes really fashionable in all classes. The fresh influx of converts may in the end have a modifying effect on the doctrines taught.

I went to evening service at All Saints' [Margaret Street] today, & came in for an adult baptism, but was too far away to see how it was done. They had the whole baptism service, and

---

[138] Pope Pius XII had stated the Roman Catholic Church's teaching on the use of anaesthetics, hypnosis, and other pain-killing methods.

the candidate said she renounced them all, and all this she faithfully believed. After it the vicar preached about it, and how it was a new life; it seems she had for some time worshipped there, but hadn't been a Church member. Next Sunday she will be confirmed, so then she will be all set for the Christian life. The vicar said that however often she might sin in future, she can seek forgiveness and be restored. I gathered he thinks it little use to seek forgiveness if not baptised. I wonder if she found it embarrassing to be preached about, but perhaps she liked it, and it was her finest hour. It's a pity most of us have it too young to feel pleased or new; I think baptism should really be at 8 or 9, when they can understand it; it might be a great romance and fresh start, and they would be too young to be sceptical, as one sometimes is at confirmation. Mother would have made us very enthusiastic about it.

What a marvellous spring day, the March sun feels like May. I hope you have enjoyed it by bicycling about a little. I ran my new car about round the parks, and took two nice young Germans from the Embassy a little way.[139] They had come to St Paul's, [Knightsbridge] as they have discovered Anglicanism and are enthusiastic about it. I introduced them to the vicar[140] after Mass. One of them said 'What a charming man: he reminds me of a witty Jesuit priest I know in the Rhineland.' In the Rhineland he said they dance all Shrove Tuesday, after being shriven. We told the vicar he should introduce Ash Wednesday ashes at Mass; he wasn't sure if the curate would like it, or if all the congregation

---

[139] Helmut Rueckriegel and a friend.
[140] Rev. D. B. Harris.

would.[141] I am sending you *Time and Tide*, with my Lent article in it,[142] as it may be helpful....

I must sit up a little later in Lent, to get my Hour[143] done as well as everything else. Is this the fast that I have chosen? Perhaps it ought to be going to Mass at 7.30 instead of 8.15 or 8.30; but I draw the line at that. Did you hear a talk about being 70?[144] People seem to feel they are very old at 70. I don't, at all, tho' I know I am.

Very much love.

E.R.M.

19 March, [1957]

Dearest Jeanie,

... I send your sermon ration for the week, including one of the Survival series by an Indian.[145] I am using up some of my daily Hour by copying out Fr Waggett's Holy Week addresses, that I began last year....

I wonder why poor Tilsley cut his throat[146]; I suppose a mental breakdown. I can't believe that any one in his sense[s] would

---

[141] Since this letter was written he has in fact introduced Ash Wednesday ashes. There have been no complaints from anyone, and much appreciation has been expressed.

[142] 'Lent Habits', *Time and Tide*, 2 March, 1957.

[143] R.M. was trying to give an hour a day to devotional reading and prayer.

[144] Probably a broadcast talk by Minnie Pallister in the 'Home for the Day' programme on 3 March.

[145] 'The Reality of Self', by Arabinda Basu, see *Sunday Times*, 17 March.

[146] Frank Tilsley, author and broadcaster, was found dead at his home, with a breadknife nearby, on 16 March.

choose that way, it would be so difficult and painful, and there are so many easy ways….

Did you hear a discussion on the 3rd programme about imprisonment the other day? I was invited to hear it, at the Aquinas Centre[147]; I never think those Disputations are v.g. It seemed to shirk the point of punishment, they talked about 'restoring the moral law', when surely the point is deterrence and prevention….

Very much love.

E.R.M.

When you feel quite recovered, can you come up one day to tea, to meet Susan Lister, who wants to meet you? She is a very charming person; she lectures on theology at King's College (London) and does a lot of speaking to women's meetings, etc.

20, Hinde House, Hinde St, W.1
24 March, [1957]

Dearest Jeanie,

Here is the fridge cheque; I'm *so* glad you are having one at last. It is necessary for the healthy life. I suppose it is guaranteed for a year, so that if it goes wrong it will be put right free. I find mine an [in]estimable benefit….

This morning, as we came out of St Paul's [Knightsbridge]

---

[147] 'The Purpose of Punishment', a 'Medieval Disputation' between Rev. Laurence Bright, o.p., and Very Rev. Ian Hislop, o.p., was broadcast on 14 March from the Aquinas Centre at the Priory of St Dominic, Haverstock Hill.

after High Mass, there was a row of men with sandwich boards picketing us, saying 'The Mass is a Blasphemous Fable ...' 'The C. of E. has no Priests', etc. etc. Perhaps to show that, though J. A. Kensit died the other day, his soul goes marching on.[148] I see we are far from union yet. Nothing would bring those men into St Paul's, except to make a row....

Very much love.

E.R.M.

31 March, [1957]

Dearest Jeanie,

Here are your sermons. When do [you] see Dr S——[149] again? I do hope he will give you something better for your blood pressure. It is one of my chief worries in my small-hours anguish, and I always hope to hear it has gone down.

Another lovely day. Too good to sit answering letters all the afternoon, but they lap about me like a great rising tide, looking awful as they toss about like white breakers, and [I] expect to drown in the end.

Now I have to go out, so n.g. writing any more. It *was* nice seeing you yesterday. Do take care of yourself.

V. much love.

R.

---

[148] J. A. Kensit (1881–1957) was the son of John Kensit, founder of the Protestant Truth Society. He took over the Secretaryship of the society on the death of his father in 1902.

[149] Jean Macaulay's general practitioner.

11 April, [1957]

Dearest Jeanie,

... I will go to Venice if you can get Dr S——when you see him next to tell you exactly how he thinks you are, blood pressure, arteries, and all. *Or* if you will give me leave to write and ask him, telling him that I have your leave, and that I much want to know before I go to Italy. I shan't, of course, write to him behind your back, as he probably wouldn't tell me—or anyhow he ought not to. If I can't get a satisfactory report, I shan't go. I shouldn't enjoy myself. When you do see him again?...

I am sending this week's *Listener* with another of Ronald Gregor Smith's talks[150]; not so good as the last one, I thought. Will there be an end of all such talks, when the 3rd Programme is shortened, the Home adapted to the Light, the Light vulgarised even further than now, 'with more emphasis on light music, and less on the spoken word'?[151] And a new programme, the Network [Three], which will be about pigeons, mostly (why?).[152] The whole object is to compete with the popularity of Television, as well as economy. It is a sad surrender to Vulgar Taste, and time we went. Another example of surrender to V.T. was in that very vulgar ... article by a Canadian woman in the *News Chronicle* about 'the English woman',[153] how she has no mind, no

---

[150] A series of four broadcast talks for Lent entitled 'The New Man'.

[151] A new B.B.C. policy of providing 'more relaxation and entertainment' had just been announced.

[152] 'Network Three' was being planned to cater for 'specialized interests', among which pigeon-fancying was specifically mentioned.

[153] 'Let's face it, Madam, you're a Mess!' by Solveig Peters, *News Chronicle*, 9 April, 1957.

conversation, is short & broad, can't dress or do her hair, can't walk, but hobbles along holding on to someone else, and smells. How *can* the N.C. publish such low, silly … stuff?

V. much love.

E.R.M.

Maundy Thursday [18 April, 1957]

Dearest Jeanie,

… I am having very crowded days this week. I went out of London yesterday to Gerard Irvine's parish,[154] to see a performance of *Everyman*, done by his parishioners in modern dress. I drove John Betjeman down, and the young German[155] from the Embassy who is so interested in High Anglicanism; he was delighted with J.B., who could tell him a lot of things. He himself is a high Lutheran; he says the Lutherans are getting higher, and have now widely adopted confession. But he says they aren't yet so high as our high churches. I thought the *News Chronicle* survey very prejudiced against the C. of E.[156] John Betjeman says it is nonsense that they don't make a lot of converts, and that they make more than Rome does. But of course Rome makes many.

---

[154] Cranford, Middlesex.

[155] Helmut Rueckriegel.

[156] The *News Chronicle* had commissioned the Gallup Poll to enquire into the religious beliefs and practices of the British. Their findings were summarized in three articles (15–17 April), the first headed 'Pagan Britain? Nonsense*. The second stated that 'the Church of Rome is holding on to its members to a far greater extent than is any other church; it is making more converts than any other church … About the Church of England only one conclusion is possible—it is in a parlous state.'

Patrick McLaughlin (Rev. Fr) says there is 'a wave of Tertullianism' in the Universities—i.e. *'credo quia impossible,'* and of course that takes them to Rome; quite a good thing for them, I think, though madly irrational. The *N.C.* says we are snobbish. Do you think we are?...

The new play (by the angry young man) that I saw last night was quite amusing,[157] and full of angry cracks against Church and State, Suez & Eden—I thought how awkward for them if he died now,[158] they would have to cut some of them out. It is very Left wing and class conscious. I must go out to Tenebrae[159] now....

Very much love.

E.R.M.

... I have some v.g. American reviews of *T. of T.*

27 April, [1957]

Dearest Jeanie,

... Here is the *Times* sermon, rather good on survival; how much better it is when preachers don't seem too sure.[160] The other

---

[157] John Osborne's *The Entertainer* at the Royal Court Theatre.

[158] Anthony Eden had just undergone a serious operation.

[159] A service said on the last three evenings of Holy Week.

[160] See *The Times*, 27 April, 1957: '... Survival of death, if it be a fact, is immeasurably more likely to be a God-given attribute of man's nature than either a reward of his virtue or dependent upon acceptance of any form of orthodox belief—to be a fact no more determined by such considerations than is birth into this life. Herein the Christian tradition, as against theories of "conditional immortality", is sound in insisting that it is not survival but

is a fuller account than the *News Chronicle's* of the bishops' protest. What a sensation if they were whipped![161] That would really lead to a crisis....

I have to go out to supper to-night, so shall miss the last part of the discussion on the Resurrection,[162] and the whole of 'What is an educated man?'[163] Remember to listen. I shall be home for Lionel Trilling (who is v.g.) on *Emma*....

V. much love.

E.R.M.

5 May, 1957

Dearest Jeanie,

... I decided that the *Life* of Baring-Gould[164] wasn't worth sending after all. It got rather dull, and I don't think is worth your time reading it. I forgot to say when I saw you, you might perhaps do some writing. It is such an absorbing way of spending one's time, when one has any. Nothing makes one happier and more

---

the nature of the life which survives that is determined by earthly probation.'

[161] The Anglican Bishops of South Africa had issued a formal protest against a new law prohibiting Church attendance by Africans in white Urban areas. They thereby risked liability to a fine of £500, 5 years in prison, or whipping.

[162] A broadcast discussion between Bible scholars as to what the New Testament writers really meant when they spoke of 'Jesus Christ being raised up'.

[163] A discussion between Noel Annan, Stuart Hampshire, and Prof. P. B. Medawar.

[164] W. E. Purcell, *Onward, Christian Soldier* (1957).

interested. Reminiscences, essays on this or that, thoughts on this & that (religious or secular). I find it a good way of meditating, to jot down ideas that occur to one on prayer, the Prayer Book, the Church, religion, or just ideas & descriptions of things seen or imagined. Or, of course, stories. I wish you would do some of this, now you have more time. Not for publication, but just as a form of interesting occupation. I couldn't do without it, however purposeless my writing extrinsically was; it helps my mind. Even reviews of books one has been reading. Do try it. For one thing, it makes the worries and anxieties of actual life slip into the background, except when they are very acute and absorbing, when writing rather deserts one unfortunately.

I have just been lunching with my German friend from the Embassy, who is very interesting & amusing company. I always enjoy his accounts of the various types of church service in Germany and elsewhere. This morning he came to Mass at St Paul's, Knightsbridge. Now I must get on with the endless business to do before I go tomorrow, including packing. I get stupider and stupider at all this kind of thing….

I shall be with friends in Venice, who will tell you at once if I am not well or become drowned or anything. Dear love always.

R.

[Venice][165]
Wednesday 9 May, [1957]

This is our pretty and economical small hotel[166]—such nice

---

[165] Postcard.

[166] *Pensione La Calcina* (Ruskin's House).

proprietress and staff. Journey was tedious, but it is lovely to be in Venice, walking about the little streets and bridges and by the little green canals. It is May, the *Mese Mariana,*[167] so a lot of fuss in the St Mary churches. We just missed a great procession to crown the Madonna del Salute, close to our inn. R.C. Church must be the most charming of the Great Myths, and the most ornate. Were I an atheist, I would join it, instead of the reasonable and sensible Anglican Church. But not in England; it would have to be in Italy, and preferably Venice. England cramps & stunts it & makes it priggish & smug & tiresome. Very cold yesterday, but today lovely sunshine, though cold wind still. Very much love. Write soon how you keep.

E.R.M.

La Calcina, 780 Zattere, Venice
15 May, [1957]

Dearest Jeanie,

… I'm glad the Christian Action letter about South Africa got into [*The] Observer*[168] I'm also glad to see that Canon Collins preached against hydrogen bombs. There is a letter in yesterday's *Times* supporting him strongly, which I enclose.[169] It is brave of Canon C, as it may mean he isn't promoted in the Church.

---

[167] '*The* month *of Mary*'.

[168] A letter appealing for funds to provide aid for those accused in the South African Treason Trial (signed by R.M., Canon Collins, and eighteen others) was published as an advertisement in *The Observer* on 12 May.

[169] A letter from John Mannering deploring that 'there are not more Church leaders like Canon Collins who are prepared to condemn this crime against all creation'.

Stepney will be excellent in Cape Town[170]; but he will be missed here…. I heard a rumour about the *News Chronicle* and *Daily Herald* and hoped it wasn't true,[171] as it would mean the end of the only London Liberal paper (wretched as it now is) and of course the Trades Unions would run it completely on Socialist lines. Little by little Liberalism recedes from view.

It is *lovely* summer weather here, really hot, and sun all day. We are v. lucky. Did you see the total eclipse of the moon on Monday evening? I am enjoying Venice very much. The two people I am with are v.g. companions. We did a lagoon expedition one day, and another today to Murano & another island. We wander about Venice looking at the lovely little canals and narrow streets, visit the beautiful churches and the beautiful picture museums. Yesterday I climbed to top of the Campanile, marvellous view.

The nights are very beautiful, with all the lights shining across the canals. On Sunday I went to 8.30 mass at the English Church, which is quite near—a nice service in a rather bleak little church which has a tabernacle on altar but no crucifixes. A Methodist girl from New Zealand spoke to me outside and asked me if I thought she could 'take communion' tho' not confirmed. I said of course, and she did. Talked to-day to a nice old retired surgeon called [W. G.] Howarth, 78, who was at King's when Uncle W. was tutor[172]; we knew a lot of the same people, and he and his wife had just read *Trebizond*.

_____

170 The appointment of Rt Rev. Joost de Blank, Suffragan Bp of Stepney, as Archbishop of Cape Town had just been announced.

171 There were rumours of an impending amalgamation of the *News Chronicle* and *Daily Herald*.

172 W. H. Macaulay was Tutor at King's College, Cambridge, 1902–13.

Lunched yesterday with a v. rich American woman[173] who lives in a palazzo with a gondola and motor boat ...

> Very much love, and love to Nancy.
>
> R.

La Calcina, 780 Zattere, Venice
18 May, [1957]

Dearest Jeanie,

... There seem to be bad storms everywhere but here—people killed in Texas and in Dagenham by lightning etc. We had a little rain yesterday morning, but it cleared up, and now is gloriously hot and sunny again. We have now done most of the essential Venice things, including two lagoon trips. We spend a lot of time strolling about the streets, admiring the things we see. Tomorrow is Sunday again, so I am going to the English church at 8.30. I'm glad we attend more to our Mass than the R.C.s do, and don't make the priest run straight on by himself [saying for instance] 'The Lord be with you, And with thy spirit' etc., which sounds so silly.

They are going to drop *another* H. Bomb soon, this time in the Pacific.[174] I think the whole thing is kept going by scientists, who are interested in developing fresh ways of making the things. It is interesting that nearly all the arguments against it seem to be that it will make us and our children unhealthy—nothing about whether it is right to do such hurt to other

---

[173] Miss Peggy Guggenheim.

[174] In May and June 1957 three British tests of 'nuclear devices' (hydrogen bombs) were carried out, all in the Pacific.

people. But I expect Canon Collins preached about that.

Very much love.

E.R.M.

La Calcina, 780 Zattere, Venice
22 May, [1957]

Dearest Jeanie,

... I am saddened by Gilbert Murray's death. Of course one ought not to be, at his age, and with that magnificent life behind him, and all the things he has enriched us with; but his going leaves the world a poorer, meaner, less idealistic and civilised place; besides, I was very fond of him, and he was very kind and friendly to me always. He wrote such good letters, full of the work he was doing, and sometimes of my books, and sometimes just friendly notes about nothing much. I always loved talking to him. And his wonderful scholarship and good works have never, I think, been so united in any one. He was a man in a thousand, both in intellectual and moral gifts, and the use he made of both. I hope they'll bury him in the Abbey. Meanwhile his memorial service isn't till June 5th, so I can go to it. Will the Oxford University Church contain all those who want to be there? I shouldn't think so. I must be early.... I hope [the service will be taken by]... either the Bp of Oxford[175] or the Dean of Christ Church.[176] ...

The Bishop of Tewkesbury, who is in Venice for 3 or 4 days with his wife and two friends, whom I met yesterday, has invited the Clergy wives of his diocese to a garden party at Cheltenham

---

[175] Rt Rev. H. J. Carpenter.
[176] Very Rev. John Lowe.

on June 18th, 'to meet Miss Rose Macaulay', as I rashly some time back said I would go, not thinking I should be printed on the invitations. They won't know why they are to meet me, and it will be rather embarrassing for them, I think. I shall pretend I am an archdeacon's widow....

The Times has a splendid page about G.M., and some good lines by Masefield about him....

V. much love.

E.R.M.

*La Calcina, 780 Zattere, Venice
26 May, 1957*

Dearest Jeanie,

Sunday again—how the days race by.... I went out to the English Church at 8.30. Certainly the R.C. Church comes out well in comparison with our bleak little unadorned church and rather plain Prayer-Book service—*how* we have improved on that in the last half century! I don't like leaving out the Prayer of Oblation, as we did this morning; it is so very good. Nor any of the other 'strict P.B.' uses. I went to a very beautifully sung Vespers in St Mark's, and a nice evening Mass in the Gesuati,[177] close here. [Two Roman Catholic friends of mine] ... (whom I met at lunch yesterday) ... he a convert, she born ... said the indulgences and miracles etc. don't bother them; they regard them as only meant for very simple people, and by-pass them altogether. I think it would be rather bothering to have a lot of things like

---

[177] The Church of the Gesuati (Santa Maria del Rosario).

that taught, which one had to by-pass as only meant for the simple. I think it is a mistake to teach the simple (who will believe it) that saying certain prayers and making certain pilgrimages will let them off so many years of purgatory. And if the priests who teach it don't believe it (though no doubt the simpler priests do) it seems to me wrong. I should say that what [my two friends] … believe seems much what we do, on the whole, except for the Pope, and a modified view of transubstantiation. I also met at lunch a delightful old Italian colonel, who doesn't speak any English, with whom I talked about what he calls 'government by the priests', whom he hates. He is R.C. by birth and bringing up, but a great anti-clerical. He says he supposes the priests are rather better than Communist rule; but he would like himself to be an Anglican, which he regards as *'moderate, gentile, educato'*, but, he said, it would be silly for an Italian to join it.

Tuesday I lunch with [my Roman Catholic friends] … and go a trip round Venice in their gondola. Tomorrow I have a trip in the Guggenheim motor launch, I hope to an island. Tuesday evening I go to *Titus Andronicus*, which Laurence Olivier is bringing to Venice for 3 days. Then on Wednesday morning I start home, arriving Thursday evening. Friday I hope to come to Romford….

I had a lovely day going to Asolo on Friday, driving in a car with Victor Cunard, to lunch with Freya Stark, who has a beautiful house & garden. Venice tends to get almost as sociable as London, after a few days in it. Of course it is a place everyone comes to, and one is liable to meet friends both visiting it and living in it. But what I like *much* best is walking about it alone, seeing all the little streets & canals & bridges & squares & churches—every step brings one to some fresh beauty; it's like living in some lovely poem. What a pity you can't be here with me. I shall miss it terribly when I am back in London, and have to step out into ordinary ugly streets, & no glimpses of green canals and little bridges and campos....

Very much love.

E.R.M.

[London]
[13 July, 1957]

Dearest Jeanie,

... Here is the *Times* sermon for last week[178] (v.g.); today's didn't seem much good, so I haven't sent it, it's about the redemption of creation in the end, including cruel animals, so I didn't think you'd care for it.[179] I don't myself care for sermons or prayers about creation of the world, as I can't suppose the world did anything but grow out of chaos, or that God was responsible.

I was shopping a little this morning, and looking at clothes, but only began after 12, when they were just going to shut; I saw no dresses I thought would do for you. If I were you I would come up and look at some materials in John Lewis's, which is the best for these. I saw some nice navy rayon etc. with white spots, which would look very nice, and if you had the top part made buttoning down the front and overlapping the skirt, would have the appearance of being outdoor, so would be suitable for street wear. If you decided to come up, I could meet you anywhere and make

---

[178] *'Laborare est Orare:* Sanctity in the Secular' *(The Times,* 6 July, 1957).

[179] 'The Redemption of Nature: Glory in the Coming Age' *(The Times,* 13 July).

suggestions. I also have a few things that might do, if you liked them; a grey costume (skirt & jacket) which looks quite nice, if you liked it. If you take a little pains, you will be a very well-turned out woman soon. I hope you won't think this too tedious a fuss; but I think it's nice to be dressed much like other people, which is all I aim at myself. Of course you would always look nice in yourself whatever you wore. Dorothea said once that the Croppers[180] used to chivy her about her clothes, which, she said, never fitted properly because she got them ready-made and they hung loosely on her. Alfred[181] too used to nag her about them, as he liked her to look nice when she came to Eton. Still, it is people's own affair how they dress, unless they are the parents of children at school and visit them. Dress has never been a gift in our family; neither father nor mother had it. Do you remember Cape's at Oxford?[182] Looking back, I see we were dressed most eccentrically.

Do you think a priest should break the seal if a murderer had confessed his crime, but wouldn't tell the police, and an innocent man was going to be hanged for it? Someone says that they can get dispensation to tell, in such a case…. Some one wrote to a paper to say that a priest is bound never to act on information received in confession, and that if someone confessed that he belonged to a gang who meant to murder the priest and his family and were waiting for them on the road they usually went home by, the priest mustn't even change the route because of it. Still, I think he certainly would. Ought he to lock up his money if

---

[180] Her cousins.

[181] Alfred Conybeare, Dorothea's brother, who was an Eton master.

[182] A drapery shop where R.M.'s mother often bought clothes for the Macaulay children when the family lived in Oxford.

someone confessed he was given to stealing it when it lay about? I suppose not. It seems confessions must be quite forgotten and ignored. *I* should have thought the priest ought to remember them, with a view to advising the person in future.

Very much love.

E.R.M.

20, Hinde House, Hinde St, W.1
29 July, 1957

Dearest Twin,

... What I think would be nice [would be] if you could come up here on Thursday (Aug. 1)[183] in time to come with me to a 1.30 service at St Peter's, Vere Street, a little church quite near me, attached to All Souls', Langham Place, and therefore no doubt Low, but seems to have a series of lunch-hour preachers; some of them are no doubt quite good. Anyhow it is a pretty little 18th century church, and I should rather like a sermon on my birthday, particularly if you would come too. If you came here first (say at 1.0) we could go together, after a snack of lunch in the flat, or better still at a small shop close by, or we could have this after the service, at more leisure. If you would like to do this, it would be very nice.

I only heard half the Iona service[184] last night, as I had to go out to supper. I hope it was good, as good as last time. I hear the

---

[183] R.M.'s birthday.

[184] An evening service at the Abbey of Iona (St Mary's Cathedral) conducted by Rt Rev. George MacLeod, Moderator of the General Assembly of the Church of Scotland and leader of the Iona Community.

Kirk is very much annoyed by Dr MacLeod, he is so High, and so unlike their dear John Knox, and they suspect him of wanting to take bishops into his system. Perhaps later on he will go where bishops are, since they won't be allowed where he now is.

There was *such* a rude and unjust article in the 5. *Express* about the C. of E. Did you see it? It was by a peer.[185] He says the difference between clergymen and laymen is that they only work one day a week instead of 5 or 6. He obviously knows nothing about it. He calls the Te Deum 'the Tedium', and thinks all clergy very dim and worthless, and that the only way of waking the church to life would be to ordain women. I suppose there will be a lot of answers, if anyone thinks it worth answering. I think those rude attacks and false statements do a lot of harm among ignorant people.

The Bp of Tewkesbury was in London for the week-end, which was very nice. He came to tea with me on Thursday, and on Friday I went to confession, and on Sunday went to hear him preach in a Royal Chapel,[186] then drove him to Paddington, so saw a nice lot of him altogether. When I talk to him, I am always converted; a pity it doesn't happen oftener. I hope he converts all the Glos. clergy. I think there are a lot of these very converting priests about the place, actually, only one doesn't always come across them. A young Oxford man told me last night that there are a lot of Moslem conversions in Oxford just now. When I said I wondered what the attraction was, he said he thought it was largely anti-women. They want to worship in a church where any women there are are in galleries behind grilles, instead of

---

[185] 'I say—Drop that ban on women as Priests', by Lord Altrincham, *Sunday Express*, 28 July, 1957.

[186] The Chapel Royal, St James's Palace.

outnumbering men on the floor, as in Christian churches. They have even got into Pusey House now, which used to be sacred to men, in Oxford. Now women undergraduates go too. A pity men are so annoyed by women in the mass....

[The end of this letter is missing]

11 August, [1957]

Dearest Jeanie,

I have now looked thro' my birthday present,[187] and find it full of good reading, both known and unknown to me. There are several William Laws, tho' none from my favourite works of his, but all are good. I have counted the days up to my birthday and yours. Your reading (Day 206) is on Belief and Doubt. Mine (213) is by Keble, and is called 'To a Lady in her Sickness', and is about the lady's dullness and dryness, which Keble thought was because she wasn't feeling well. Today's is good, from the *Theologia Germanica*. I ought to write the dates in, as it is hard to count every time. Is it Leap Year, because this would put each day later, of course? It would be an interesting occupation to compile such a book; there is room for many more such. One could do it as a sideline, whenever a piece of religious or moral writing struck one, without sparing much time from one's regular work, and gradually one would have collected 365. I think I should give more attention to particular days than Baillie has; in fact, I should do it round the church year. We might collaborate in it, to get it done faster, as our earthly time gets short.... Thank you *so* much

---

[187] John Baillie, *A Diary of Readings* (1955).

for this book, I am delighted with it, and how nice to get a post-birthday present....

The new parking rules which the Ministry of Transport is meaning to bring in soon have been published.[188] It will be very expensive to leave one's car in the scheduled streets of which Hinde Street is one. 6d. for [the] first hour, 1/- for two hours, after that 10/-, so that 2½ hrs will cost 11/-. I think there will be too much revolt by motorists to let them bring it in; people without garages who live in London will be ruined; and the garage rents will be put up even higher, of course, when people will be so eager for them. Those circularised are asked to state their objections in letters to the Ministry, and no doubt every one will. I am lucky to have a garage, tho' it will be a nuisance putting it in there every time I have had it out, then getting it out again, as my mews gets very crowded with cars & lorries. What the new rules will do, I hope, is to prevent those outside London from driving up every morning, parking in some street while they go to their offices and shops, and not going home till 6.0. Hinde Street is now full of such cars. If the cost will be 11/- daily, most people won't do it; train & bus would cost them much less. But Londoners will be in a fix. Perhaps it will drive many Londoners to live in the country.

I am getting more and more interested in N. Shute's *On the Beach*, and am longing to know if the radio-active disease will get to the people in a few months. They are all planting trees, buying things for their future lives, and going on as usual. The disease has the symptoms of cholera, but is incurable, and you die in a few days. I won't tell you what happens.

---

[188] In the annual report of the London and Home Counties Traffic Advisory Committee.

It was v. nice to see you on Friday, looking so smart in your spotty dress, but you must dye your hearing-aid cord blue or navy.

V. much love.

E.R.M.

20, Hinde House, Hinde St, W.1
14 August, [1957]

Dearest Jeanie,

Many thanks for yours, and for *Race Relations.*[189] I will send them something. But, after hearing the Bishop of Jo'burg,[190] I feel that African race relations have got past anything money can do, and can only be improved by mutual good feeling and justice....

I hope you managed to hear the 'Brains Trust' at lunch time. It was quite good. All but Violet Bonham Carter were far too tolerant of Trades Union violence—as she said, they seem a privileged class. All this violence is very dreadful. And why on earth are homicidal maniacs allowed to leave their hospitals 'on parole' and murder children without being caught, then return to their hospitals still free to take walks? Do you think that poor little boy[191] was killed by the same one who murdered the little

---

[189] An official journal of the South African Institute of Race Relations in Johannesburg.

[190] Rt Rev. Ambrose Reeves had recently been speaking at a meeting of the South African Church Institute, also preaching at St Martin-in-the-Fields.

[191] Allan Warren, aged 7, whose body had been found at Loughton, Essex, on 11 August. On 25 October H. H. Edwards, of Wanstead, pleaded guilty to the murder and was sentenced to life imprisonment.

girl and boy lately?[192] But, from tonight's *Evening Standard*, it seems that his uncle Colin is under suspicion. Perhaps he is known to be mad, tho' not shut up. But wouldn't his relations have known that? How dreadful madness is!…

I suppose I should choose 'Love one another', as the essential Christian approach. Certainly not 'Come unto me all you that labour', like that lazy schoolboy.

I think I shall read *Enigma*, Arnold Lunn's book about M.R.A.[193] I think its aims are to encourage more thinking about goodness—the four virtues—and to make people aim at them more vigorously, and think they are all that matters. I am interested that a R.C. should approve of it so much….

> Very much love.
> *E.R.M.*

25 August,[1957]

Dearest Jeanie,

Here is yesterday's *Times* sermon. Also the second bit of Old Age from the *Church Times*.[194] I think it might suggest more pastimes for the old—raffia work, painting, sketching, patience, compiling anthologies of their favourite quotations, etc., etc. But

---

[192] The bodies of Royston Sheasby (aged 5) and his sister June (aged 7) had been found near the Bristol Mental Hospital on 1 July. On 13 September, at the resumed inquest, a verdict of murder by some person or persons unknown was recorded.

[193] Sir Arnold Lunn, *Enigma: A Study of Moral Re-Armament* (1957).

[194] The second of three extracts from On Growing Old by Sybil Harton. The theme of the second instalment (*Church Times*, 23 August, 1957) was that old age should be, above all, a time for prayer.

perhaps the whole book does. I may take to sticking scraps, pictures, etc., on a screen, when too old to write. There are endless sedentary pursuits which are amusing & soothing.

I see there is supposed to be a R.C. plot to convert England to the Church by radio. It seems there are a great number of them in useful places on the B.B.C. and TV, who are prepared to allow as much R.C. religion as they safely can, and it is all aimed at conversion, the R.C. Radio Guild says, not merely for their own flock. I wonder what effect it will have. It will be interesting to see. I hope it will be a counter-attraction to the Evangelical school. That is the school of Christianity I would least rather see getting popular, tho' I suppose it does encourage right conduct. Middle and High Anglicanism will never, I fear, do much conversion here; it seems, like Liberalism, too much of a middle way, and what people like are extremes. I suppose I shall hear next week at Oxford how international Lib: is getting on.[195] …

I have been reading Maisie Ward's *The Wilfrid Wards and the Transition*, volume 2, called *Insurrection and Resurrection?* [196] about the death of the Modernist movement, in which her father[197] took a great interest, but was on the whole against it. Tyrrell, Von Hügel, Abbé Bremond, and other Modernists come into it. M.W. says the movement is now quite defeated. I wonder if it will ever rise again. The R.C. authorities are so careful about it that when a French book about 'The Religious Thought of Von Hügel' was

---

[195] The 10th anniversary congress of the Liberal International was to be held in Oxford on 29–30 August.

[196] Maisie Ward, *Insurrection versus Resurrection* (1937).

[197] Wilfrid Ward.

published some years ago, the English version[198] had to have all the parts about Modernism cut out; as this was one of his major interests, it must read oddly. But he had to be made out absolutely orthodox.[199] ...

Did you hear the discussion between two educationists the other day on public schools?[200] Both thought that a good education was too important to be bought for one's children when many parents can't afford to. I wonder if it is really more unfair than other advantages for one's children being bought. This idea of exact equality is growing....

Very much love.

E.R.M.

20, Hinde House, Hinde St, W.1
[4 September, 1957]

Dearest Jeanie,

... I got back from Oxford on Saturday, seldom having heard so much hot air blown off in 4 days. Foreigners really are very airy. They propose resolutions like sending telegrams to Russia telling them to get out of Hungary, and think they have proposed something useful. However, they enjoyed meeting other Liberals, and enjoyed talking and seeing Oxford, which was looking very

---

[198] Maurice Nédoncelle, *Baron Friedrich von Hügel; a Study of his Life and Thought* (trans M. Vernon, 1937).

[199] Nédoncelle, in a foreword to the English edition, states that it is 'almost identical with' the French one. A 26-page section of his first chapter, on Von Hügel's life and work, is headed 'The Modernist Crisis'.

[200] 'The Future of the Public Schools', a broadcast conversation between Anthony Crosland and Sir John Wolfenden.

lovely in sunshine…. I stayed at a nice hotel near Magdalen (where the conference was), with a pleasant staff, and a schoolboy doing porter's work for the holidays, who told me how pleased he was to meet me, as they had been doing me (among other literature) at his school, so he was eager to carry my suitcase upstairs. I talked to Dr Micklem,[201] but hadn't time to ask him about the Congregational Church. I must consult him later. Today I lunched with Douglas Woodruff, the editor of *The Tablet*, and discussed the R.C. Church 1922–37, about which of course he knows a lot. I discuss the C. of E. with Susan Lister … and others. I do know something about M.R.A. and Quakerism, of course…. But Douglas Woodruff tells me that it [Moral Rearmament] is now out of bounds for R.C.s so they can't go any longer for holidays at Caux.[202] It is silly of the Pope, as apparently it sent R.C.s back to their church duties when they had grown neglectful.

I have been reading a novel in which a wife's husband, an artist, disappears during the war and is reported killed, and she presently marries again and has two more children, and after 11 years she hears from Italy that her first husband has been living in the house of an old countess, blind, but she can't keep him any more. What would you have done? And what would be right to do? What she & her second husband agree to do is that she should go out and live with him, with her two elder children, leaving the 2nd family with the 2nd husband. She loves the second one best. I think I should have divorced the 1st for desertion, as he had deliberately given himself out for dead, being tired of his old life. He was quite a bad & selfish man.

---

[201] Rev. Nathaniel Micklem.

[202] The Swiss headquarters of Moral Rearmament.

I am now reading *Angel*, by Elizabeth Taylor, which is amusing, about a bad but best-selling novelist. I have Ivy Compton-Burnett's new one,[203] which I will bring. I also read *Behold your King*, by Naomi Mitchison, the story of Good Friday, vivid, but has faults of style. I'm glad to see that it rejects the idea of Mary Magdalene as a harlot, for which there is no evidence at all…. I must now go out to hear Edith Sitwell read her poems, to restore an old R.C. chapel in a country house, the only chapel in England where Mass has been said continuously for over 400 years.[204]

V. much love.

E.R.M.

20, Hinde House, Hinde St, W.1
15 September, [1957]

Dearest Jeanie,

… Yes, I go to Oxford [again] tomorrow, till Monday … but I *may* come home on Sunday evening, very likely, as I have Monday engagements. The latest of these is an evening reception on a Turkish ship, to which the Embassy has invited me. I think it wise to keep in with Turkey, so shall very likely go to this. I like to make friends with the mammon of unrighteousness—not that they are more unrighteous than most other governments, and less than some we can think of. I prefer to keep in with them all….

On Sunday I attended 10 o'clock Mass at [the] King's Weigh

---

[203] *A Father and his Fate.*

[204] Dame Edith Sitwell gave a poetry reading in aid of the Stonor Chapel Restoration Fund on 4 September, 1957.

House[205]—a nice service, very like ours in words, but the minister, Dr Daniel Jenkins (a very learned man, I am told) celebrated in a black gown only, and stood facing us, and no candles on the altar, and of course no crucifix. A very small congregation, about 6 or 7, I should think, all communicants, including me.

I must go to some other services there sometime. I have been reading a book about Congregationalism; they say they began in 1185 *[sic]*, which seems strange.[206] I have started a new group, called Inter-communionists, which I hope you will join. I shall make my communion in all the non-Anglican churches near me which have it at a possible time; in time I may even work up courage for St James's round the corner, but at present I feel that would be bad manners as they wouldn't let me if they knew.

The thing is not to hide the fact that one is (probably) Anglican, in the Nonconformist chapels, or it would be useless as propaganda; I mean, I behave exactly as I do in an Anglican church, so that anyone noticing it would think 'I see Anglicans communicate with us. We ought to communicate in *their* churches too.' So gradually it will become common form on both sides, and the fences will lapse.

I agree with the Wolfenden Report. I don't like to see these unseemly goings-on in the streets, it looks very ugly & common.[207]

---

[205] The Congregational church in Duke Street, W.I, not far from R.M.'s flat.

[206] Congregationalism came fully into being during the years following 1640; its early beginnings can be traced back to the middle of the 16th century.

[207] The report of the Departmental Committee on Homosexual offences and Prostitution, published on 4 September, aimed at 'cleaning up the streets' of London and other big cities by greatly increasing the maximum penalties for soliciting in the streets by prostitutes.

I don't in the least mind grown men in private doing as they like together—why not?[208] The whole business, homo & hetero, seems, when one thinks of it, a little unseemly, but the whole animal race appears to be so made that it seems to be an essential part of love (anyhow for males), though one may feel, with Sir Thomas Browne, that it is a pity nature did not invent 'some nicer way than this of coition'.[209] But we are as we are, and love is what it is, and it seems it can't only be kept for reproduction purposes.

I think sitting up part of the night might be all right if you really slept and rested for a corresponding time in the day—but would you? Otherwise, it would be much too tiring; even for me.

Very much love.

E.R.M.

20, Hinde House, Hinde St, W.1
20 October, [1957]

Dearest Jeanie,

I enclose some religious reading for you, from *Church* and *Sunday Times*. (Ignore the Byron poem, which is carnal not spiritual.)[210] Do you think any of the other animals will ever

---

[208] The report proposed a relaxing of the law on homosexuality, and urged that there should be no penalty for consenting adults.

[209] See *Religio Medici*, II 9: 'I could be content that we might procreate like trees, without conjunction, or that there were any way to perpetuate the world without this trivial and vulgar way of coition.'

[210] The *Sunday Times* was running a series of articles on 'The Mystery of Life', and R.M. had sent the second, 'From the Atom to the Saint' by the Archbishop of York, Dr Michael Ramsey (20 October). Inset in the article was

evolve into thinking and potentially religious beings? There really seems no biological reason why man should be alone in this. I don't know what scientists say about it; I must ask Julian Huxley, whose special thing is biology.

I handed the jazz Mass cutting to Fr Harris after church, but I fear he won't try it.[211] He said he had heard it performed, and decided that it would shock the congregation, who are many of them old-fashioned. I told him it would attract a quite new congregation, young and skiffle-minded.... I said he ought to be avant-garde from time to time, as the old will die out and there must be a new generation to take their places. He said he would talk to the organist, Dr Latham, about it. But we *are* rather stick-in-the-mud at St Paul's. St Thomas's [Regent Street] (Patrick McLaughlin's church) was far more experimental....

I will post you Vol 1 of *The Early Church,*[212] if you'd like to read it. Then Vol 2 when you've read it.... It is interesting, but one doesn't, I found, want to read it all, there's so much apocryphal literature described, not all worth study. I like the account of the Gospels and their origins.

I am just off to the Tate Gallery to see the paintings by chimps.[213] I have found *Manservant and Maidservant* [214] and will bring it for you to look at, to see if you know it or not. I think it is

---

the *Sunday Times'* usual poetic item, on this occasion Byron's 'Juan and Haidée' from *Don Juan*.

[211] The 'jazz' setting for the service of Holy Communion, composed by Rev. Geoffery Beaumont, was much in the news at this time.

[212] Philip Carrington (Abp of Quebec), *The Early Christian Church* (2 vols, 1957).

[213] This exhibition of paintings by two chimpanzees (Congo, of the London Zoo, and Betsy, of the Baltimore Zoo) was held at the Gallery of the Institute of Contemporary Arts, not at the Tate Gallery.

[214] By Ivy Compton-Burnett (1947).

one of the best, much better really than *The Father and his Fate,* which is almost *too* impossible in plot.

Very much love....

E.R.M.

20, Hinde House, Hinde St, W.1
30 October, [1957]

Dearest Jeanie,

... I had been just going to write to say that unfortunately I can't come this week, as I have the Cranford Folk Mass on Friday evening, and on Saturday have to draw the lottery at a St Paul's sale. Anyhow it would have been difficult to come, as I suddenly have to do a longish *Spectator* review of a Life of Jowett[215] by Monday, so ought to work all the spare time I have till then. I am looking forward to the Folk Mass. It won't be very perfectly done, as the performers aren't much, nor the musical instruments, in fact I think they will only use a piano; but the congregation will join in, when they pick the tunes up, which people are v. quick at doing, mostly, and I shall get the idea of it. I will report on it.

I heard the Dick Sheppard programme,[216] but thought, as there are so many recordings of his voice, they should have had some; his voice and manner of preaching was so charmingly characteristic, and no one else could possibly convey it. No, he hadn't a lot of common sense, tho' more than one might think, and could be very shrewd, especially about people. As to being

---

[215] Geoffrey Faber *Jowett; a Portrait with Background* (1957).

[216] 'Dick Sheppard, The Human Parson', a programme broadcast in memory of Canon H. R. L. Sheppard (d. 1937).

like Christ, certainly his love and understanding of people was, and his power of sacrifice, but less judgment, no doubt. He would never have abused the Pharisees in that violent way that I'm sure Christ *didn't* (the Evangelists must have put that in, being themselves annoyed with the Pharisees). Dick would have asked them in to drinks and made friends with them and been calling them all by their Christian names in a minute or so, and would very likely win some of them round to his point of view, tho' of course many would have strongly disapproved and disliked his ways, as people did the Peace Pledge Union.[217] Dr Matthews[218] and he were very fond of each other, though so utterly different. His pacifist programme was firmly based on what he kept repeating, 'I must not kill my brother', and the consequences of it had all, however terrible they might be, to be subordinate to that. I thought at the time, and still think, he was right, whatever the outcome might have been, and might be now. But he was quite often ill-judged in his methods, and worked himself to death of course. He was unique, I think, and it is nice to have known him....

No flue yet. I feel like the psalmist, with 10,000 falling beside me but it shall not come nigh me,[219] perhaps because of inoculation, perhaps because of my righteousness. With you, it must be righteousness. Do keep it up! Constance Babington Smith says we must both be stronger after Pleshey;[220] she is a nice mixture of

---

[217] See above, p. *95n.*

[218] The Dean of St Paul's.

[219] See Ps. 91, 5–7: 'Thou shalt not be afraid … for the pestilence that walketh in darkness … A thousand shall fall beside thee, and ten thousand at thy right hand: but it shall not come nigh thee.'

[220] After a Retreat at Pleshey conducted by the Bp of Tewkesbury.

great simplicity and real ability. Her air-photography book[221] is being serialised in the *Sunday Times* (some of it) thro' December. She is a great dear, and radiantly happy about her book promising so much success…. I hope she won't have her head a little turned by fame & money.

I thought Canon Warren Hunt[222] wrong about Lazarus not having improved at all after death. He showed real unselfish concern for his brothers, and might in the end develop a wider pity and generosity. 'As we die, so we stay' seemed to be Canon Hunt's belief.

V. much love.

E.R.M.

Guy Fawkes [5 November,] 1957

Dearest Jeanie,

… Do you remember your minute of silence each morning at II. O for Little Lemon?[223] I'm afraid the Russians have quite done for themselves with the English now. They tell us reassuringly how comfortable Little Lemon is, and how he'll soon be shot out, won't become a satellite on his own (I should like him to

---

[221] *Evidence in Camera; The Story of Photographic Intelligence in World War II* (1958).

[222] Canon W. Warren Hunt, Vicar of Croydon, who was giving the current broadcast talks in the 'Lift up your Hearts' programme.

[223] After the second Soviet satellite, carrying a dog named Laika ('Little Lemon') was launched on 3 November, officials of the National Canine Defence League made an official protest to the Russian Embassy in London, and called for a minute's silence daily on behalf of the dog in the satellite.

fly round the earth yelping) but will be parachuted gently to earth and picked up. But this morning a Soviet scientist blundered, and said something about 'if the dog is still alive then', so obviously they know he'll die soon.

If they'd any sense, or wanted to please us, they would have called him a rat or guinea-pig, then only a few children with guinea-pigs would have minded. Dear me, how clever they are! The next thing will be the moon, and quite soon. Perhaps they'll send Zhukov there. Would you volunteer, if you were offered £10,000 for missions? Would you think it right to?…

The Folk Mass was quite attractive, I thought. I drove down Fr Derry and Fr Jeffery (whom you talked to, and who is going back to Grace Dieu)[224] and Gerard Irvine's brother, a clever young barrister who attends the Annunciation Church [Bryanston Street] and is amusing company. We had an enjoyable evening; tho' Fr Derry, who is musical, doesn't think the music very good, nor do most musical people, but it suits me quite well. Fr Jeffery said no use for Africans, who prefer hot Jazz and rhythm, like many young people here. Myself I prefer neither really, but something more classical. However, this is worth trying.

I went on Sunday to the All Saints' [Margaret Street] patronal festival mass, with the Bp of Tewkesbury preaching and a fine procession, the Bishop blessing us to right & left all round the church and people falling on their knees as he passed. The church was packed out, with lots standing. Then in the evening I went to mass at the Weigh House, where Dr John Huxtable

---

[224] Rev. R. M. Jeffery, who had worked in South Africa from 1946 to 1955, became Principal of the Grace Dieu School, Pietersburg, in 1958.

preached a magnificent sermon, great waste really, with only about a dozen people there. He was most impressive, about the Table prepared for us in the presence of our enemies (Ps. 23) who prowled in the background waiting their time to get us again and sneering 'I shall get you in the end.' My blood ran cold, he was so dramatic. I wonder if Congregationalists are dwindling; so very few people go there. After the sermon and prayers they had the communion, Dr Huxtable consecrated the bread and wine, and a lay helper took them round to us in our seats. As I had been [to an] early [celebration], I couldn't practise intercommunion this time. Before the service the minister said it was free to all denominations.

Fr Harris … is worrying in the November *Parish Mag.* why more don't come to Sunday evensong, and what he can do to entice us. Jock Henderson used to have discussion meetings after church at the vicarage, which people liked; I went to several, but the level of intelligence seemed rather too low for a sensible discussion of the book we were reading. However, it was popular, if rather dumb. I doubt if Fr H. would have this, discussion not being in his line, but he contemplates a social gathering sometimes. I would like a discussion of the sermon, as I have often told him. People would have lots to say about that, I think, even the less intelligent of us. I wish he would try it. I would like him to cheer up and not feel discouraged about his congregations. All the same, I can't often go to evening church, I am too busy, and rely on Sundays to get some work done without interruption. This Sunday I had to finish reviewing the Life of Jowett, a most interesting work, for *The Spectator,* and get thro' a great many letters. Work first, worship later if time, I think must be my rule. You might like to read Jowett's Life; the part about *Essays and Reviews* (1860) and the extraordinary excitement and hostility against it, and the heresy prosecutions for statements we all accept today, makes very interesting reading.[225] I suppose in another 100 years things that shock orthodox Christians today will all be accepted except by a few die-hards....

Very much love.

E.R.M.

[p.s.]

A correspondent in *The Tablet* this week says Anglicans can't be considered by Catholics as belonging to the Church—I suppose the Christian Church.[226] This seems to me to be going too far, and if I was the editor I wouldn't print it. I wonder if Canon Mortlock (against whom the letter was addressed) will answer it, or think silence better.[227] I don't suppose the writer is very educated—at least he puts the name of his house in quotation marks, which is usually a sign of this.

Wednesday [20 November, 1957][228]

... Yes, I think the Church would be *made* if a Bishop went up

---

[225] The opposition to *Essays and Reviews*, a collection of essays by seven authors (including B. Jowett), who believed in the necessity of free enquiry in religious matters, culminated in the synodical condemnation of the book by the Church of England's Lower House of Convocation in 1864.

[226] See *The Tablet*, 2 November, 1957.

[227] A letter from Canon C. B. Mortlock headed *Anglicans and Catholics* had been published in *The Tablet* of 26 October. He did not write again, but the correspondence continued until 14 December.

[228] Postcard.

for the dog. I hope the R.C.s won't get in first. I'd send one of those East Anglian bishops, who are so evangelical—no, I wouldn't, I'd send a very High one (any except Tewkesbury, who can't be spared). I wished you had seen with me the TV interview between Muggeridge and Alec Vidler, the Dean of King's. I went to my Club to see it. It was v.g. I took notes of it. I also wrote to the B.B.C. to say they must have it on sound radio. Dr V. answered M.'s questions, about the creeds, Articles etc. None of them are to be taken literally, all are *symbols* of truth. (Tell Miss B——this.) ...

Much love.

R.

27 November, [1957]

Dearest Jeanie,

I am so very sorry about your flu.... Nancy said it began quite suddenly, which this Asian [kind] always seems to. I know a man who started for his office at 9.0, feeling quite well, walked to the underground, still feeling well, and suddenly collapsed just as his train drew up, fortunately before he got into it. He took a taxi home and went to bed with a temp. 103, which had come on quite suddenly. He stayed in bed 3 days, and then was able to go about again. I have heard of several which began equally suddenly, sometimes with a faint, as Dorothea's did. I do hope you won't get up too soon ... N. says *she* is quite safe from catching it, because she isn't afraid of it! This is what my old char used to say when I begged her not to come near my bed when I had flu and tried to make her smell Vapex. 'You don't catch it unless you're afraid of it', she said, and no number of times of being proved wrong would shatter this dogma, which uneducated people always seem to have. It is no use telling them that it is often caught quite unconsciously, from sitting near someone in a bus as they won't believe it. I notice that the Dales[229] say this whenever any of them have flu or a cold. But anyhow it is certain that flu isn't catching after the temp, is down, or has been down for a day, so Friday will certainly be safe. I should be disappointed not to come. When I do, shall I bring you *Jowett,* and an interesting book (older) about the Oxford movement, by J. Lewis May—very good about all the leading people.[230] I have been reading several books lately partly about that, as it was raging in the mid-century at Oxford. Its effect on poor A. H. Clough was disastrous; for a short time he was carried away by 'Newmania', but very soon rallied and reacted against it, having a v.g. rational intellectual mind, and having been trained by Dr Arnold, who disliked the whole business. But his earlier faith was shattered by all the discussion and argument, and his work went to pieces owing to lack of attention to it, and he only got a 2nd instead of the 1st every one expected of him. Later he swallowed the Articles, which they then had to do before matriculating, and got an Oriel Fellowship, and lectured there for 6 years, but the Articles were very indigestible all the time, and he was very honest, and after 6 years he threw them up, together with his job, and left Oxford, which was very sad. He was a very attractive character; I have just been reviewing two large vols of his letters, and those to him.[231] They

---

[229] The Dale family in the broadcast serial story 'Mrs Dale's Diary'.

[230] James Lewis May, *The Oxford Movement, its History and its Future: a Layman's Estimate* (1933).

[231] *The Correspondence of Arthur Hugh Clough, edited by Frederick Mulhauser,* reviewed by R.M. in *The Listener* (5 December, 1957).

are full of interesting things and people. However, I am selling them, while still clean, as they apparently cost £5:5....

I have been invited by Lady Ravensdale to a gathering about Penhalonga, addressed by Fr Huddleston, to raise money (some huge sum[232]—why does *everything* need such astronomic sums? It seems too ambitious; surely a little at a time would be better) and will I bring with me some 'rich tycoon'. I know none, or none who would finance a missionary house in S. Africa. I don't move among millionaires. I get hundreds of appeals all the time, for this & that. People seem to start things in faith, and then have to beg in order to go on. We have become a nation of hitch-hikers, thumbing every one for lifts.... I met Mr Gaitskell at dinner, and liked him. It was at the Ian Flemings ...

Very much love,
E.R.M.

20, Hinde House, Hinde St, W. 1
3 December, [1957]

Dearest Jeanie,

... I had a very interesting Sunday evening again at my club seeing two programmes, the 'Brains Trust', on which ... Sir Ifor Evans was nice, and also James Morris, and I always like [A. J.] Ayer. But I enjoyed much more the 'Christian Meeting Point' programme, on which the Indian Mr Pande (Methodist) was seen at his leper college *[sic]*, and being interviewed by C.

---

[232] £50,000 or more was the target for the appeal launched by the Community of the Resurrection in May 1957 to provide education of a higher level at its mission schools in Penhalonga, Southern Rhodesia.

Mayhew, about how he felt towards God.[233] He said he had no direct perception of God, not being a mystic, no visions or anything, but felt God all the time in his work, and in his relations with other people, especially the lepers, to whom he is devoted. He was a very nice, smiling man; we saw him also in the leper chapel, taking a service and preaching, and with his wife and young son afterwards. The last part of the programme was an interview between Mr Mayhew and Fr Hugh Bishop, C.R., when they discussed the two Christian ideals shown by the Franciscan last Sunday and Mr Pande this Sunday, one mostly prayer & worship & monastic life, the other service and work. Fr Bishop said the two sides of Christianity depended on each other, and must weave in and out; he thought the work would become dry and stale without prayer, and the prayer rather sterile without the work. He is an excellent interviewee. I quite see why religious people don't go to evening church as much as they did; TV is so much more interesting and full of ideas. It is rather sad for the clergy, who naturally like a full church and a full collection; perhaps they all ought to hold services and discussions on TV, and have it in church, on a large screen. That would fill the churches all right.

I didn't see about the worker priest; what does he work at? There is a fashion for this just now, started by the French. I haven't yet read Canon Moore Darling's book about his experiences when in the factories talking to the workers.[234] The whole

---

[233] The B.B.C. Sunday programme 'Meeting Point' (1 December) consisted of the second of 'Two Christian Portraits', in which Christopher Mayhew interviewed Rev. C. C. Pande, Methodist Minister of Bankura, West Bengal.

[234] E. Moore Darling, *Highways, Hedges and Factories* (1957).

252

business of religion is in a state of great transition just now, and very interesting. If the Church wants people to belong, it's got to drop the present rigid system of set services.

Did you hear the religious Brains Trust on Sunday?[235] Rather foolish questions, on the whole, like the one about, in view of the sufferings of people in concentration camps (as if people hadn't suffered far worse than that in former ages), has the Atonement lost its meaning. People often seem to turn slightly mental when speaking of the Atonement; I wish we had less of it. It is a Hebrew idea carried on into Christianity, based on the sacrifice of animals to the glory of God, and had better be let drop now, surely. But it does seem to mean something to a lot of people. To me, nothing, and it spoils a number of hymns etc. for me. Advent, on the other hand, gets to mean more and more; perhaps because of so soon dying. Fr Harris preached so well on Sunday about Christmas, and not making it an orgy of present-giving to each other but sending the money saved to refugees and others in need. I think he had got some of his ideas from a Xmas article I wrote in *The Spectator* which had pleased him.[236] Is it part of my mission, do you think, to give the clergy good ideas? I wish the R.C. ones were more open to them. Really it seems scarcely credible, their view of the Christian Church. They leave their pamphlets in Grosvenor Chapel sometimes, to convert us, called 'Reasons for being a Catholic', and so on. Fr Derry says an Anglican wrote an answer, called 'But I *am* a Catholic',[237] but this is like a red rag to a bull to them, and no use at all. When they say

---

[235] A 'Christian Forum', in the B.B.C. Home Service series 'The Way of Life', broadcast on 1 December.

[236] 'Saturnalia', see *The Spectator*, 22 November, 1957.

[237] Oscar Hardman, *But I am a Catholic* (1958).

'Catholic toleration of Anglicans has been carried to its very limits', as someone in *The Tablet* did,[238] what do you think he meant to do about it? He sounded like Hitler, 'my patience is exhausted', and we know what *he* did about it. We can't be saved without baptism, they keep saying; it is such a wild notion that one wonders if they are really unbalanced, or if their minds are so feeble that they really can believe that love of God and moral struggle can't save. I wish I knew one of them I could talk to about such things without upsetting them. I shall listen this evening to the Greek church on divorce.[239]

I am glad you find J. L. May interesting.[240] He is rather too sold on unity, I think, but good on the people in the movement. They must have been exciting times. But what a terrible state of mind the majority were in about ritualism and popery! We have certainly improved.

I saw a film about Tarzan this afternoon, but not v.g.[241] I am told *The Ten Commandments* aren't v.g. either, in spite of the Red Sea dividing and drowning Pharaoh's army and chariots, as on the posters. How very religious the Jews were! Melting down all their precious gold ornaments in order to have a golden calf to worship in the desert; it was really rather touching, tho' stupid....

Very much love.

E.R.M.

---

[238] See *The Tablet,* 30 November, 1957.

[239] R.M. is referring to a broadcast on the Orthodox Church and Divorce, by Iulia de Beausobre (Lady Namier). See *The Listener,* 12 December, 1957, 'A Religious Justification of Divorce'.

[240] See above, p. 244.

[241] *Tarzan and the Lost Safari.*

I still brood over the Dame business.[242]

If you invest your £1000 well, you will have a little more to give away annually.

20, Hinde House, Hinde St, W.1
New Year's Eve, 1957

Dearest Jeanie,

This is to send my love for 1958. I shall be going out soon to a watch night party, tho' we shall not watch much, but see the new year in with babble & revel & wine. I don't know why we don't have a Mass for it.

I am busy with the Articles, reading Newman's *Tract 90* on them, and Pusey on Newman. Newman & Pusey both quite disobey the preliminary order of 1562 about not putting one's own interpretation on them,[243] but sticking to the sense and literal meaning as put down, on pain of punishment. 'Dr Jenkinson' (who is Jowett in Mallock's *New Republic*[244]) preaches in a sermon 'Even if we do come across some incident in the history of our religion which seems, humanly speaking, to subserve no good end at all—such as our own 39 Articles—let us not suffer such to try our faith, but let us trust in God, believing that in his secret councils He has found some fitting use even for these'…. When I have more time, I will look up which I

---

[242] In the 1958 New Year Honours List R. M. was appointed Dame Commander of the British Empire. When this letter was written she had just been invited to accept the honour.

[243] See 'His Majesty's Declaration' preceding the Articles of Religion in the Book of Common Prayer.

[244] W. H. Mallock, *The New Republic* (1877).

don't believe, and perhaps can tell you on Friday.

The news of my Dameship has reached the Press, which rings me up for photographs, but I won't have this. I think the list is sent to the papers two days before Jan. 1st. I am told that, as regards literature, it is a rather dull list, which tends I am afraid to concentrate interest on me, as Dames are considered interesting. Well, I hope it will soon blow over. People ring me up to say how pleased they are, which is nice of them. But I am afraid I shall also have to answer a lot of letters.

I enclose the *Times* sermon, which I like. It is what I have felt always, after childhood, that the Bethlehem legends, on which Xmas tends to concentrate, are irrelevant to me, and I expect it is true that they cause disbelief in the Incarnation in many people. On the other hand, no doubt many others find their faith strengthened by them....

Very much love, and a good year to you both....

R.

20, Hinde House, Hinde St, W.1
Twelfth Night [5 January] 1958

Dearest J.,

I send the Epiphany sermon in *The Times, a* v.g. one, I think. Also, as I know you don't take the *Sunday Times,* a photograph they published of me typing, or rather pretending to type. I look very industrious! Do you ever hear any of 'Woman's Hour'?[245] On Wednesday at 2.0 they begin with New Year Honours guests;

---

[245] A daily broadcast programme.

256

they asked me to speak at it, but I am lunching elsewhere at that time, so they asked me to record a few remarks tomorrow afternoon, for transmission on Wednesday. They say they will ask me a few questions, which is easier than speaking without stimulus. If you listen, tell me what it is like. I believe it is repeated (perhaps more fully) next Sunday at 9.10 or so, in the morning, on the Home programme 'Home for the Day'. I don't think I can hear that either, as I shall be staying in Dorset and probably shan't be able to listen. I think they said they would ask me about things I like and don't like. If so, I shall probably say I like beautiful country and buildings, driving through romantic scenery, swimming in warm seas when no one else is doing so near me, good company and talk, listening to good music, including a well sung and orchestrated Mass. I shan't include the things every one likes, such as nice food & bed, being loved & flattered, watching people happy etc., reading interesting books. I shall say I dislike crooning, especially vulgar and silly love songs, repairing things that have gone wrong, such as my car, my clothes, etc., religious intolerance (I don't mind other intolerance nearly so much, as it isn't paradoxical), industrial towns, ugly and monotonous rows of houses, etc. I shan't mention the obvious things, such as cruelty & wickedness & oppression & cold. But whether there will be time for all these I don't know. The more vulgar and silly newspapers, I might add. I don't know who else will be speaking.

I go on getting cartsfull of kind letters daily. It is nice to get them and read them, tho' less so to answer them. I have laid in a lot of convenient cards, with flowers on them, but do feel I must write many letters too. I wish more people would type theirs. When they don't I often revenge myself by hand-written answers, of which they have to make what they can. Such a nice one from E. M. Forster this morning. I bagged 4 bishops (perhaps more, I

257

forget), 2 ambassadors, and of course most of my literary colleagues, and too many wires signed with names I can't identify, tho' sometimes the postmark helps. I see how neglectful I have usually been in writing congratulations. Some years after he became a Knight Hugh Walpole told me I hadn't written to him about it; he was a pettish man.

I have been asked to a Foyle lunch on 31st where the Soviet ambassador is to be the chief guest[246]; the long telegram which invites me says there will also be present statesmen, scientists, writers, actors, industrialists, athletes, and philosophers; but I don't expect they'll all come. Perhaps I shall sit between an athlete and a philosopher, which will be like a banquet in 4th century Athens, only they wouldn't have asked any dames.

I'm sorry I shall be away on Friday. I go to Dorset for the week end, with my 4 gentlemen friends at Crichel,[247] and any one else they may have asked. I hope the weather won't be very cold. In cold weather there is no place like home. Luckily our management has postponed the operation they threatened on the boiler, so we keep warm. I hope you do, but I wish you too had central heating.

Next Monday I am asked to a sherry party at the clergy house of St Mary's, Graham Street, one of the most extreme churches (no chalice unless you wait on for it) to meet some young men who it seems were persuaded into Anglicanism by the *Towers of Treb*. I feel very proud of this. Next thing should be to persuade them into intercommunion with dissenters. I went to the Weigh

---

[246] Mr Malik was guest of honour at a Foyle's Literary Luncheon in honour of Russia's scientific, artistic, and literary achievements.

[247] Raymond Mortimer, Edward Sackville-West, Eardley Knollys and Desmond Shawe-Taylor.

House again on Sunday evening, and stayed on for the communion. I like the Epistle, very short (in the 1928 P.B., I mean).[248] We used it on Sunday at St Paul's.

Jan. 7. We have the famous Mr Stott lifting our hearts this week: he is the most influential Low vicar in London. I thought him poor yesterday, but good today. Tho', as he was religious enough at school to pray often alone in the chapel, I don't quite see why it was news to him to be told of Christ; he should have been told about that before, both at home and at school. But tomorrow he will no doubt 'accept' him.

Now I must go on wading thro' my letters and cards. Writing to you is a restful interlude....

E. M. Forster says 'What a silly title!' He is right.

[No signature]

20, Hinde House, Hinde St, W.1
17 January, 1958

Dearest Jeanie,

... I enclose our abolition [of nuclear weapons] papers, also the [Church] Unity Week notice; I only got to half this meeting[249] as I had to go first to a wedding reception. Neither abolition of nuclear weapons nor of Church divisions got far, I'm afraid. The [abolition] committee discussed and talked too much

---

[248] The Epistle for the Second Sunday after Christmas given in the 1928 Prayer Book consists of one verse only, II Cor. 8.9.

[249] A meeting held at the St Pancras Town Hall on 15 January in connection with the Week of Prayer for Christian Unity.

about differences in wording of our propaganda, instead of making plans. But there is a large public meeting on Feb. 17th, with several good speakers. The Unity meeting was nice, every one very polite and charitable to one another but no definite plans laid. The Methodist speaker[250] was v.g. Afterwards some of us went and had supper at a neighbouring restaurant; I was with Gerard Irvine and another priest and two women from Gerard's parish. The Bishop who had presided[251] came over & spoke to us, also the Methodist, both very nice. A R.C. reporter went to visit the Methodist & the vicar of St Martin's [-in-the-Fields][252] for the *Catholic Herald*, and wrote a nice ecumenical polite account of what they had said to him. The Methodist, Mr Spivey, he said, had a crucifix in his study, and laid great emphasis on sacraments, as Wesley did. Mr Austen Williams laid more stress on the Good Life. But it was quite a nice useful article to have in the *Catholic Herald*, and I hope will do good to the more intolerant R.C. writers in it. The editor[253] is a v. nice man.

Thank you so much for your letter. I don't believe Dorothea is right about R.C.s and communion, but I will find out & let you know, and if it is true will certainly go.[254] It might be the turning point of our lives, like being converted and accepting Christ. Perhaps however it would be rash, as our C. of E. communions might after that seem empty....

---

[250] Rev. R. V. Spivey.

[251] Rt Rev. Ivor Watkins, Bp of Guildford.

[252] Rev. S. Austen Williams.

[253] Michael de la Bedoyere.

[254] Dorothea Conybeare had maintained that no Roman Catholic priest has a right to 'turn anyone back from the altar', whether a heretic or a 'notorious sinner'.

I hear there is no Scottish Episcopal church in London so can't join it. Yes, Belloc was boring and revolting about the Church. Enough to keep anyone out of it.

V. much love....

E.R.M.

24 January, [1958]

Dearest Jeanie,

… When next I come we will have a mutual 'Frankly Speaking'. I should be hopeless at it in public, I am much too shy. Violet B. C. was splendid.[255]

I thought Unity Week as silly as ever. Simply shadow boxing; drawing red herrings such as 'getting together'. When it comes to intercommunion, they all say there must be sacrifices on both sides. I see no need for any sacrifices at all; just an announcement from the heads of each church that in future intercommunion with every one else was o.k., and no nonsense about the Pope, bishops, orders, elders, and whatever else they've got. I like the article about Dr Fisher[256]; it is true that he seems sometimes to blow both ways, on many subjects. But I think he wants the right things. I doubt if he'll get round to stopping nuclear weapons; he is one of the many who think them a good deterrent that will never be used. He doesn't seem to see that even in the

---

[255] 'Personal Questions' were put to Lady Violet Bonham Carter by John Connell, Margaret Lane and Anthony Wedgwood Benn in the broadcast programme 'Frankly Speaking' on 21 January.

[256] 'He is the Great Reconciler' by Geoffrey Murray (*News Chronicle*, 21 January, 1958).

background they are savage. Like announcing that, if people do this or that crime, they will be burnt alive. It would no doubt deter, and would probably be never used, but it would be like having some awful savage standing at the ready in a corner; *quite out of keeping with civilisation....*

I am now quite sought after by royalty. I have been commanded to dine with H.M. and the Duke of Edinburgh on Feb. 18th. I hope I shall behave rightly. Today I have an invitation to dine somewhere else and meet the Duke and Duchess of Gloucester, also on 18th. I won't reply that unfortunately I can't because I am dining with the Queen that night, tho' it is tempting.

I thought Janet Adam Smith very understanding on the 'Critics' about *The World my Wilderness.*[257] She is one of the two literary editors of the *New Statesman....* The others[258] were, I thought, quite polite and honest, and I more or less agreed with their views. Of course even if it hadn't been by me, Arnot Robertson wouldn't care for a book about ruins, or about ideas; she is all for people and nothing but people. The only thing she liked, she said, was a remark I made about the cook. However I don't think it matters what the 'Critics' say about a Penguin, [when the novel itself was] published so long ago. What I don't like is the picture of Barbary on the cover, they've made her so hideous, and I feel the Penguin audience wouldn't care for that.

I am reading a lot about Newman, besides this new French

---

[257] It had just been re-issued as a Penguin.

[258] The other 'Critics': E. Arnot Robertson, Harold Hobson, Stephen Potter, and David Sylvester.

Life which is v.g.[259] A strange man. *Nothing* is quoted that he ever said or wrote in letters which isn't about religion. It must have been very monotonous, and tedious to those of his friends whose interests were different. But an extraordinary number of them just then had the obsession too.

I go on getting furious illiterate letters about Anglicans thinking they have Mass. It is an interesting psychology. They sound like snarling dogs with a bone when they think someone else has a bone like it; or perhaps a woman with an exclusive model dress, learning that others have it too. It seems very shocking & unchristian. I'm glad we don't write to Nonconformists in that strain, furious because they think they have communion services. I am told there is a great element of bitterness imported by ignorant Irish priests who hate the English. Gerard Irvine was told the other day, apparently in good faith, that of course Protestant priests always repeated what they heard in confession, as they weren't vowed not to. Nothing he could say convinced the man who told him; he had been told so by his priests, and was sure. Such hate is uncomfortable. I wonder if one day the R. Church will suddenly see the light and realise that it is very wrong. I enclose an article[260] by Dr Micklem ('Ilico') that I like. May I have it back, sometime, please.

Very much love. Do stay in & keep warm, like me.

E.R.M.

---

[259] Louis Bouyer, *Newman, His Life and Spirituality* (trans. J. Lewis May, 1958). See R.M.'s review in *The Spectator,* 31 January, 1958.
[260] From the *British Weekly.*

Long Crichel House, Wimborne, Dorset
[14 February, 1958]
St Valentine's Day

Dearest Jeanie,

I looked for you on Tuesday after the ceremony,[261] and also in the audience room when I came into it after my own bit was done, but I couldn't see you. I expect you came out before the end. I had to wait till it was over, as all the others did. We all met beforehand in another room, as you did before your investiture, and received instructions. I knew several knights—Julian Huxley, Jim Butler, Steven Runciman, the Master of Pembroke,[262] and also met the Bp of Gloucester,[263] whom I liked. His knighthood isn't much use to him, and none to his wife, as they won't be called sir and lady, which is rather dull … The Queen was very charming, and said nice words to us all. When I got home the *Evening Standard* rang up asking what she had said to me. I said 'nothing'. I was half afraid of seeing a heading in the *Standard* 'The Queen snubs Dame Rose', but luckily there wasn't.

I meant to write earlier, but have been living such a lethargic life in this comfortable house, lying in bed till lunch time nearly, then lunch, then a short stroll of about ¼ mile, then back to more lethargy. Raymond Mortimer is alone here this week, and after the morning, when he works, we talk and read, and it is all very nice…. I am reading a lot of interesting books here. Very much love….

Your loving *E.R.M.*

---

[261] The investiture when R.M. received her D.B.E.
[262] S. C. Roberts.
[263] Rt Rev. W. M. Askwith.

Dearest Jeanie,

Thank you so much for yours, and for returning the Abbot.[264]The young man[265] at the Faith Press, who are publishing the book, thought I hadn't enough conveyed his charm, which seems to have been almost hypnotic, so I read it again and thought I hadn't, and put in a few remarks to improve it. I also altered 'manic depressive' to 'paranoiac', which I am sure is the right word, and what he was. I hope the author of the book, Peter Anson, will think it all right.[266] He was really very fond of the Abbot, though brings out his faults clearly. I should like to meet someone who was under him at Caldey,[267] but I fancy they are all dead now, except Anson. I can see he might have been fascinating, but I should have been repelled by all that fondling & kissing that went on, as well as by all the extravagance.

I enclose a letter from Dorothea…. I like Fanny Macaulay's remark to John Cropper about how the paper he made might be used for R.C. tracts.[268] I sympathise with her distaste for these.

---

[264] *Abbot Extraordinary,* Peter Anson's memoir of Aelred Carlyle, for which R.M. was writing a foreword.

[265] Robin Denniston.

[266] Peter Anson comments that in his own view R.M.'s foreword lays undue emphasis on the Abbot's eccentricities and shows little appreciation of his good points.

[267] In the 'Benedictine Community' on Caldey Island.

[268] According to legend, T. B. Macaulay's sister Fanny and John Cropper, a Quaker who was connected with the manufacture of paper and also of

I am coming in for a lot of Lent addresses just now. We had the Bish. of Kensington[269] on Sunday, and he was excellent. On Sunday evening at St Paul's Fr Harris has started questions and answers instead of regular sermons, and asked us to put questions into a box for answering. A very dull question about church organization was dealt with. The curate told me he was answering next Sunday one about prayer, that he had asked himself, which doesn't seem to me fair. I put in one. I think it will be a popular service, tho' the TV religious competition on Sunday evenings is heavy, of course, and will always keep a lot of people at home, till they alter the time of the religious discussion to later in the evening. On Wednesdays [at] lunch-time I see St Cyprian's [Clarence Gate] is having an 'Any Questions' service, which I may go to sometimes when free. I think TV has put the church on its mettle, which is all to the good. I'm afraid I can't come this week, by the way, as on Friday I dine somewhere to meet the Duchess of Kent, whom I missed by going away before. I hope she is as beautiful as she looks in her photographs....

The rocket site news gets more & more disgusting.[270] People write letters about nuclear [disarmament] and ask me to join in signing them, but I seldom do, as they don't usually say what I think about it. It's no good saying nuclear weapons aren't deterrent, they probably are, but are just wrong and cruel and uncivilised, which is the point. Burning people alive for stealing

---

gunpowder 'for industrial purposes' had been discussing the ethical problems involved in the latter case.

[269] Rt Rev. Cyril Eastaugh.

[270] Details of an Anglo-American agreement on the establishment of missile sites in Britain were published on 24 February.

would be a deterrent, but no one now would dream of it as a possibility, we have got past it. But not yet past the dream of mass
bombing. I suppose we shall one day. Constance thinks Christ
didn't disapprove of war, but I can't remember that he ever mentioned it, and he certainly would have disapproved, it seems to
me.[271] I am reading the Bp of Cape Town's *Uncomfortable Words,*[272]
which I bought, and will give them to you later.

25th.... This fashion for violence at meetings is alarming. The
Rent Act one seems to have been terribly brutal.[273] I *feel* like
throwing chairs & tables, but refrain. I suppose many young men
enjoy violence for its own sake, on whatever pretext; a very
alarming symptom.

Very much love.

E.R.M.

20, Hinde House, Hinde St, W.1
12 March, [1958]

Dearest Jeanie,

... Re religion, I think it would be interesting to note down,
day by day, the religions, when known, of the people we meet.

---

[271] Christ's *acceptance* of war was what I meant; see Mark 13.7, 'And when ye
shall hear of wars and rumours of wars, be ye not troubled: for such things
must needs be.'

[272] Abp Joost de Blank, *Uncomfortable Words* (1958).

[273] A meeting at the Holborn Hall on 24 February, when the Minister of
Housing and Local Government (Mr Henry Brooke) was to speak on the
new Rent Act, had ended in uproar and brawling.

If we both do that, and perhaps get Dorothea too (I think it might interest her), we could be a kind of research institute. (Omitting those we only meet in church, and the clergy.) This week I met: *Monday*, Lunched with a non-religious man (called in my list m.); *Tuesday*, Lunched with a non. (m); also present 1 R.C. m. (from cradle), 1 non.m.… 1 F. non (lapsed French R.C), 1 m. (lately down from King's, I think non, but don't know), and 2 girls not met before, so don't know. In evening went to church with Anglican priest (no, of course I am not counting these) and his brother, a lawyer, also Anglican (extreme). *Today* I have had communication with couple upstairs, both non. Also in this block of Hinde House are 3 Jews, I *think* practising, but I only know one of them well enough to ask; she is Sara, the hairdresser on ground floor. The single Jew has that little token like a snail that they put outside their doors sometimes,[274] so I assume he practises. *Tomorrow* I am going to lunch with a non couple, and will note whom I meet, but usually most are nons there, and mostly literary or political. I had a middle aged Durham carpenter the other day mending my window, and I gathered he was non, from something he said. I find there is a good deal of connection between religion and churchgoing. All believing R.C.s go to Mass (unless excommunicated by un-confessed mortal sin) as not going to Mass on Sundays (when possible) is a mortal sin, a R.C. friend told me. There is a list of these. Lying isn't, unless complicated by some mortal-sin motive, or mortal in its effects on someone. I think fornication etc. is and must be

---

[274] A very small scroll inscribed with the ten commandments.

confessed before communion.[275] An R.C. (m) told me the other day that he had had a great relief once, some years back, when he made his confession in a strange church, & confessed a great many bad things at some length, and when he had done the priest said a few words in Latin and then absolved him without remark and when he got outside the box he noticed that it was the box for Spaniards, so he concluded the priest hadn't understood a word of what he had said. I suppose he would know some English, but not enough to follow an English confession. Another time, said this talkative R.C. man, he confessed to a priest who took him for a priest, and was very severe on his sins, till he said suddenly before the end of his lecture, 'You *are* a priest, aren't you?' When he said no, the priest's attitude changed, and was quite tolerant and indulgent and he only got the usual nominal penance. I suppose it is right to be sterner with priests.

I will bring on Friday my reports up to then. I expect both you and Dorothea meet more religious people than I do, as literary people seem on the whole apt to be non…. Thank goodness I have at last finished my wretched foreword to Peter Anson's book about the abbot…. [He] was a most shocking character—someone who knew him advised P.A. not to write his life, but 'let him be forgotten'….

Very much love.

E.R.M.

---

[275] A Roman Catholic authority comments that R.M.'s rendering of her friend's remarks is open to serious misunderstanding.

20, Hinde House, Hinde St, W.1
[17 March, 1958]
St Patrick's Day

Dearest Jeanie,

Many thanks for C.S. Lewis's letter[276] which I return. It gives quite a reasonable answer, I think. When I read the book I didn't get it all, e.g. about her [Orual's] jealousy of Ungit for being beautiful and good. But I read it rather quickly and probably not very carefully, being slightly hampered by its unplaceable period & people.

I am sorry you were worried about me; I was a little tired on Friday, but quite well now. I suppose all our memories are getting muddled; mine is. It is a nuisance, losing things and forgetting appointments and to answer letters etc. But what I'm afraid of is getting the part of my brain muddled which I use for writing. So far I think it is all right, but if it begins to fail, and I find myself unable to put my words together properly, and [start] writing awful sentences, and general low-grade nonsense of the kind I don't like in many writers, I shall give it up. I don't actually remember any writers who have gone to pieces in that way thro' age, so perhaps it doesn't happen, tho' one's intellect certainly

---

[276] This was a letter from C. S. Lewis to Dorothea Conybeare, who had asked him to explain the title of his book *Till We Have Faces*. He pointed out that it was a quotation from a remark in the book itself (p. 305), 'How can they (i.e. the gods) meet us face to face till we have faces?' 'The idea,' he continued, 'was that a human being must become real before it can expect to receive any message from the superhuman; that is, it must be speaking with its own voice (not one of its borrowed voices), expressing its actual desires (not what it imagines that it desires), being for good or ill itself, not any mask, veil or *persona.*'

fails in business & other matters. But I am relieved to notice that most elderly people go on writing much the same as before….

Do you hear 'The Way of Life'?[277] It seems rather bitty and silly to me. I like more sequence. I was a little disappointed in John Huxtable last week. He wasn't bad; but I heard him preach such a very good and unusual sermon one evening in the King's Weigh House, and these morning talks are rather commonplace compared with that. I went to the Weigh House on Sunday morning for their communion service. It is very nice, and very like ours, but we sit in our places, tho' sometimes we go up to the rail, which I much prefer. Fr Harris on Sunday evening answered my pulpit question about intercommunion; he explained the Church rules about the need for confirmation, and endorsed them, which I suppose officers of the Church must, in public. But he didn't really answer about our going to dissenting churches. However, I go and like it, tho' not really so much as our sung Masses. I suppose what some Anglicans would say is that something happens to the bread and wine when consecrated by a priest ordained by bishops which doesn't happen when not. I wish we knew the earliest history of the development of this view. There is no evidence of it in St Paul's references to the service. I expect it was thought of pretty early, to enhance the position of the clergy.

Very much love….

E.R.M.

Soon after this Rose had a fall and broke her right wrist and femur. For two weeks she was in Charing Cross Hospital, then University College Hospital. Towards the end of April she was home again.

---

[277] A weekly religious broadcast programme.

30 April, [1958]

Dearest Jeanie,

... Today I went to the Orthopaedic[278] for arm and hand treatment, by radio *[sic]* heat, and massage and exercises, and also a little leg treatment. The therapist had heard from Mr Trevor[279] that I had mended quickly, and she thought the same herself. She said I should do hand and wrist exercises, and use my hand, as it has got v. stiff and swollen, so I use it much more freely now. She says there is no danger of it coming unstuck. Tomorrow my help comes, so between us we shall get the flat much cleaner. Yesterday I had a nice god-daughter[280] to tea, and she did a lot of washing up. She is an interesting girl, and interested also in religion, and can discuss it quite intelligently. Like many of her age she reads a lot of C. S. Lewis.

Did you hear 'Lift up your Hearts' this morning? I didn't agree that Christians tend to be alike. St Francis, whom he[281] referred to, was extremely different from Savonarola, or St Bernard, or St Jerome. And I don't suppose the old lady who spent 60 years lying in bed talking cheerfully and knitting (she ought to have got up long ago I expect) was like the enterprising girl who went as a missionary to India. I liked the Royal Academy dinner speeches

---

[278] The Royal National Orthopaedic Hospital.

[279] David Trevor (Orthopaedic Consultant Surgeon to Charing Cross Hospital and the Royal National Orthopaedic Hospital), who had operated on R.M.

[280] Mary Anne O'Donovan.

[281] Rev. Donald Mason.

last night, especially Kenneth Clark's and the President's.[282]

V. much love.

E.R.M.

20, Hinde House, Hinde St, W.1
10 May, 1958

Dearest Jeanie,

… Yes, Dummelow[283] is very orthodox; a brother of Mother Selina[284] would be likely to be, I suppose. Gore's commentary[285] is more critical, but I expect even that sticks up for the credibility of the 4th Gospel on the whole. I will look up what it says about it. You might look what D. says about Mary Magdalene. I find this is often a test of whether a critic has examined the Gospel allusions to her and [those] to the 'woman who was a sinner' and came in to the supper and who was, they said, unknown to Christ; or whether they have accepted a Church tradition (started by Gregory the Great) without evidence. Gore says there is no evidence that she was a sinner; 'seven devils' usually means fits or mania in the Bible. If critics repeat this tradition without question, it usually means that they will accept others, more important, without question either. I don't know what the best recent commentary is, or what is the latest view about the 4th Gospel….

---

[282] Sir Charles Wheeler.

[283] John R. Dummelow, editor of *A Commentary on the Holy Bible* (1909).

[284] Selina Dummelow became a Deaconess and was one of Margaret Macaulay's friends.

[285] *A New Commentary on Holy Scripture, edited by* C. *Gore, H. L. Goudge and A. Guillaume* (1928).

I went to St Paul's [Cathedral] this afternoon to see the new high altar, which is very splendid, the canopy all gold and decoration and angels and a tall Christ standing at the top, and gold leaves scrolling round the pillars.[286] A woman who had come up from Lancashire to see it was almost in tears of admiration. Her mother had told her it wasn't worth the fare, but 'I've seen something better than I've ever seen in my life!' she said. She had never seen St Paul's before. I also saw the 2 new National Gallery pictures.[287] The Reni is n.g., but the Poussin is attractive, the Israelites dancing round the gold calf in touching joy, and Moses coming down the mountain to them looking furious and just about to break the Tables. It was rather a shame, they had taken so much trouble and it was a beautiful creature and they liked it so much.

Did you listen to *The Square Search* the other evening?[288]I thought it odd that a quite decent & kindly pilot should condone the cold-blooded attempted murder by another pilot of three men because he thought one of them had been getting off with his wife. All the good pilot said was, what a lot he must have been through. I should have reported him and got him sacked as a dangerous criminal. He had also deliberately wrecked two expensive planes.

V. much love.

E.R.M.

---

[286] A new high altar at St Paul's Cathedral, to replace that destroyed by bombs in 1940, was consecrated by the Bishop of London on 7 May.

[287] Guido Reni's 'The Adoration of the Shepherds' was bought by the National Gallery in 1957; Nicolas Poussin's 'The Adoration of The Golden Calf in 1945.

[288] 'Square Search', a broadcast play by Redmond Macdonogh.

17 May, 1958

Dearest Jeanie,

… I went the other night to the Layman's Trust meeting at the Albert Hall, described as a Christian Social Challenge.[289] The speakers were all good, Fr Huddleston and Manuela Sykes the best I thought. Fr H. saw me in the audience and came at the end to chat; he said he tried to come and see me in hospital, but went to Charing X after I had left it, what a pity. Tomorrow the new C. R. Superior[290] is preaching at St Paul's, Knightsbridge, I think I shall go there. Today there were May processions from various churches about the streets, in honour of Mary, who balanced rather unsteadily on her perch.[291] I should have been glad to see her topple, but couldn't throw any thing, as police were near. They (not the police but the processors) were singing Hail Mary as they walked, very monotonously. A pity no Protestant Truth champions turned up. There will be some more processions tomorrow. The Layman Trust speakers, with their emphasis on social justice and mercy, were much better representatives of Christianity. I liked the 'Lift up your Hearts' this week. What a lot of things the speaker[292] had done….

I see that the Kirk is getting very restive about the idea that

---

[289] A Mass Rally of the Layman Trust Society on 15 May. The purpose of the society is 'the linking of citizenship with Christianity'

[290] Rev. Jonathan Graham, who had succeeded Rev. Raymond Raynes as Father Superior of the Community of the Resurrection.

[291] On 17 May outdoor processions were part of the annual festival of the Society of Mary, an Anglo-Catholic organization.

[292] Janet Lacey, of the Inter-Church Aid and Refugee Service Department, British Council of Churches.

they should have bishops, and Anglican elders. It does seem silly, when all that is needed is intercommunion, without any attempt to get a similar church. I like to see bishops in church very much; the Bp of Kensington turned up at G. Chapel the other morning to confirm someone and took the 8.15 mass after it, and to see his golden mitre and crozier added great dignity to the service....

Very much love.
E.R.M.

20, Hinde House, Hinde St, W.1
27 May, [1958]

Dearest Jeanie,

The buses still out, and probably no hope of [a] meeting this week.[293] They *are* selfish & mean; and now trying to stop the coaches by calling out the petrol tankers. Well, no doubt they will have their reward. I hope you had a nice Whitsun. I drove to Sussex on Sunday and spent the afternoon with John Lehmann, who has a cottage & a wood & a small lake. I came home in comparative quiet, because of Whit Monday next day. It was my first long drive since my fall, and my hand survived it quite well, tho' ached rather. Everyone seems to be breaking their femurs just now, it seems an epidemic; I visited someone in hospital with it yesterday.[294] ... I hope she will get better ... quickly; she is coming on

---

[293] A bus strike which had begun in London on 5 May did not end until 21 June.
[294] Lady Juliet Duff.

my cruise.[295] So is Lady Diana Cooper....

The Times is having a correspondence about intercommunion, the first few days of which I enclose (mixed up with one about the Kirk, by mistake apparently).[296] I will send later letters as they come up. Anglican opinion seems sharply divided. I rather like the last letter.[297] I imagine the masses see no reason at all why we shouldn't all communicate together, or indeed with Rome, as an English woman tried to do in a Spanish church not long ago, but her acquaintances and husband told her to sit down at once. Besides believing it to be right and Christian, I also feel that it would be a pity for (say) the C. of E. & the Kirk to try and adopt one another's organizations, as neither would feel so happy that way. Much better be as different as we like, and allow intercommunion with all Christians. I certainly don't want elders, and they don't want bishops. I feel that kind of approach to a similar organization might lead to minimising Anglican ritual and ornament, which I shouldn't at all like, and perhaps making the Scotch use our P.B. more, which *they* wouldn't like....

What *is* De Gaulle up to? How is he able to 'take over the government' like that, in the face of its present members?[298]How

---

[295] R.M. was planning to go on a cruise to the Greek Islands and the Black Sea in August.

[296] This correspondence originated in comment on a leader about relations between the Churches of England and Scotland in *The Times* of 17 May. A letter from Peter J. Harrison (22 May) was chiefly concerned with Intercommunion, and others on this subject followed.

[297] A letter from E. B. Sims, whose views on Intercommunion coincided with R.M.'s.

[298] This was just before General de Gaulle was voted back to power (after the Algerian insurrection and the Corsican revolt had led to the resignation of the Prime Minister, M. Pflimlin).

odd the French are, politically. I'm sure he will do a lot of harm, and may bring about civil war. If so, which side would G.B. support, for I can't imagine we should keep neutral. Nor America either. Nor Russia. 'Massive support' would roll in for all sides, and I dare say an H-bomb would go off.

Very much love.

E.R.M.

20, Hinde House, Hinde St, W.1
31 May, 1958

Dearest Jeanie,

Thank you for your letter & enclosures…. French affairs seem to be settling down under de Gaulle, but I expect there will be a lot of trouble and violence in Algeria and Tunisia. People just back from Paris say it is very quiet, and the French shrug it away as unimportant, but are probably ashamed of it. I sent you some more intercommunion letters yesterday. Public opinion is certainly for it, and the cons are having a rough handling.[299] It looks as if the Kirk would turn down the Report; they are stiffening against episcopacy.[300] Much better drop the whole thing, and just throw down the communion barriers where they exist. I can't imagine why the Kirk should have bishops. It would split it in two, as most of them would never accept them; George MacLeod

---

[299] *The Times* published three letters in favour of Intercommunion on 29 May.
[300] The 'Bishops' Report' (which examined ways of bringing together the Churches of England and Scotland, and recommended the appointment of 'Bishops-in-Presbytery') was debated in the General Assembly of the Church of Scotland on 27 May.

would, but it is thought he would rather like to be one….

Did you see that Bishop Morris, the head of the 'English Church in South Africa', protested to the Archbishop about asking Makarios to Lambeth[301]? … I hope Makarios won't come as there would certainly be unpleasantness; he might be attacked, and General Spears says he will get him arrested and imprisoned for murder.[302] In any case he might be mobbed & shouted at & stoned, as the Czars used to be when they came over after atrocities at home.[303]

How very silly we are; some people here have now formed a 'Committee for the defence of French democracy'. I wonder what they plan to do to defend it….

I wonder if *The Observer* tomorrow will correspond any further about hell fire.[304] A rather futile subject, as every one really knows that the Biblical writers thought of real fire and that we don't any more…. Now I've just heard 'Lighten our Darkness' on the wireless,[305] but turned it off when he talked about 'the good book'

---

[301] Rt Rev. G. F. B. Morris, Bishop of the Church of England in South Africa (elected in 1955), had protested against the invitation of Abp Makarios to the Lambeth Conference, on grounds that he was associated with 'violence, treachery, and murder'.

[302] Major Gen. Sir Edward Spears had written to the Abp of Canterbury protesting against the inviting of Abp Makarios, adding that if the Abp came, he hoped to help relatives of men who had been murdered in Cyprus to arrange for his arrest.

[303] R. M. here re-echoes her misconception of the English reaction to the visit of Nicholas I of Russia in 1844, see above p. 184*n*.

[304] The final letter in a correspondence on 'Everlasting punishment' was published on 1 June.

[305] A broadcast programme of Evening Prayers conducted by Rev. Ronald Falconer.

and 'folk'. I wish people wouldn't talk like that about religion, it debases it rather and will do it no good with listeners, who are becoming more intelligent. Did you hear the 3rd Programme talk on the Church? I thought [it] interesting.[306]

How vulgar and spiteful these R.C. propagandists are about the C. of E. I'm glad we don't talk like that to the Press about them, though we do privately to one another. I think all that happened to the Church Enquiry Bureau was that they thought of starting one and decided not to after all, as they didn't think there would be enough demand.[307] I expect they were right; very few people would write and ask about the C. of E., which most people think they know quite enough about already, whereas very many are curious about Rome, and (in this country) great numbers are attracted by it, because it is strange to them and romantic. Lots, when they get to know it, don't like it much and don't join, or soon leave. But there is a much more admiring feeling about it here than in R.C. countries, where the majority belong, but complain of it. There have been several attacks on it lately, in Irish and French books by lapsed R.C.s who didn't like their education in Jesuit schools. I imagine that when the C. of E. quite disintegrates, its former members will mostly either become agnostic or R.C. and the fight will be 'between irreligion & Catholicism', as the R.C.s say it is now. I doubt if dissent will ever be powerful again. The Scotch Church Assembly says the Romans treat people like infants, the Anglicans like adolescents, and they themselves like civilized adults; hence they won't be

---

[306] 'The Church and England', a talk by Rev. Joseph McCulloch.

[307] On 17 June, 1958 the Abp of Canterbury (Dr Fisher) admitted, during a debate in the Church Assembly, that the Church of England Enquiry Centre had ceased to function owing to financial difficulties.

ruled by bishops.[308] I like bishops, their golden mitres shine so finely, and their croziers. We had Bishop Hamilton[309] this morning at St Paul's [Knightsbridge]; he used once to be vicar there. He preached well, about the division between Christians and non-Christians, if they ever came to be sorted out, which I agree with him is whether they believe that Christ was in any sense God or not. He is a thoughtful bish., but rather slow perhaps; he is reputed the best-looker on the Bench….

Very much love.

E.R.M.

20, Hinde House, Hinde St, W.1
12 June, [1958]

Dearest Jeanie,

… I sent you a card from Stonehenge, where I spent an hour on the downs in sunshine looking at the stones.[310] Then my companion took over the driving and drove me home, which was restful, as I don't like to drive for so long with my present hand, tho' it doesn't damage it really. I am driving to Cambridge tomorrow for the night, but that is a much shorter way. The Conference[311] should be interesting, as some good speakers are there.

---

[308] This comment was made by Rev. Prof. W. R. Forrester of St Andrews in the General Assembly of the Church of Scotland on 27 May.

[309] Rt Rev. E. K. C. Hamilton, (1890–1962).

[310] R.M. was on the way back to London after a week-end at Long Crichel House.

[311] A Christian Action conference held at Westcott House, Cambridge.

If I had 7 yrs alone in prison, and a ball-top pen, or still better a typewriter, I should write a long and very successful book recording my reactions & thoughts & occupations each day, something like yours, no doubt, and, like yours, showing my degeneration into imbecility and morbidity.[312] It would make a lot of money when published, probably more than yours, as I should start with a known name. But I dare say yours might be better.

I will send you the two books I am now reviewing later. Both are small books, one by Lord Altrincham,[313] one by Peter Kirk,[314] son of the late Bp of Oxford. Both are about the C. of E., both making criticisms & suggestions, but P.K. is a much firmer member of it. When at Oxford he says he got discontented with it and had a good look at the R.C. and Quaker Churches; at first he was pleased with Rome, but after a time he saw he could never join it, owing to its narrowness, bigotry and erroneous belief that it was the one true Church, besides Mariolatry etc. He admired the morality and good works of Quakers, but wanted something more articulate; he couldn't worship without any stimulus of words, music, etc., and also likes sacraments. He then decided to stay C. of E., and now much prefers it to anything else, and thinks there is the greatest potentiality of good in it, anyhow for him. He is sensible about disunion, feeling that every one must stay in the Church which best shows & helps him to be Christian, and that differences are quite a good thing. He believes in apostolic succession as a help to the value of sacraments, and I don't

---

[312] This is à propos of *Seven Years Solitary* (1957) by Edith Bone, a former Communist who was imprisoned in Hungary for seven years.

[313] *Two Anglican Essays* (1958).

[314] *One Army Strong?* (1958).

agree with him in everything. Lord A., on the other hand, makes a fuss about the things in the creeds, Prayer Book and Bible that he can't believe; he is a little childish about it, thinking it keeps many people out of the Church. Of course in the case of clergy he is partly right. But I get bored with all this literalness, like those humanists telling us we must believe in material hell fire because it is mentioned in the New Testament,[315] as if Christianity wasn't allowed to march with the times and re-interpret from age to age, like any other system of thought. Because every one believed in material hell torments 2000 years ago (and even much later, like Dante) is no reason at all why anyone should now. Peter Kirk says one very odd thing; that his father the Bp never told him that he was brought up a Methodist, but let him think he had been C. of E. always. I suppose his grandparents were dead, or was he never allowed to meet them? He discovered by looking thro' his father's papers after his death that he changed to C. of E. at Oxford. It would seem to me almost impossible to keep it dark from one's children, considering how enquiring children are; you would think Peter would ask how many times on Sundays his father had to go to church, and what church was it, etc. etc. I wonder if his mother too was in the dark. Peter says he is puzzled as to the reason, but it was probably snobbery; many people did say he was rather a snob. I should have been nervous about its coming out and making me look silly & deceitful....

Very much love.

E.R.M.

---

[315] R.M. was probably thinking of letters from Margaret Knight and Colin McCall (Secretary of the National Secular Society) in the recent correspondence on 'Everlasting punishment' in *The Observer.*

20, Hinde House, Hinde St, W.1
16 June, [1958]

Dearest Jeanie,

Thank you so much for yours, and interesting piece on Cyprus by Cameron.[316] How menacing it all is. Turks v. Greek Cypriotes would be a very barbarous and savage war, horrible to contemplate; neither Turks nor Greeks bar any holds in war. If only we can save it from coming to that.

My Conference was really worth while, I think. We discussed a number of things (I enclose the programme), and had a lot of it in the garden, in lovely weather. Quite a bit of Church thrown in, H.C. for any one who liked to come (Canon Collins doesn't fence the Anglican altar), and other prayers for those who didn't like to, as most of the non-Anglicans didn't. I went on Sunday morning to a very attractive Children's Mass at Little St Mary's. Adults communicated, some with infants (in their arms or kneeling by their sides) who got blessed by the priest, and the bread and wine brought up by two children, and five children kneeling at the rail holding candles, which they raised high during the elevation. A very good church training for them.

All the conference speakers were good, the best were Canon Collins on Nuclear bombs and Mervyn Stockwood on the general position of Christianity today. I am glad he is on the Commission for revising the Canons, Liturgy, etc.,[317] as he is on the right lines about it. As he put it, he hopes the revisers will 'play ducks &

---

[316] See *News Chronicle*, 10 June, 1958. James Cameron's article was entitled 'A tough baby lands in Mr Lloyd's lap'.

[317] R.M. means the Liturgical Commission for the Revision of the Prayer Book, which is not concerned with the revision of the Canons.

drakes' with a great deal of it…. Canon Stockwood … thinks the Church will never pull much weight till … assumptions [such as the Genesis view, which assumes that man was once perfect and fell] are got rid of & no one can taunt Christians with believing nonsense. Also the [Thirty-nine] Articles must be torn up, or most of them. He is a very energetic and purposeful man, and speaks excellently. I believe he fills the University Church every Sunday in term with undergraduates and dons—and no doubt elderly women too, tho' he spoke with scorn of a Church which 'only appealed to elderly women and children'. I sometimes feel quite ashamed of being one, as Dorothea used to say she did when Fr Waggett was at Great St Mary's. The clergy seem very friendly when one talks to them, but all the time I suppose they are feeling that one is rather contemptible and not worth while. I wonder about old men; but of course fewer of them go to church.

The Bishop of Willesden[318] spoke in favour of retaining nuclear bombs as a deterrent; he feels quite hysterical about Russia and the threat of Communism, which he says is 'wholly of the devil'; and better keep the bomb, & even use it if necessary, than risk Russian occupation. Canon Collins replied to him very well, saying all I think about it. Afterwards we formed groups, and discussed it, and each group made a report of our conversation, which was read aloud later on, after the Bishop had gone, so our group reporter could say that 'The group found the Bp of Willesden somewhat onesided and even hysterical in his views.' The Bp of Jo'burg[319] unfortunately couldn't come; I am going this evening to his meeting[320] at the Central Hall [Westminster]

---

[318] Rt Rev. G. E. Ingle.

[319] Rt Rev. R. A. Reeves.

[320] A meeting organized by Christian Action.

when he will tell of his African experiences. The Racialism discussion was entirely about Africans v. Europeans, which seemed a pity, as there is so much other race hate, but we had a Kenya man, Mr [Joseph] Murumbi, there, so he kept it to that. The only blot on the proceedings was the speech of an English worker in Kenya, who had asked if he might come and give his point of view, tho' he doesn't belong to Christian Action. He made a most embarrassing speech, about how we ought to know the reasons for Europeans not liking to mix with Africans or share their lavatories etc.; it was a question of two levels of civilization and hygiene (meaning obviously syphilis) and it was very unpleasant to mix them. Mr Murumbi was present of course, and every one was very angry. Canon Collins replied to it, pointing out that when one was in a foreign land, such as Italy e.g., one had to adapt oneself to its lavatory arrangements, tho' no doubt every one preferred those they were used to. Mr Murumbi also spoke, but avoided the lavatory question. I liked Fr Corbishley,[321] the R.C., whom I sat next at dinner on Saturday; but his talk wasn't very practical, too much about Thomist views on war etc., and how every one is 'equal', which is obviously untrue. Does it mean in character, brains, or what? But almost the best was Janet Lacey, who manages the Refugee Church Aid,[322] and gave a most interesting account of refugees everywhere, and the general situation. Such a nice large beneficent woman. She did 'Lift up your Hearts' lately, and I liked her then....

Very much love.

E.R.M.

---

[321] Rev. Thomas Corbishley, s.j.
[322] See above p. 266n.

I liked Edith Bone's account of her 7 years in prison.[323] She is wonderfully courageous & tough. The worst part would be the filthy floor, I think.

20, Hinde House, Hinde St, W.1
19 June, [1958]

Dearest Jeanie,

… I am sorry to miss you tomorrow, but shall be at Stonehenge, spending first part of the night at Amesbury, where I have booked a room, and going on to Sunrise on Stonehenge (there probably won't be any) about 4 a.m. I am writing about it in my novel,[324] and thought I had better get it right. I shall like to see the Druids at their sun-worship; I saw a booklet giving their prayers to the Great Light. No sacrifices are allowed. Then I have breakfast and drive back to London along, I hope, nice quiet morning roads.

Thank you for cuttings. [James] Cameron is a v.g. commentator, and writes well always. I fear his pessimism is justified. No one seems to have a hope. The Turkish ambassador here says Turks are feeling very anti-British, so are the Greeks. Macmillan may as well save his breath this afternoon for all the good he will do.[325]

Bp Reeves spoke very well, and very fairly, giving credit to the South African government for spending millions on housing and

---

[323] See above, p. 272n.

[324] *Venice Besieged.*

[325] The Prime Minister was to present the British plan for Cyprus to Parliament that afternoon.

schools etc., for Africans. How silly the papers are for only reporting interruptions at meetings.[326] The Bp ignored them all and went on talking thro' them. Lord Pakenham, when he spoke, answered interrupters & made them look silly, which may be better. He begged us all to see the question in the highest light we knew, if we didn't happen to believe in a God. A young man shouted 'The highest light is the British Empire.' Lord P. commented 'An understandable view, but, if I may say so, a little parochial.' On the 27th I promised to attend a Women's anti-bomb meeting. I refused at first, as I don't approve of sex segregation on public questions, but later said I would, as it is important to stir up ordinary women about it. They have a good platform list.

Geoffrey Murray in the *News Chronicle* was rather unfair and sensational about Lord Altrincham's not very good little book[327]. He doesn't, e.g. say the clergy in general have 'a rapt Druidical air', but only that when they file into church they have. His book is often silly & ill-mannered & crude, but I think is worth while. He thinks the communion service involves a theory of atonement which he dislikes … but I didn't like, in my review, to snub him for his efforts for reform. I will send or give you the book. We *must* meet next week (not Friday). When we do, you might suggest some good religious books for me to speak about to the Mothers' Union (mostly officials and Bishops' wives, not so much the common run) on July 9…. No, I shouldn't canonize Newman, tho' apparently the Vatican means to presently. After all what were his

---

[326] Interruptions by hecklers when the Bp of Johannesburg addressed the recent Christian Action meeting were reported in detail in *The Times*.

[327] *Two Anglican Essays,* see above p. 272.

saintly deeds? I should saint Fr Damien,[328] Schweitzer, and any who have given their lives up to difficult work for other people at great personal sacrifice.

V. much love.

E.R.M.

20, Hinde House, Hinde St, W.1
16 July, 1958

Dearest Jeanie,

Many thanks for yours and cutting. I cut out for you from *The Times* Dr Chavasse's angry abuse of pacifists in his sermon to Territorials.[329] But I can't find it. I enclose however a reply from me, from which you will gather the kind of thing he said.[330] He certainly *was* 'bloody-minded', tho' I agree that a clergyman shouldn't call him so in the pulpit.[331] He says the Peace Pledge

---

[328] The Leper missionary (1840–89).

[329] The Bp of Rochester, Rt Rev. C. M. Chavasse, preaching on 13 July at a Territorial Army jubilee service at Rochester Cathedral, had said that total destruction and possibly a lingering death for any survivors would be a lesser evil than serfdom under a totalitarian domination. He said pacifists preached that it was best to save one's skin at any price, and attributed to them the responsibility for the 'stupidity and iniquity of the second world war'.

[330] A letter from R.M. to *The Times* in defence of pacifism was published on 15 July. She called the Bp of Rochester's accusation about 'saving one's skin' 'an exact reversal of the fact'.

[331] Jean Macaulay had sent a cutting from the *News Chronicle* of 14 July, reporting that the Rev. R. C. Gaul, of Rand, Lincs., had said from his pulpit that 'the Bishop of Rochester is bloody-minded enough to see no difference in principle between bows and arrows and the H-bomb.'

Union caused the 1940 war. What nonsense. It never had the slightest effect on the Government's defence policy. The war was caused by Hitler's mad aggressions and our desire to stop them. The Bp of Jo'burg told Canon Collins the other evening that bishop after bishop at the [Lambeth] Conference got up and spoke for the H-bomb. I now of course have got a lot of letters, some from agreers, some from not. I shan't answer most of them. I only have one thing to say about it, and I've said it in my letter—I don't think it is civilized either to make or use the things. As to Cantuar, can he be going rather mad, with the pressure of this Conference and all he has to do?[332] If God's plan is for the human race to perish, why choose such a wicked end? Another flood, or great quake or pestilence, would be more moral. If the former, who would you select for the Ark? No animals, I expect. I don't think the Noahs were really worthy, they weren't a very nice family. William Clark said yesterday that he doesn't think we shall get our cruise. I was rather discouraged, as he is the very well informed political correspondent on foreign affairs for *The Observer.* But I hope he is wrong. How very impertinent all this rushing of troops into Lebanon is.[333] Really the small states mustn't start calling the big ones in to save them from their

---

[332] In *The Fearful Choice: A Debate on Nuclear Policy conducted by Philip Toynbee* (1958) Abp Fisher had commented that he was convinced it was never right to settle any policy simply out of fear of the consequences. He said that for all he knew it was within the providence of God that the human race should destroy itself by means of nuclear war, adding that there is no evidence that the human race is to last for ever and plenty in Scripture to the contrary effect.

[333] After the Army revolt in Iraq, President Chamoun of Lebanon had appealed to the U.S. for forces to help maintain security, and 1500 marines landed at Beirut on 15 July.

revolutions; they must manage them for themselves. If we had a revolution here, we should never dream of sending for Lebanese help, nor even, I hope, American, tho' their planes are on our shores already. I suppose we shall go in ourselves before long. How nosey the nations are about each other's quarrels, as if we hadn't enough of our own.

I was glad Frank Pakenham wrote to defend Canon Collins in *The Observer,*[334] it will have cheered him up. I am lunching with Lord P. in the House of Lords next Wed. Rather amusing to see the other Lords at their food.

I'm so sorry you have caught radio activity. Mine is much better now, but I still feel lassitude. This evening I am going as John Betjeman's guest to a City dinner.[335] Decorations to be worn, so I shall for the first time don my pretty D.B.E. But I fear I shall be a poor hand at the food and drink....

Dorothea writes that Fr Wood (St Clement's) used to say that communion 3 times a year is all we are mostly 'ready for'. Rather surprising, from him.[336] Rochester doesn't think we need go much at all, but he is Low.[337]

---

[334] In *The Observer* of 6 July 'Pendennis' had written of Abp Fisher '... he is unexpectedly self-critical, and (unlike Canon Collins) often admits he is wrong.' The following week a letter from Lord Pakenham was published saying of Canon Collins 'I have found him very different from that, and full of Christian humility.'

[335] A dinner given by the Grocers' Company.

[336] Canon E. G. de S. Wood, Vicar of St Clement's, Cambridge from 1885 to 1931, was an Anglo-Catholic who advocated the daily Eucharist.

[337] The Bp of Rochester (Rt Rev. C. M. Chavasse) at a recent Diocesan Conference had recommended twice-monthly celebration of Holy Communion, once in the morning and once in the evening.

20, Hinde House, Hinde St, W.1
24 July, 1958

Dearest Twin,

This is to send my love for tomorrow, tho' I shall see you later. I forget which year you will be entering on; I prefer to forget that about both you and me, so don't tell me. Our age grows too formidable. But, whichever year it is, I do hope it will be a good one for you. Perhaps your sight will be improved in it by the cataract operation; I hope so. Anyhow, I hope we shall meet a lot.

Did you hear my voice (but not in the sung parts, as that was confined to the choir and clergy) in the High Mass from All Saints' [Margaret Street] on Sunday at 9.45? I don't expect so. But I was there, and felt I was broadcasting. It was a beautifully done service, and I expect came over well. I liked Fr Ross's[338] sermon, too…. My City dinner with John Betjeman was fun, as his company always is. We drove back to his flat in the City together afterwards, and he talked about the things no one else but you and Dorothea ever wants to talk about (anyhow with me) such as confessions, beliefs, communion …

I am so glad you enjoyed 'Frankly Speaking'.[339] I thought my interrogators[340] very intelligent and civilized and easy to discuss with. Why does——say I 'made short work of them'? I don't know what she means. Nor by saying that she and a friend of hers were disappointed that I showed no 'faith'—didn't like H-bombs but had nothing to recommend instead, etc.

---

[338] Rev. K. N. Ross, Vicar of All Saints', Margaret St.

[339] R.M. had been interviewed in this programme on 20 July.

[340] William Clark, Nicholas Fenn, and Alec Robertson.

etc.——never will, I fear, think I show 'faith'. It would sound conceited to tell her of all the clergy and laity who found it in *Trebizond*, which I meant to be about the struggle of good and evil, its eternal importance, and the power of the Christian Church over the soul, to torment and convert.... [She] found none of that in it ... she only thought I was 'mocking'___I expect we are too different. A young woman I didn't know came up to me at the Empire Hall & told me reading *Trebizond* at a crucial moment in her life had decided her for the right course, and she had always wanted to tell me. ——would be puzzled by this, and by the clergy who read bits of it to doubting ordinands, with successful results. But to tell her this would sound like conceit.... I have had several letters about 'Frankly Speaking'. Roughly, the educated ones liked it, the non-educated didn't. Some of these were angry that I didn't like Sabbatarianism; others thought I spoke lightly of serious things. I suppose it relieves their annoyance to write, but I wish they wouldn't. But I am told the B.B.C. gets angry letters and telephone calls all day from people who haven't liked a programme. What a lot it must cost them. And they are usually poor people; I expect the rich just switch off. I think the poor feel they have paid for something and aren't getting their money's worth, so complain and feel better.

Lying. I think generally wrong, except in the case of small polite lies about being pleased to see people, sorry we can't, etc. But some lies I should think right; e.g. if it was the only way to save a victim from his pursuers or aggressors. I should certainly say I didn't know where he was, even if I did. I might also lie to save someone being badly hurt by something said about them. I don't think I should bother about lying for my country, even if I knew what lie would help it. Nor for my Church. If I could by a lie abolish the use of nuclear weapons, I would, but I can't think of any lie which would achieve this, can you? This would be to save the human race. I don't see why a woman's character should be shielded more than a man's. I shouldn't try to shield either unless something very terrible would be done to them if unshielded. I don't call it lying to say I believe something in order to remain a clergyman, as religious belief is too uncertain and shifting a ground (with me) to speak of lying or truth in connection with it. One believes in patches, and it is a vague, inaccurate word. I could never say 'I believe in God' in the same sense that I could say 'I believe in the sun & moon & stars.'

Did you hear, by the way, the story of Darwin & the *Beagle* voyage?[341] I wonder if clergy and other Christians really told him that 'immutability of species' was stated in Genesis. I can't think where. I don't remember anything about it at all, do you? If it became a religious doctrine, I wonder why, and when? But their whole conversation, including the Ark story, sounds too fantastic to be true. I must look it up.

Yes, Trebizond in my novel stood in Laurie's mind for the Christian Church. I thought I made that clear. I think the questioners asked did it stand for an ideal city or something, and if I had had longer notice I would have been able to explain more at length. These snap answers are unsatisfactory.

My House of Lords lunch with Lord Pakenham was amusing, but the part of the debate we heard afterwards in the Lords was deadly dull, all about motor car testing, tho' they had meant to discuss the Middle East, I should hate to be a life peeress.

More tomorrow when we meet. What a difference it makes to

---

[341] 'The Voyage of the Beagle' by H. A. L. Craig, a 'dramatized reconstruction of some events in Darwin's five-year cruise', was one of the broadcasts to mark the centenary of the theory of evolution.

life to be able to say that! It is one of my greatest pleasures.

Very much love, from your loving *Twin.*

20, Hinde House, Hinde St, W.1
2 August, [1958]

Dearest Jeanie,

    … I said I would look up my birthday collect (for St Peter's chains). It is a nice one: 'O God, by whose power blessed Peter the apostle was loosed from his chains, loose us, we beseech thee, from the chains of our sins, and mercifully put away from us all evil things.' A good introit, too. The Lesson, of course, is about Peter coming out of prison. The Gospel is the one R.C.s like so much, about 'upon this rock I will build my church'. I wish we had this feast in the B.C.P. Perhaps Lambeth, or the Commission on liturgical reform more likely, will put in a few more Saints' Days….

    I hope you are getting on with the Church Diet.[342] I should think you were almost out of the Abbots now, and almost on to Abel. What a lot you will know when you have finished it—except that at 90 you may not take it all in so well….

[No signature]

Three weeks after this Rose set off on her last trip abroad, a cruise to the Aegean Islands and the Black Sea, starting from Venice and ending with a second brief stay there.

---

[342] *The Oxford Dictionary of the Christian Church*, which R.M. had given her.

20, Hinde House, Hinde St, W.1
17 August, [1958]

Dearest Jeanie,

... I leave for Venice Thursday 11 a.m.... Mind you cable in case of illness or anything.

I am sending you a mixed packet of papers—some bits from *Sunday Times,* Father Ross's ... views on future life as I am investigating what people think about this, and an answer from *Catholic Herald* about what it is permissible to believe about evolution and the method of Eve's birth. I don't expect any one does believe it, actually. By the way, I looked up the Greek for Matt. 5, 32, and Knox's trans. is a quite impudent invention.[343] The Greek word means 'apart from', *not* 'whether or not'. It always seems odd that, knowing it would be read by Greek scholars who know what the original says, Knox should have the audacity to mistranslate as he does. Still, I suppose he was between devil and deep sea, and better be despised by scholars than rebuked by the Vatican and perhaps have his trans. withdrawn....

Poor Fr Derry failed to get anyone to take the Grosvenor Chapel services today, so nobly returned from his holiday in Devon for today, and has just gone back there again. I think he might have left it untaken when he found no one he wrote to could come. I told him he could probably have got a Free Church

---

[343] R. A. Knox, in his translation of the New Testament, renders this passage as follows: 'the man who puts away his wife (setting aside ... unfaithfulness) makes an adulteress of her'. In a footnote he comments, 'The Greek word here translated "setting aside" has commonly been taken as meaning "unless she is unfaithful", but it can also be interpreted as meaning "whether she is unfaithful or not".'

minister to take the early mass, tho' I suppose they have their own services at 11.O. I should do this in his place, and risk reproof by the Bishop and congregation.

> Very much love....
> Your loving *E.R.M.*

Venice[344]
25 August, [1958]

Perfect weather, charming little pensione—I am breakfasting in the garden under vine trellis. I had a comfortable journey. Venice seems full of acquaintances. Yesterday I went to the little Anglican church at 8.30, and mass at St Mark's later. I have seen a lot of things I wanted to see. This morning I shall go and bathe on the Lido. On Wednesday the *Hermes* sails from here for Greece & Black Sea. I pray I shan't miss it!... Yesterday I kept Uncle Regi's[345] centenary! He can never happen again.

> V. much love.
> *E.R.M.*

S.S. Hermes[346]
29 August, [1958]

... We are just back from Delphi, where we had a heavenly afternoon and evening. Very hot, and some steep climbing, but so

---

[344] Postcard.

[345] R. H. Macaulay (1858–1937), R.M.'s uncle and godfather.

[346] Postcard.

beautiful. Now it is dark, and at midnight we go through the straits of Corinth, for Athens & Daphni. It is a very successful cruise, with such nice people on it. I am glad to have got to know better Lady Diana Cooper, a very charming and beautiful person. The crew are all Greek, and talk hardly any English. The Chaplain[347] is Low Church, and works in Rochester Diocese. However, he held an early celebration for St John Beheaded this morning, which he said he could not have done in his own parish. Last year the chaplain had daily mass and compline in the evenings. A Presbyterian passenger says they only have communion 4 times in the year. The Lambeth Report was dull, I thought. But sensible on birth control[348]....

V. much love.

E.R.M.

Venice[349]
14 September, [1958]

Back in Venice, after a wonderful voyage. I think the Greek islands (3) were the most delightful of all—marvellous bathing, temples on mountains (I rode up on a donkey), charming little towns where one bought mementoes, hot sunshine. Trebizond

---

[347] Rev. G. R. W. Beaumont.

[348] The Resolution on Family Planning (in the Report of the 1958 Lambeth Conference) asserted that the responsibility for deciding the number and frequency of children has been laid by God on the consciences of parents. This 'requires a wise stewardship of the resources and abilities of the family as well as thoughtful consideration of the varying population needs and problems of society'.

[349] Postcard.

was like coming home. Russia like a ridiculous fairy story, full of sanatoria & resting workers. Istanbul wonderful from the sea, not so attractive inside; ship life entertaining and comfortable, such nice people. Of course Venice is better than anything else.... I have to write an article on the cruise for the *Queen* magazine now.[350] ...

Very much love.

E.R.M.

20, Hinde House, Hinde St, W.1
22 September, [1958]

Dearest Jeanie,

... Life is closing round me again, now that I can no longer live like a lily of the field but must toil & spin. No doubt it is better for one, mentally and morally. And it is nice to get daily early Mass again and have it properly taken. If one lived in the country and had no choice of churches and a Low Church vicar, one's spiritual life would have to be very intense if it was to remain alive.... If I was a clergyman I would live in Venice, try and get the job of regular chaplain to the English church, and spend the week trying to convert the natives, tempting them with clouds of incense and a great number of images and processions. Tho' actually I believe non-R.C. processions aren't allowed there. But anyhow the English would come, or some of them, and I should quietly seduce some Italians, perhaps with little presents....

It was lovely seeing you again. V. much love.

E.R.M.

---

[350] See *The Queen*, 30 September, 1958, 'The New Argonauts'. 287

25 September, [1958]

Dearest Jeanie,

... I didn't hear about the people sitting outside Aldermaston, and don't know what good they hope to do.[351] That is the worst of *The Times*, it ignores so much folly that one likes to hear about. For other reasons, the evening papers probably also would ignore this, thinking it anti-nuclear-weapon. The *News Chronicle* is the best paper for these enterprises. J. Cameron today is v.g.[352] He puts things so well and incisively.

My distaste (general, of course, by no means universal) for the Low Church way of celebrating Holy Communion is that it so often seems to me slovenly and unceremonious, and the service read too slowly and expressively, the priest seeming to put his own personality into it instead of saying it in a level, colourless way so that one gets the meaning without emphasis or the intrusion of personality. Also, I naturally prefer the order of prayers (and the additions) that I am used to and take for granted. And I prefer the celebrant to pray facing the altar, not facing either south or towards the congregation, except when addressing us. If I found the Low way as good (for me) as the High, I would go to St Paul's, Baker Street,[353] much my nearest

---

[351] The *News Chronicle* (22 September, 1958) reported that members of the Direct Action Committee against Nuclear War had been picketing the Atomic Weapons Research Establishment at Aldermaston for 9 weeks continuously.

[352] Jean Macaulay had enclosed a leader by James Cameron (*News Chronicle*, 22 September) on a 'new order for teen-agers' in Communist China: 'Youth to work by day, study by night.'

[353] R.M. means St Paul's, Portman Square.

church. (Except that it only has Sunday services, another defect of Low churches.) As it is, I am very lucky to have Grosvenor Chapel so near. Even if I had to walk I can do it in 13 minutes, and in the car it takes about 5 or 6 only. And All Saints' is very little further (tho' earlier). Fr Derry ... is educated, intelligent, and ... preaches well. And the Chapel itself is a charming one. So I am v. lucky....

I asked Gerard Irvine the other day what he thought about life after death. He said he thought purgatory would be a state of trying to get used to being with God, which would inevitably be painful at first, and to some people very tedious and unrewarding. After a time he thinks one would get used to it and it would cease to be painful and one would get to like it, or else become quite worn down by it and at last crumble away.[354]

V. much love.

E.R.M.

20, Hinde House, Hinde St, W.1
[29 September, 1958]
Michaelmas

Dearest Jeanie,

... A young man who was in the German Embassy[355] and is now in Bonn is staying here for a few days at the Embassy and wanted to see me, so he and I and Gerard Irvine drove about on Saturday showing him extreme Anglican churches, which he

---

[354] Gerard Irvine points out that the observation beginning 'or else' is an addition by R.M. to what he had said.

[355] Helmut Rueckriegel.

likes; he nearly joined our Church when in London (he is a high Lutheran) but when sent back to Germany could find no English churches at all high, which are the only kind he likes, so now is on the verge of Rome, at present hesitating because his father doesn't like it. We did our best to persuade him into C. of E. but our influence will wear off once he is back in Germany, and he will pope soon…. I took him yesterday to St Mary's, Bourne St, about the highest church in London, which he liked. The preacher (the vicar[356]) said we needed things to remind us of the church festivals, which we might otherwise forget—such as Easter eggs, gooseberry pie on Whit Sunday, midnight Mass and carols at Christmas, hot cross buns on Good Friday. He said if hot cross buns didn't remind him what day it was, they would choke him. His idea was that all these symbols are [in the nature of] sacraments, calling us to Church life. Do you remember the young man whose faith died and who was going to keep Good Friday like an ordinary day, but when his cook came in & asked him what time he would like lunch, he came to himself, exclaimed *Lunch* on Good Friday!" and rushed off to the 3 Hours …

Today I am remembering your Baptism, but have forgotten mine, which was noted in my baptism Bible that Miss Currey[357] gave me and illuminated with the text about 'remembering always our profession', but got burnt[358] in '41 so now I can't ever remember it. I don't think mother used to remind us of our days, which I should have thought she would.

What do the people round Aldermaston sit on? What would

---

[356] Rev. F. E. P. Langton.
[357] One of R.M.'s godmothers.
[358] When R.M.'s flat was bombed.

you do to call attention to the Jane Furse [Memorial Hospital] (say)?[359] I should drive round and round Manchester Square all day, never stopping, as I prefer to be under cover. I suppose I should have to have a flag about my Cause.

The book about U and non-U speech[360] was merely, of course, a study in the different words used by different sections of people; it was not meant to be about differences in outlook. That would be a much more difficult and profounder research, and probably not nearly so accurate. Anyone can hear the language differences and the different accents; the differences in mind and character caused by different educations are much more complex, and are complicated by differences in character between members of the same social class.

I didn't hear the 'Brains Trust'. But I think there is something in their view that spying shouldn't be done in the interests of other countries against one's own. After all, one accepts the benefits of social welfare, police protection, etc. etc., given by one's country, so it would seem mean to work against it while doing that, except when one thinks it very wrong in its policy, or a very corrupt government as Vichy was. But I wouldn't spy against Britain just because of Cyprus, Suez, Nuclear weapons, etc. Gerard Irvine, who was in Greece lately, had a conversation with Makarios, who called on the Archbishop of Athens while he was there. They got on quite well. Gerard told him that many of us

---

[359] The missionary hospital in the Transvaal where Jean Macaulay nursed in 1938–9. Subsequently she was always a keen supporter.

[360] A. S. C. Ross, Nancy Mitford, Evelyn Waugh, 'Strix' [Peter Fleming], Christopher Sykes, and John Betjeman, *Noblesse Oblige* (1956).

regretted what Cantuar said about him,[361] and M. replied that he himself regretted some of the things said about us.

I am sending you the *Dome*,[362] which I picked up in a very extreme church in—on Saturday. I don't know how wide its circulation is. It was their congregation who marched to Walsingham to atone for their new vicar, who had dropped some of their cherished rites. I ought to march to Walsingham to atone for my nearest church,[363] which has no weekday masses and only once a month on Sundays. Instead, they leave me notices about speakers from Keswick who function there. We certainly have a wonderful variety in the C. of E....

Very much love.

E.R.M.

Do read *Evelyn Underhill,* if you can get it.364 It is interesting. She was ... very self-absorbed, and concerned with her spiritual state. There is an allusion to going to see 'Deaconess Margaret' from Haslemere, but probably not Margaret, whom she would call 'Sister Margaret' I think. Anyhow, M. would have mentioned meeting her.

---

[361] Abp Fisher, when asked (in a television interview on 25 June) why Abp Makarios had been invited to the Lambeth Conference, replied 'He is by tradition one of the officials invited ... I had to invite him ... I know as well as anybody what a bad character he is ...' Later, after leaders of the Greek Orthodox Church had protested against the reference to 'bad character', he sent a cable of apology.

[362] *A newspaper for 'Anglican Catholics'.*

[363] St Paul's, Portman Square.

[364] Margaret Cropper, *Evelyn Underhill* (1958).

6 October, [1958]

Dearest Jeanie,

… I enclose … an article from the *Times* Cyprus correspondent, saying that murder of women was planned by the Eoka leaders in order to infuriate the troops and provoke them to violence which they can then complain of. What a vicious circle it has all become.[365] …

Yes, I think the Lambeth Report is pretty unimportant, and says nothing but platitudes. Perhaps these were all they *did* say. They are hampered by disagreements among themselves, of course; e.g. about Nuclear weapons. (By the way, I am surprised you thought D. Soper[366] was for these; he has always been a pacifist.)

… I have a letter from P. Anson saying the book[367] is going well, tho' the Abbot of Prinknash was very vexed that a life of their disreputable but honoured founder should have been written at all. Their attitude towards him seems very ambivalent. They know how bad he was in many ways, but want to honour him all the same, and have enshrined his relics in the foundations of a huge Benedictine church they are building. They would rather he remained a pious legend than be revealed as a very faulty man. It makes one wonder how many of the saints of the Church were similarly built up; it is an interesting thought. The

---

[365] One Englishwoman was killed and another seriously injured by Eoka gunmen in Famagusta on 3 October. The subsequent search for the murderers was carried out by British troops who (according to the *Times* Cyprus correspondent) 'were in the grip of sheer cold rage'.

[366] Rev. Donald Soper, Methodist minister.

[367] *Abbot Extraordinary.*

Tablet review (by an oblate of Prinknash) calls P. Anson 'waspish' towards Carlyle.[368] I thought he should have been considerably more so. I shall look forward to seeing the *Cath. Herald*. I am glad P.A. got in his Life before there was a pious one by some Prinknash monk.

I sometimes wish fools wouldn't talk so much on the wireless, I must say. One gets very sick of hearing them at it when one switches on. I suppose their egoism supports them thro' it and persuades them that they are liked. Anyhow, they get paid. In private life, we ought to talk in our natural manner whenever we like, so long as our natural manner isn't (it often is) too spiteful and unkind. Private *folly* in talk does no great harm. Anyhow one can't be always stopping to think 'Is what I want to say sensible?' or one might be quite silent (as I am when I am among people who discuss things too high for me).

Very much love, & do take care.

R.

20, Hinde House, Hinde St, W.1
27 October, [1958]

Dearest Jeanie,

Many thanks for yours and for sending Andrew Duncan-Jones.[369] I think the condemnatory and self-righteous verses in

---

[368] *The Tablet*, 4 October, 1958.

[369] In a letter to *The Times* (13 October, 1958) on the Revision of the Psalter, Rev. Andrew Duncan-Jones pointed out that a knowledge of the Bible is of much greater importance than 'leaving out the bits we don't like'. R.M. then wrote to him asking about the interpretation of one of the Psalms.

the Psalms can only be used about one's own worse self, and when it comes to helping them and giving them kindness, it makes nonsense, as in Ps. 35, v. 13[370] etc. It is obviously an offended human being who speaks. But the simple denunciations and resolves to do injuries to one's foes can be applied all right in the sense I mean. I told A. D-J. when I answered him[371] that I didn't think they were true to the mind of Christ, and that I felt rather the same about some parts of the Gospels, in which the Evangelists seem to have let their own annoyance colour their reports.

I was rather exhausted on Friday, and began to think I was breaking up. But on Saturday I started a bronchial chest with slight temperature, which explained it. The temperature didn't last long, and now Dr B——has sounded my chest and given me something for it, so I am really all right again. I spent Sunday morning in bed, which is rather nice and peaceful, except that I had about 50 letters to write. I enclose Trevor Huddleston's exasperated letter to *The Times*,[372] the [Times] Saturday sermon, and an interview with Aldous Huxley,[373] at part of which I was present, as it was at dinner with Julian H. They must have gone on with it after the women had left the room.

When I have prepared my talk on 'Sacrament and Image', I

---

[370] 'Nevertheless, when they were sick, I put on sackcloth, and humbled my soul with fasting: and my prayer shall turn into mine own bosom.'

[371] When she answered his reply to her enquiry.

[372] Protesting at the 'non-interfering* attitude towards apartheid which Great Britain had adhered to in the voting of the political committee of the U.N. General Assembly.

[373] 'Conversation with Aldous Huxley' by Cyril Connolly, *Sunday Times*, 19 October, 1958.

will show it you.[374] It is an interesting subject, tho' vast, of course, and one can only touch on it. Gilbert Murray has a passage about what the statues of the gods were to the later educated Greeks—fables, but a way to the apprehension of the true God.[375] He quotes Maximus of Tyre, who said 'God, who is greater than time and eternity and all the flow of being, is unnameable, unutterable, not to be seen by any eye. But we, unable to apprehend his essence, use the help of sounds and names and pictures, of beaten gold and ivory, etc. etc., yearning for the knowledge of him. Why should I pass judgment upon images? If a Greek is stirred to the remembrance of God by the art of Pheidias, an Egyptian by paying worship to animals, another man by a river, another by fire, I have no anger for these divergences, only let them know what is divine, let them love', etc.[376] Someone else wrote 'God is invisible, but the mind of man demands a visible symbol.'[377] And so on.

I am not sure that I will come this week, as my cough may be catching, and I am also rather tired. But I am picking up fast, and taking good medicines. I told the chemist he must label my tablets and medicine with their names and what they cure. He said there was a law against this, as patients might guess what illness they had. I said that if my doctor hadn't told me that, I should change him, and that Dr B. always does. He thought that if someone had a heart in [a] poor state, doctors should say it was muscular strain. I never heard anything sillier. The poor patient might drop dead from running for a bus, owing to not having

---

[374] R.M. was to give this talk to Cambridge undergraduates on 6 Nov.

[375] See Gilbert Murray's *Five Stages of Greek Religion* (1925), chap. II.

[376] R.M. has abbreviated the quotation as given by Gilbert Murray.

[377] The notes for R.M.'s talk suggest that this is a quotation from Erasmus.

been warned. I told Dr B. afterwards and he quite agrees with me, and says of course there is no such law; how could there be?

I have a long letter from Dorothea. She says that Mabel (widow of Bruce [Conybeare][378]) thinks no one could guess from *Trebizond* what religion, if any, I had. That seems to me so odd. On the other hand the clergy think I am very Anglican, and Fr Ross of All Saints' [Margaret Street] asks me to open the All Saints' historical centenary exhibition next June. I can't of course. He would probably be shocked if he knew I was an intercommunionist. A friend of Dorothea's[379] who heard our Religious Brains Trust at Bognor[380] was rather shocked by my suggesting this as my contribution to our discussion about the way to union. I dare say the Bish. of Chichester[381] was too; but the Presbyterian[382] and the Methodist[383] agreed with me. So does D. but she thinks lots of Anglicans wouldn't.

The white smoke has gone up ![384] I hope at 6.0 we shall hear who he is. Several cardinals have died of excitement since the

---

[378] R.M.'s first cousin.

[379] Jessie Boy dell.

[380] This was a 'Christian Town Forum', organized by the Bognor Regis Christian Council, which took place on 7 October, 1958. The Question Master was Adrian Hill, of the B.B.C. Television Sketch Club, and the team consisted of the Bp of Chichester, R.M., a Methodist and a Presbyterian.

[381] Rt Rev. Roger Wilson.

[382] Rev. Kenneth Slack.

[383] Dr Harold Roberts.

[384] From the stove in the Sistine Chapel, the traditional signal that the election of a new Pope has been made.

conclave began.[385] Now the news is announced,[386] and none of the favourites have won. I expect the younger ones all voted for one of 76 in hopes their turn would come in 2 or 3 years. I know nothing about him, but hope he is rather mad and will utter strange things.

Deep fog coming down again.

Very much love.

E.R.M.

It was three days after this letter was written, on 30 October 1958, that Rose's death took place, suddenly, after a heart attack.

---

[385] Cardinal Celso Costantini died in Rome on 17 October, just befor the Conclave, and Cardinal Edward Mooney on 25 October.

[386] Cardinal Roncalli had been elected Pope John XXIII.

Appendix

Venice Besieged

Venice

A Fragment of a Novel

T *he idea of a novel with Venice as its setting had been taking shape in Rose's mind for more than a year before she died. During her stay there in 1957 she was already jotting down some rough notes. But various writing commitments kept her from starting on the book until she was in hospital after her accident in the Spring of 1958. Before her death she had completed the first chapter, 'Midsummer Moon', which gives a dramatic beginning to the plot (a road accident near Stonehenge), includes a satirical sketch of the doings of latter-day Druids, and introduces some of the main characters. This and Rose's miscellaneous notes provide many clues as to how the novel might have developed. They show that 'Venice Besieged', like 'The Towers of Trebizond', was to combine flights of fancy with familiar scenery and facts, and suggest that in parallel with the main plot (evidently involving blackmail) there would have been a portrayal of conflicts at a deeper level of consciousness.*

It appears from the notes that the theme of a beleaguered city held several allegorical meanings for Rose. 'Venice Besieged' represents not only mankind encompassed by the powers of spiritual evil, and civilization threatened by

313

barbarism, but also the individual soul locked in desperate warfare with itself, barricading itself against the torments of a guilty conscience. There are also hints that the eventual overcoming of the deadlock was to be, first of all, by means of a cataclysmic disaster. A terrible destruction had to take place before new life could begin. Rose had, in this context, apparently been toying with the idea of a second Deluge, caused by a great tidal wave sweeping in from the Adriatic and submerging the lagoon islands and then Venice itself Clearly the portrayal of this allegory and also the main plot were still evolving in her mind; on the other hand, she had already visualized the personalities of several of her characters in some detail.

There was to be a bouncing ingénue, Sukey Bun-Flanagan, daughter of a nouveau riche father and an aristocratic mother, owners of several Venetian palazzi; and there was her friend Emily Hyde, 'pretty and white and round', whose fiancé, Henry Tarrant, a barrister-novelist, takes to drink after the accident in which he killed a cyclist. Then there is their friend Peter Luckles, who subsequently collided with the dead cyclist and was accused and tried for manslaughter; and Danby, a cool, enigmatic writer in her late sixties, sardonically amused by the foolish conversation of her friends. Obviously, as in the 'The Towers of Trebizond', there was to be a strong flavour of religion, and also an unusually talented animal, this time a budgerigar which could memorize and repeat telephone numbers.

Chapter I

Midsummer Moon

Peter Luckles rode his Vespa from Great Gussage in Dorset towards Stonehenge in Wiltshire on the night of June 20th-21st. The sky was overcast and dark, the windless air was laden with fugitive drifts from the sultry day. The road twisted between broad grass verges and hedges pink and white with dog-roses and honeysuckle; beyond them the downs heaved rounded shoulders against a brooding sky.

Peter Luckles rode in a mellow dream, and sang, from time to time, snatches of opera. Taking a sharp bend on its off side, the Vespa crashed into a pedal bicycle and overturned. Peter, having passed out, came to, and he was lying beneath his Vespa, with the pedal bicycle and its one-time rider in a grim tangle of buckled wheels and blood beside him.

'Oh Lord,' cried Peter. 'Oh Lord, what have I done?' Trying to sit up, he fell dizzily back, and lay still, breathing heavily, supposing that someone would before long arrive. He guessed rightly, for the roads to Stonehenge were by no means empty to-night. A car

315

presently appeared, stopped, and emitted three people, all eager to assist at an accident, for the world has greatly altered since the days when priests and Levites passed by on the other side, and now it is all the police can do to keep the crowds back. So one of them drove on to Amesbury to fetch the personnel essential to incidents, such as doctors, police, and ambulance, while two remained on the troubled scene, endeavouring to recover the injured and comfort them with the coffee and champagne they had brought with them for their sustenance through the night. The pedal cyclist was past this, he lay in stupor, or else was it death; but Peter, whom they already knew, copiously drank, and the more he drank the more his mind cleared and the blackness of his situation impressed itself on him, so that soon he was groaning aloud. His friends, who were a brother and sister called Tim and Sukey Bun-Flanagan, tried to cheer him up, but they knew him to be in a pitiable case which could have no happy issue. They could only murmur dubiously, 'I expect hell come round soon', and 'They never look where they're going, these pedallers', and 'They never have their lights on', and similar consolations.

Peter only sighed. His friends, while they made their sympathetic partisan comments on the situation, plied him with more drink, firmly, painfully and mistakenly massaged his ankle, which appeared to be broken, tried to get his victim into a less comfortless posture, and conned over in their minds the probable tale of their unfortunate friend's iniquities. Distressed by his mournful plight, and by the alarming inanimateness of the poor cyclist, to whom such plights are a recurrent occupational disease, Sukey blinked away tears. She was a sympathetic girl of great natural kindness.

Presently there arrived from Amesbury two policemen, a doctor, and an ambulance. The policemen and the doctor sized up

316

the familiar scene. The doctor knelt down by the cyclist, examining him for signs of life, and finding none. It was apparent that yet another pedal cyclist had got the worst of yet another encounter. The doctor presently said, 'Back broken. Dead for at least an hour, I should say.'

The police took measurements and photographs, and the poor cyclist was placed in the ambulance. The police then turned their attention to Peter. The doctor said he had broken his ankle, and bound it round with something.

The police said, with their poker-faced severity, 'May I see your papers?'

'No papers with me,' said Peter.

'Name and address?'

'William Smith. I live in Iceland.'

'British citizen?'

'No. Icelandic.'

'Over here on a visit?'

'Yes. To see Stonehenge.'

'Is that your own machine?'

'No, it belongs to a friend.'

'They drive on the right in Iceland, I take it?'

'Yes. Oh yes, always.'

'Will you kindly turn out your pockets, sir?'

Peter groped in his pockets and produced a wallet, a handful of coins, a ball-top pencil, a cigarette case, a lighter, a handkerchief, a dog's lead, and an empty whisky flask.

'Come, come,' said the policeman, and drew from Peter's breast-pocket a couple of letters. One envelope was addressed 'The Hon. Peter Luckles, 13b Shepherd Market w.1,' the other, in a less literate hand, 'Hon. Luckles, White Barn, Great Gussage, Dorset.'

'We shall have to charge you, Mr Luckles,' (he pronounced it Luckless) 'with giving false information to the police. I should advise you to answer the ensuing enquiries accurately. Are your insurance certificate, driving licence and motor licence in order?'

'What's the good of my telling you? You know damn well they're not.'

'Anything known?' said one policeman to the other.

'Quite a lot,' said the other, and addressed Peter. 'You will be charged with riding dangerously, riding under the influence, riding an unlicensed machine, without an operative driving licence, and causing the death of a man. You will now accompany us in the ambulance to the Amesbury police station, where you will be formally charged with these offences, and will enter a hospital for the necessary treatment. But first we should like your account of the incident.'

'Well, I was on my way to Stonehenge …'

'After dinner, no doubt?'

'Naturally after dinner. Hours after. I dined with friends at Little Gussage.'

'And had plenty to drink there, I take it.'

'Well, they did me all right. I wasn't drunk, if that's what you're getting at. I was quite capable of riding the Vespa.'

'It appears not, doesn't it. And you're slurring your words now. What made you take that bend on the off side?'

'How should I know? I didn't know there was anything in the way. The next thing I knew, I'd crashed, and was lying in the road all tangled up with a push bike. Of course I'm damned sorry about him, whose-ever fault it was. But he hadn't got his lights on, and no one could've seen him, poor chap.'

'Well,' said the policemen, putting away their notebooks and looking impassive, 'that will be all for now.'

Peter's three friends said they would accompany the ambulance to the police station, for they did not like to desert him in his dark hour. They were allowed to do this, and when Peter had been charged and taken to the hospital for treatment, they drove on to Stonehenge and joined the great crowd who were milling round the stones in the dark. Some sat on the grass drinking beer and tea and playing gramophone records, some on the tops of the stones obstructing the view so that no one behind them would see the Druids when they arrived. The fence round the circle of stones was well broken by those who had surged through it. Among these was the party whom Peter and his three friends had arranged to join. When they heard of poor Peter's latest mischance, they all agreed that it could scarcely look worse for poor Peter. Riding with suspended driving licence his unlicensed, uninsured Vespa, quite drunk, taking a blind corner on the off side and killing a cyclist—it might well be manslaughter and prolonged incarceration. As they were all fond of poor Peter, they were shocked and saddened and drank some more. It was about half past three and quite dark still. The Druids would not be there until after four. People were eating and drinking out of paper bags and beer bottles, and throwing the empty bottles at the stones. Gramophones played jigging music, and there was rocking and rolling. But Peter's friends sat on the grass against one of the sarsen stones, and sadly drank. They were Bill Hammond, and the two Bun-Flanagans, and Henry and Emily, whom they had joined. Henry and Emily were engaged, and had driven over from the house of Henry's parents at Tarrant Hinton. Henry was a lawyer and a novelist; he was very distinguished-looking but by now quite drunk. Emily was pale, round-faced and wide-eyed, and she too was now intoxicated. Both had reached the quietly morose stage, and were taking an irritable view of the proceedings. When the dawn began, it was chilly and grey, and the stones looked still more rude and unpleasing than in the dark.

The Druids were perceived to be arriving, and there was a general rush towards them. White-robed and hooded, some oak-garlanded, they did not suggest the Ku Klux Klan, nor even, really, such Druids as Caesar and Tacitus and Nennius had known, spell-hurlers, potent magicians and enchanters, wielders of the sacrificial knife, bards and priests of the sacred groves, bloody and learned men; no, these Druids seemed innocent, mild, affected, performing their innocuous rites with prim correctness, feeding the sacred fire with sacred oak boughs from the sacred groves, uttering mystic words, joining hands and beseeching the sun to arise, but in vain, it did not arise. The Druids did not seem to mind; they were no doubt used to this, and had probably never seen it arise, which, for heliolaters, made a frustrated life. But they went on about the Sacred Purpose and the Divine Harmony and the Three Desirable Objectives which all Druids ever strive to uphold; they seemed to invoke the Great Spirit, and rather suggested Red Indians or the Ethical Society; in fact, they were pretty sissy. There seemed to be some implication that earlier Druids had planned and built Stonehenge, a notion in which they had been encouraged in the past but now not at all, for they had been long told that Stonehenge was built a millennium and a half before any Druids entered Britain, but they did not listen much to this, and did not care for archaeologists. So they innocently pomped it among the great stones as if these were their temple, reciting their spells the while, and obviously intent on the good and noble life, in spite of being so phoney.

'Where are the wicker images?' a hopeful child enquired of her parents.

'What wicker images, silly?'

'The ones the Druids had, to burn people in.' For it was this holocaust that she had been allowed, she thought, to come and see, so delightfully, in the very middle of the night.

'Oh, they don't burn people now, they've learnt better. Besides, the police are here.'

'Won't there be human sacrifices, like the book we do at school says?'

'No pet, not to-night.'

'Why are they lighting a fire on that stone?'

'That's Druid magic, that is. Look, that's Mr Popplethwaite from the draper's in the High Street lighting it.'

'Will they sacrifice an animal?'

'Dear me no, Mr Popplethwaite wouldn't consider doing a thing like that.'

'Well, will they chase early Christians, like in the pictures?'

'No early Christians here.'

'Why aren't there?'

'Afraid of the Druids, I shouldn't wonder.'

Hope dwindled. The expedition was apparently for nothing in particular, only to see the big stones by night and Mr Popplethwaite playing games with fire and water. The child, raised on her father's shoulders, yawned, drifting into sleep. The Druids went on with their strange rites, speaking the while of the Golden Age, the Triad, and the Word that had been made known to their forebears. They were prolix and high-minded, but few people could hear what they said.

The friends of Peter Luckles did not try to; they thought poorly of the whole business, sitting against a sarsen stone on the grass and drinking. Three of them had brought with them Druid costumes, which they had thought would be amusing to put on, but the idea no longer seemed good. The outsize stones looked as uncultured as ever, in spite of all the work lately done on them. Those who wrote them up said they were polished, but this did not seem to be noticeably the case.

'The wrong shapes, the wrong sizes, no elegance, no architectural unity. What, after all, do they mean?' they complained.

'Religion, human sacrifice, bloody death. Like all ancient temples,' Henry grumbled.

Emily, who viewed religion, human sacrifice and bloody death with the greatest apprehension, and only liked ancient temples for their elegant and noble shapes and their sculptured ornament, blenched at Stonehenge. Why had the Bronze Age inhabitants of Britain been so little accomplished that, at a time when their contemporaries overseas were building Mycenae, Tiryns, Knossos, and all that, all they could manage was to transport great slabs of rock from one part of Britain to another, cut and polish them inadequately, and stand them on end in circles? So much labour, such huge, uncultured achievement, like the uncouth gestures of giants.

'Bloody cannibals,' Henry said, as if the builders of Stonehenge had been capitalists and he a Soviet orator.

'My uncle Danny is a cannibal,' said Sukey. 'He sells things to cannibal chiefs in Africa and goes to their banquets, and they often have human dishes. Uncle Danny rather likes them, they keep up his strength. He says if ever he lives in Europe again, he'll have to contrive something, or he'll waste away.'

The rain began; it had a persevering look, tumbling out of slate-grey skies. There was a rush towards the car park across the road. Henry stopped his quiet drinking and said, 'We'd better get back. I'm leaving my car in Amesbury for the night, the steering wants seeing to. Can you take Emily and me to Tarrant?'

'Very wise of you, Henry,' said Bill. 'Meet us outside the George.'

The others all got in, Bill and Emily and Sukey and Tim, and, when they had fought their way out of the car park, they drove off into the wet dawn, and presently Henry joined them outside the George.

Two miles out of Amesbury Sukey said, 'That's the bend where Peter met the bicycle.'

'Stop,' Tim said. 'I want to look for my lighter.'

He got out, and Henry got out too, and they searched the road and the green verge.

'All right,' Tim said presently, 'here it is.'

Henry went on looking about.

'Peter may have dropped something,' he said, moving his torch about the edge of the road. But nothing was there, only the rain-splashed dust and the green wet verge and a frog that hopped in the ditch. The smell of honeysuckle and dog-roses and cow-parsley and rank ditch mud hung on the air above the crushed and flattened grass where Peter and his Vespa and the cyclist and his Rover had lain tangled and smashed, and the others had sat by them plying them with Thermoses and flasks and vain comfort, and the police with their questions and notebooks had, experienced and grave like recording angels, summed up the scene.

If any of them had left anything there, it was no longer there now. Henry got into the car; they drove on through the melancholy night and the soft midsummer rain.

'What's the worst they can do to poor Peter?' Sukey asked of Henry, who as a lawyer might know, though under-briefed and meaning to stand soon for Parliament as a Socialist, or perhaps a Tory.

'Oh, he won't get much,' Henry said. 'Perhaps six months, for all those crimes—no driving or car licence or insurance, dangerous driving while suspended and drunk, misinforming the police, and all his past driving record. The fact that the poor chap died doesn't add much actually.'

He did not pronounce 'actually' at all well, and the others thought how wise he had been to leave his car in Amesbury.

Bill said, 'But surely the fatal crime was to kill a man. It could be manslaughter, I suppose.'

'Don't be silly,' said Henry, indistinctly. 'That's finished.'

'Still,' said Bill, 'I should have thought it could be two years, given a vicious judge.'

Henry, wrapped in thought and drink, did not answer.

Sukey said, 'Poor old Peter. He must have had a hellish time, lying there for an hour by himself with the dead chap.'

'An hour?' said Henry.

'Well, the doctor said he must have died at least an hour ago.'

'I wouldn't give that,' said Henry, 'for what doctors say about times of death. Did Peter say he'd been there an hour?'

'I shouldn't think Peter had a clue,' said Tim, 'the way he was.'

Henry and Emily were dropped presently at Tarrant Hinton, where they were staying with Henry's parents. The midsummer night had not agreed with Emily, who was pale and shivering now that her mild intoxication had abated. She looked wan and plain, and had no word or smile for her friends as they parted. She and Henry had fallen out and were estranged; perhaps, thought Emily, for good.

Henry said to her 'I shall be going to Amesbury early for the car,' and Emily replied, 'I shall catch the 11.15 from Salisbury,' then went up to bed.

One cannot sleep in the midsummer dawn, the day coming

inexorably on. Emily lay awake and restless and heard the noisy birds, slept awhile, and woke a little before eight. Henry's amiable mother had put a portable wireless in her room; she turned it on, and it spoke about the weather, of how a weak cold front was advancing from the east, and would reach the western counties before evening, and how there would be scattered showers and bright intervals. Then it said, changing the subject, 'Here is a police message. An accident occurred on the A 345 road two miles from Amesbury last night, between a motor cyclist and a pedal cyclist. The pedal cyclist was killed. Anyone who saw the accident or can give any information about it is asked to communicate with the Chief Constable, Salisbury 1212.'

Emily turned it off. She dressed and packed and went down to breakfast, where Henry's parents were eating away, but Henry had gone to Amesbury in the bus. Emily said she had to catch the 11.15 from Salisbury.

'Why not wait for Henry to drive you up this afternoon?' said Henry's mother.

Emily said she had a luncheon engagement. Henry's mother said to herself, and later to Henry's father, 'They've fallen out. Henry was as cross as a bear this morning.'

'Oh I shouldn't think they had,' said Henry's father, who was reading *The Times*.

'I wonder what it was about,' said Henry's mother.

'Well, if they have they'll soon make it up,' said Henry's father, 'so it won't matter what it was about.' And he went on with *The Times*, while Henry's mother rather wished her sister Peggy was staying with them.

The coroner's jury at the inquest on the cyclist decided that he had been killed in a collision with the motor cycle of Peter

Luckles somewhere between one and one-thirty on the night of June 20. They added a severe corollary about dangerous and intoxicated driving. Mr Luckles was committed for trial at the next Assizes, allowed bail, and taken to his parents' home to mend his broken ankle and consider his plight. A plight indeed it was. At first his father was almost too vexed with him to do anything about engaging counsel for his defence, for he felt that a spell in prison would be just what Peter needed and deserved. But his wife prevailed on him to get their son defended, though Peter himself was too depressed to care much; he felt that he was certainly doomed, and rightly so, for he had killed a man. His friends tried to cheer him up in vain. They suggested that Henry Tarrant might be engaged in his defence. But Henry, though known to be brilliant, was also known to be drinking pretty heavily just now, and his defence of a drunken driver would make an unfavourable impression on the court, so Henry was ruled out. They got a sober, sensible barrister, who would do his best for this probably hopeless case. He asked Peter to tell him all he knew about the accident, but found that Peter did not know much. He had started from the house of his friends at Gussage All Saints at, he supposed, about half past one.

'Surely before that,' said the lawyer. 'According to medical evidence the cyclist had been dead for at least an hour when the doctor examined him at 2.30. The distance from Gussage All Saints is about twenty-three miles.'

'Well, it may have been at one, I dare say. Does it matter?'

'It might. Because, even if you started at one, you would have done the twenty-three miles in about twenty-five minutes, which is an incautious pace on a dark night along an unlit road for someone in the condition you were. It would add to the impression of reckless riding, which it's our job to lessen. I should certainly not tell the court that.'

'But the Vespa always does a pretty good lick. It has a good headlight.'

'I know. They dazzle everyone else on the road. Do you know the number of people—drivers, walkers and cyclists—who are killed by dazzling headlights each year? Of course they shouldn't be allowed. If they weren't, drivers would have to go slow and there'd be a damned sight fewer accidents. But anything for speed, these days.' Disgust with headlights and with speed tightened the lawyer's face. 'So for heaven's sake don't go saying things about headlights and good licks. Good headlights are feared and hated; you'd get more sympathy if you'd only had sidelights on. All the members of the jury who have been dazed and dazzled and endangered by headlamps are liable to see red at the thought of them. I am myself. And judges see redder than anyone. I'm afraid you may get old Arbuthnot.'

'Afraid?'

'Yes. His wife was crippled for life by a crash. He was driving, and the other car didn't dip its lights. He's never got over it. So the less we say about speed and headlamps the better. You must surely have left Gussage some time before one.'

'I told you, I don't remember. My friends might.'

'I shan't ask them. If they confirm your time, it would be bad, and one can't ask them to lie.'

'Oh, they wouldn't mind. I'd do it for them.'

'I dare say. But I think we'll leave them out of it, and not stress the time. You've more than enough counts against you without that. Unfortunately this man Jim Higgins was known as a very experienced cyclist. He seems to have been a nice chap, riding from Cranborne to meet his wife and children at Amesbury and take them to Stonehenge to see the Druids.'

Peter groaned. 'Those damned bloody Druids. They still cause as many deaths as they used to five thousand years ago.'

'Well, come, hardly five,' said the lawyer, who was rather a pedant.

'Oh, what's it matter. The point is they've killed Jim Higgins, and they'll get me put in jug. All that ballyhoo in the middle of the night. I should never have gone near them; I might have known.'

The lawyer reflected that there were so many things that Peter might have known that they had better be getting on with them. He turned the conversation on to some of them. The case for the defence looked such stuff as dreams are made of.

Chapter II

Sir Barty Bun-Flanagan—a rich tycoon whose father had migrated from County Cork to Chicago as an enterprising youth, made a great deal of money from a chain of bakeries, and finally died in Surrey—had so much money that he was being progressively ruined by taxation, so he took to salting his wealth away on the Continent, buying palazzi in Venice (he would have liked a chain of them, but could only get two), a villa near Nice, a castello on Capri, and a fine hotel on the Costa Brava, so that his British income tax and sur-tax were considerably mitigated. When people asked him if he did not ever want to visit County Cork, the home of his ancestors and indeed of many of his living relatives, his answer was 'No'. His father had instilled into him a profound contempt and distaste for the land of Eire and all its ways, and he had endeavoured to pass these on to his children, forbidding them, so long as they lived under his roof, to have anything to do with the distressful and backward country where their grandfather had as a lad made bread and buns in Skibbereen.

Sir Barty, on account of being so rich, was married to a Viscount's daughter, who was the life and soul of a women's paper, and often spoke on 'Woman's Hour' about such matters as the problems of adolescence and how parents should treat their children. One thing she said was that they should give them a lot of liberty, as this saves trouble and friction and creates confidence. So she let Sukey go abroad with her friends whenever she liked, and Sir Barty provided her with financial contacts so that she did not lack, and the only country she might not go to was Ireland, where they might meet their relatives and pick up ideas. He did not know, though his wife did, that Sukey and Tim had been to County Cork one summer, and visited Skibbereen and met a number of relations, some of whom were nuns and some priests and one the manager of a bakery.

So, when Sukey asked her parents if there would be any objection to her bringing Emily Hyde to the Palazzo del Vigno in July, they said that would be all right.

Sukey said to Emily, 'When shall we go? Shall we wait till we hear what happens to poor Peter?' and Emily said, 'All right, yes.' But when Peter was committed for trial at the Assizes, after the coroner's jury had said that he had killed the cyclist, Sukey and Emily did not wait any longer, for the Assizes which would try Peter might not sit till September....

Rose's consecutive narrative breaks off here. But the scribbled contents of a notebook marked 'Novel Notes 1957' suggest the general direction she meant it to follow when the scene of action shifted to Venice; they also hint at the deeper themes which were in her mind.

Novel Notes 1957

'Glimpses of a motiveless malignity.' 'Stories of hauntings, of subtle spiritual influences, of the elemental powers that preceded man's coming to earth, of possession, of evil let loose in the form of a werewolf of sheer human malignity—in the conviction of mystery and horror, moving in a world only just beyond the apprehension of the physical senses.'[1] Haunting from deserted lagoon islands, and from ruined parts of house. Continual ambush, pressing in of evil and barbarism. Sins, pushed out of consciences, relegated to the marginal darkness, kept at bay, lay constant siege. Car accident, killed someone, never discovered. Frauds, cruelties, deceptions, malice, lies, selfishness. Purgatorial swamps.

'We despise one another. We both know what the other is like. We couldn't live together. We should always be afraid the other was doing that kind of thing again. I couldn't live with someone who knows I did that.'

Lagoon islands. Wild primitive creatures there, swim to Venice, or come in fishing boats. People and animals besieging civilization. As in old house, partly ruined and discovered attics full of strange life.

'Was that a footstep?'
'I don't think so.'
'I think it was a footstep.'
'Just one footstep? Like Man Friday's on the sands?'
'Oh, you can make fun. There are odd things in this house.'
'Odd things in all houses.'
'Some odd form of life.'

---

[1] After these two quotations R.M. had jotted down, 'Ghost Stories of Joseph Sheridan Le Fanu (1860s)' and 'Ingoldsby Legends'.

'All forms of life are odd. Life is odd. Don't *fuss*.'

'If it's coming closer. Laying siege. What then? Like a tide, will it reach us and drag us back with it?'

'I shouldn't think so.'

'If sirocco blows, you hear boom of waves breaking on Lido shore. If it gave way, sea would roll in on city, sweeping palaces and churches to destruction, as Tintoretto has pictured in Santa Maria dell' Orto.[2] Lido never more than ½ mile wide—near Pellestrina, only a hundred paces. They put up palisades, later stone walls...,'[3]

On mainland stood [the cities of] Venetia: Aquileia, Altinum, Padua, and many more. Rich nobles lived there. Then came the Goths (406) and they all fled. Returned [to the mainland] after Alaric's death. But fifty years after Alaric came Attila the Hun, the Scourge of God, and they fled again.... *The first fugitives, blind with terror, stumbled ashore on a sand bank, crying 'The Huns are upon us.'* ... *Verlorensein* (sense of being lost and consequent blind panic) ... The cities fell. Citizens from Altinum built on Torcello. Islands united in federation, against the common danger of the great families; some were Frankish and from the West, others Greek and from Constantinople.

The Franks in 9th century under Pépin[4] took the nearer islands one by one, till Venetians left Malamocco and fled to Rialto ... where enemy could not reach them. Siege of Rialto.

---

[2] This refers to Tintoretto's painting of the Last Judgment in the Church of the Madonna dell' Orto.

[3] See Horatio Brown's *Life on the Lagoons* (1884).

[4] Pépin (777–810), son of Charlemagne and King of Italy.

Pépin's ships grounded in sand; he had to give up attempt, and retire to Ravenna. Rialto was fortified, and became seat of Government. It, and islands round it, were beginning of modern Venice. Buildings, churches, houses, begun. St Mark taken for patron saint, as he had once been shipwrecked on shore of Rialto. Devotion to him grew. His body was in Alexandria. Two Venetian merchants stole it (about 828. See mosaic of C.13 on façade of Basilica). Taken to ducal palace till a church could be built for it.

Venice of C.9. Currents and rivers not yet all controlled by stone-faced canals. Long stretches of mud, on which tide threw up seaweed. Piles had to be driven in, side by side, forming a surface. Buildings on them still stand. St Mark's was roofed with thatch.

… Ebb and flow of tides twice a day. At high tide lagoon surface is water, at low tide mudbank, cut by innumerable channels. Sea sweeps impetuously through Lido port, with Atlantic *[sic]*, Mediterranean and Adriatic at its back. Spreads through channels in mudbanks, till they brim over and flood whole lagoon. Tide flows on past Venice and Murano to Campalto, Mestre, Fusina, on mainland. Laguna Viva and Laguna Morta. Sea-lavender spreads shimmering veil of blue. Boats have to keep to channels, even at high tide. Five main waterways, defined by *pali*[5] along their margins.[6]

A few sand ridges above surface of lagoon…. *Venice will disappear into sand and water….*

---

[5] 'Posts'.

[6] See Horatio Brown's *Life on the Lagoons.*

Great tidal wave in Adriatic submerges islands; their wreckage swept into Venice—boats full of lunatics; wooden buildings, people, animals, trees, crops, flung onto Venice. Adriatic sweeps into the lagoon....

What animals swim in canals? Rats, cats, dogs, ducks, wolves, fishes, crabs, sea creatures during flood; pigeons, one with dry twig in beak, perched on Campanile. Lower storeys of houses, palazzi, shops submerged. Children drowned, some ride dolphins. '*Simo, Simo.*'[7] Monkeys ...

Campanile sticks up, and the domes and houses. All the debris of the islands flung into Piazza. Piers, bridges, calles, campos, all submerged. Piles of wrecked gondolas in the Bacino. Fragments of Austrian cannons. Sea slowly sinks, inch by inch.

'The world of Chaos has become real to us. What takes shape before us corresponds absolutely with that state which to the Christian is Hell, and it is this that has become part of the inner world of Man's soul.'[8]

[In] Hieronymus Bosch's Hell pictures 'We see dark gulfs, empty stretches of earth and sea that seems to tell us how utterly God has forsaken them, the desolation of empty cities, strange hideous places.... Above all we see ruins, we see them continually'.[9]

'As thou long since wert pleased to buy our drowned estate,

---

[7] 'Snub-nosed, Snub-nosed'. According to Pliny the Elder (*Natural History,* IX, 7–8) dolphins particularly liked to be called 'Snub-nose', and some became tame enough to allow boys to ride on their backs.

[8] See Hans Sedlmayr's *Art in Crisis* (trans. B. Battershaw, 1957), p. 166.

[9] See *Art in Crisis,* p. 187.

Taking the curse upon Thy self, so to destroy
The knots we tyed …
So let Thy grace now make the way
Even for Thy love …'

(Vaughan)[10]

'The Protestant is left to God alone. For him there is no confession, no absolution, no possibility of an *opus divinum* of any kind. He has to digest his sins by himself…. Bad conscience has all the unpleasant characteristics of a lingering illness which makes people chronically uncomfortable. But because of this the Protestant has a unique chance to realize his sin to a degree that is beyond the reach of Catholics, since confession and absolution are always at hand to ease excess of tension. The Protestant is left to his tensions, which can go on sharpening his conscience. Conscience, and in particular a bad conscience, can be a gift of heaven, a veritable grace if used in the interests of the higher self-criticism…. When we have done something that seems inexplicable, we need the sting of a bad conscience and the powers of discrimination that go with it, in order to discover the real motives of our behaviour. Only thus do we become capable of seeing what motives dominate our actions. A bad conscience spurs us on to discover things that before were unconscious, and in this way we can cross the threshold of the unconscious and take cognizance of those impersonal forces which make us the unconscious instrument of the mass-murderer in man. A Protestant … is defenceless against God and no longer protected by walls or communities and he has a unique opportunity for

---

[10] Henry Vaughan (1622–95).

335

immediate religious experience…. The experience may well crystallize into a new God-image, into an access of religious feeling. It requires considerable courage to accept oneself just as one is, to face up to oneself. Also, the approach to the unconscious may give rise to panic terror. When his personal experience of God threatened to become too dangerous, Angelus Silesius[11] almost fell over himself to get into the Catholic Church in order to escape the unconscious powers…. The non-Catholic *interiorizes* heaven and hell, and feels religious experience more profoundly in his own soul.'[12]

Kurt Leese[13] asks, 'Is a new *Götterdämmerung* about to begin?'[14]

Conversion. Odd phenomenon. Not really Anglican; nothing about it in Prayer Book, whose liturgy and collects aren't in tune with it, but with a slow and fitful trying. Really a nonconformist approach; language strange to Anglicans. 'Trusting in Christ's death.' 'Accepting Christ.' Not trying to get nearer to him. 'Four years ago I became a Christian; I accepted Christ. Now I know I am saved by His blood. I may sin again and again, but my sins are no longer held against me, I am redeemed.' Such language has no meaning to ordinary church people. What is history of this view? Why have nonconformists inclined to it?

---

[11] Johannes Scheffler (1624–77), mystical poet and controversialist.

[12] This is a free rendering of a passage from C. G. Jung's *Psychology and Religion*, as quoted by Hans Schaer in his *Religion and the Cure of Souls in Jung's Psychology* (trans. R. F. C. Hull; Routledge & Kegan Paul, 1951).

[13] Protestant theologian, b. 1887.

[14] Hans Schaer quotes this from Kurt Leese's *Die Krisis und Wende des christlichen Geistes* (1932).

'How wonderful!'

'Do you drive a car, bicycle, ride, bathe, travel, work, go upstairs, go on buses and trains, dine out, see plays, read, write, etc. How wonderful!'

'Why yes. Don't you?'

'Oh yes, *I* do.'

'It seems an ordinary human activity, surely—not really wonderful, would you say?'

And, when put like that, they could not say why they had thought it wonderful. But Danby knew that they thought it was odd of her, at her age, to be doing anything at all except sitting in a bath chair, for they supposed she must be well on in her sixties, and finished but for getting into her coffin. It would never do, they thought, if the elderly were to get about, competing with the young for places on buses and trains, taking up the road with cars and bicycles, the sea and swimming pools with elderly swimmers in need of rescue, the publishing houses with the stupid books they have written, the theatres with plays, the cinemas and restaurants and parties with people who no longer need to enjoy themselves, for this is a thing they should have finished with years ago; they have, in fact, had it.

'I don't,' said Danby, 'see why I shouldn't go on behaving like an ordinary human being, and doing what I like.'

'It's wonderful the way you know how the young talk.'

'Not in the least. They talk all round me, and it seems to me more or less the way we all talk. Do people begin to talk in a quite different way after they are forty? I didn't.'

'But then you're wonderful.'

Danby left them to it; she was tired of them.

Blackmailer, who suspected accident. Someone they know …

Danby offers everything, her love, all she has, except the truth … : 'You must tell me the truth (you must sell me the truth)'…

Quiet, cynical man called Francis Park, a writer, who had been ill reviewed and mocked by Guy, and is in love with Danby…

Children: Jane, Guy's sister, and Chris (10 and 9), whose friend Jimmie had been killed. Determined to discover who did it …

Henry and Emily lose figure [of number plate] off car which stranger finds in road and blackmails them with.

Budgerigar repeats telephone number he hears most often. It is found by friends of owners, who recognise number, and know who rings it….

Venetian Ghosts: Hobhouse,[15] Byron, Shelley, Corvo,[16] Leigh Hunt.[17] Lady Blessington.[18] Henry James. Sisters in *Aspern Papers* (in which campo was house?). Horatio Brown.[19] Lady Layton.[20] Doges, Popes. Marco Polo, Browning, Ruskin, Hare,[21] Colleoni.[22] P.E.N. Congresses. Hemingway. W. D. Howells[23]…

---

[15] J. C. Hobhouse, Baron Broughton (1786–1869).

[16] 'Baron Corvo', the pseudonym used by F. W. Rolfe (1860–1913).

[17] J. H. Leigh Hunt (1784–1859), essayist, critic, and poet.

[18] Marguerite, Countess of Blessington (1789–1849), authoress.

[19] H. R. F. Brown (1854–1926), historian of Venice.

[20] R.M. probably means Lady Layard, wife of Sir Henry Layard (1817–1894) who became the *grande dame* of the English colony in Venice.

[21] Augustus J. C. Hare (183 4–1903).

[22] Bartolommeo Colleoni (1400–1475), Italian soldier of fortune.

[23] William D. Howells (1837–1920), American man of letters, and U.S. consul in Venice 1861–65.

Sukey was in love with Byron, and hunted for all his Venice dwellings, especially the one with animals on ground floor (Palazzo Mocenigo)[24] … [In the] *Casa Mocenigo (Nuova)* 'Byron's room' is room where he worked; mosaic floors, valuable pictures … Front door only by gondola (or swimming). Large courtyard, where he kept the animals? He slept on ground floor. View over canal. Rather dark upstairs room, large, beautiful. Engraving of it with Byron sitting at table, in Drawing Room Scrap Book (Album) 1847. Also poem about him by Lord John Manners.[25] Sukey knows it by heart, and quotes it. Also 'I rode one evening with Count Maddalo.' Lido no longer 'a desolate waste'[26] …

'I should have liked to follow him about as his page. I wouldn't want to sleep with him, but if he wanted me to I would do it. But it would spoil things for me. All this going to bed

[Sukey] hoped that Emily, having lost Henry, won't turn to Byron 'on the rebound'.

'You can have Shelley,' she said.

'No thank you,' said Emily. 'He must have been a nice, angelic bore. I couldn't use him.'

Sukey sighed. 'I was afraid not. Well, of course there's always [T. S.] Eliot. You do adore him, don't you? So do I. We can share him.'

---

[24] In 1818 Byron lived in one of the three adjoining Palazzi Mocenigo on the Grand Canal which are known as *Casa Nuova,* to distinguish them from *Casa Vecchia,* the nearby palazzo originally belonging to an older branch of the Mocenigo family.

[25] 'The Mocenigo Palace at Venice'; see *English Ballads and Other Poems* by Lord John Manners (1850).

[26] See Shelley's 'Julian and Maddalo'.

'And I've got John Cleveland,[27] too,' Emily said....

'I wish I was a Catholic, like the Bun-Flanagans always used to be. Catholics see visions and spirits and phantoms. If I was one, I might see a vision of Byron in Venice, coming out of Palazzo Mocenigo with a lot of his animals. Perhaps he'd see me and smile, or wave his hand. Or he might frown and shoo me away. But anyhow I should have seen him. My aunt in the convent near Skibbereen sees visions. She told me she saw the Virgin Mary one day, in a blue cloak, and she said my aunt was to pray for Pa and me and Tim, that we should all come back to the Church. So she has prayed ever since for us, but it's done no good so far. She asks Mary to give us the gift of faith. Wouldn't it be awful if I suddenly got it? I should never dare to tell Pa.... The church doors are like women's magazines, all in a fuss about what we ought to wear. Long sleeves, long skirts, high necks. Goodness, one can't pack special clothes to take abroad just to go into churches. Why are Catholic churches so clothes minded? Anglicans aren't, are they?'

'No, they couldn't care less what we wear.'

'Well, if ever I look like getting the gift of Faith, just remind me of this clothes business and I'll snap out of it. I wish they'd tell me what to wear, but they don't seem to bother about that. Do you think it's Mary's fault, and that she tells them about correct church fashions? I don't believe Jesus Christ would have cared, do you? I mean he was kind of simple and fair-minded, and he didn't make special rules for women. In Malta, girls and women are told to dress in a Mary-like manner. Like in the pictures of her, I suppose. It would look terribly odd.'

---

[27] John Cleveland (1613–58), Royalist poet, see R.M.'s *They Were Defeated*.

'Our towns are copied fragments from our breast,
And all man's Babylons strive but to impart
The grandeurs of his Babylonian heart.'[28]

VENICE:[29] *Malamocco,* engulfed by sea at beginning of 12th century. *Torcello,* once full of churches, palaces (all gone but the cathedral, church and campanile which stand alone among yellow fields, vines, and gardens, peasants' houses and thatched boat shelters) now the cemetery of an older life. [It was once] *Altinum novum,* [the home of] refugees from Altinum [one of the cities] destroyed by Attila. Tragic ghost at its heart. Cicadas. Once important city. Some medieval traces left of the old piazzas, calles, churches, canals. The main canal still spanned by the ruined bridge of the Diavolo. But 'the gran' piazza with its little group of buildings' is all that is left…. The neighbouring islands were named after [the] gates of Altinum. After [its] destruction the fugitives returned to bring to Torcello the stones of destroyed city. Pulpit steps of duomo, Greek relief. Madonna in the apse. *Murano.* San Donato and its pavement, [which] rivals S. Mark's— 'beauty of designs, harmonies of precious marbles, porphyry and verd-antique, serpentine and *marmo greco* and Verona'— [but is] much ruined and despoiled. Madonna in the apse, grander than the one of Torcello in her dark robe worked with gold, the feet resting on luminous fire. She draws us to worship. Murano was pleasure-ground of Venetian nobles. But fell with the fall of Republic[30]; 'palaces snatched away piece by piece, fell

---

[28] See Francis Thompson's sonnet 'Correlated Greatness'.

[29] The following notes are based on passages in *Venice* by Beryl de Selin-court and M. S. Henderson (1907).

[30] The Republic of Venice was abolished by Napoleon in 1797.

into irrecoverable ruins'. Only one still has remains of splendour—the Cà da Mula. Glass works begun at end of nth century. Convent front of San Cipriano, brought here from Malamocco in C.9. Its façade 'stands up nobly from tangled garden. Central arch has Byzantine tracery; above it is frieze of Renaissance Roman-Byzantine symbols sculptured in stone discs in walls of cloister' …

San Marco mosaics: Precious marbles and stones; *diaspro* (radiant and full of light); *breccia adriana di Tegoli,* harmony of greens; *porpora* (red); *verde antico* (green); *diaspro sanguinoso,* dense green spotted with crimson—sanguinary jasper. *Miracoli*[31]: Coloured marbles of walls. Choir raised above nave by marble steps. In choir, great cross of porphyry and serpentine in apse. Company of sea youths and maidens. On pillars, birds, lizards, ears of corn, serpent. Slabs of marble in walls, Carrara cream and white, *marmo greco,* Verona red; dusky gold and colour of ceiling. *Ancient houses,* by Ponte Widmann, and Ponte *Pasqualigo.* We leave the Miracoli on our right, cross Rio Santa Marina and Rio San Giovanni Grisostomo, and pass into Rio del Teatro, with [the site of] *Marco Polo's* palace on our right. 'This corner is one [of the] most beautiful in Venice. Rich in palaces and fragments of ornament, and strange interplay of lights from ways that converge here. No spot in Venice so full of ancient mystery, the gloom, the light, the sound of water ways.' *Palazzo Gussoni,* Rio della Fava. Early renaissance. Rich sculptures. Stone barbican supporting upper storey overhanging Calle della Fava. At juncture of Rio della Guerra with Rio del Palazzo is *Casa dell' Angelo,* with sculptured angel on wall. Remains of fresco under projecting roof, with figures of women (Tintoretto). *Cannaregio* in north

---

[31] The Church of Santa Maria dei Miracoli.

Venice, with Campanile of *Madonna dell' Orto* (white statue) looking out over city and lagoon. Abbazia della Misericordia and garden of *Casa degli Spiriti*. Abbazia is one of most beautiful ruins in Venice. Built 939.

'And of course,' said Emily, 'you had a rather queer family, your uncle, Danny, being a cannibal in Cork.'

'In the Congo. I expect we *are* rather queer.' Sukey looked complacent. 'I'm sure Pa is. You knew his father came from a back street in Skibbereen.'

'Why?'

'Well, wouldn't you? A front street in Skibbereen is dull enough, but a *back* street—you couldn't even see the traffic from my grandfather's bakery. So he came away, and never looked back. But it's made Pa rather queer, knowing about Skibbereen and how awful it was, and always frightened it might pull him back, or us. So he never lets us go there. Tim and I went over secretly last year, and really it was quite fun. But not to stay long in…. Cork is very religious, and it's full of crazies. My great aunt that's a nun in Malta is as queer as a coot. But of course she's a right to be, at her age.'

'Do not adultery commit; advantage rarely comes of it.'[32]

Sukey on going to bed with men: 'Ma says it's common, and Pa says he'd wallop me. Ma says she expects they take a pretty poor view of it in Skibbereen, and she says Pa has Skibbereen in his blood, though he hates it. She says it's all under his skin, fretting him— and scaring him, and that's why he won't let Tim and me go to

---

[32] From 'The Latest Decalogue.' by A. H. Clough (1819–61).

343

Ireland. Perhaps it's under my skin too, because I'm not much sold on this bedding business. Are you? Ma says she thinks you'd be too proud for it. Besides, you go to church. Well, I don't know. It's funny about men, they don't seem to be so proud in that way. Tim isn't; is Henry?'

'No, Henry's not proud,' [said] Emily [and] thought, 'Going to bed is cosy and comforting, you can forget everything else, it wraps you round in forgetting like music and drink, and religion can too. Religion, music, love, drink—they could wrap you round in dreams, you can hide in them, till everything seems a dream.'

'I'm going into San Marco for Vespers,' … [said Sukey].

'Then you're too proud to sleep with people.'

'Is it proud? It's just that I don't believe I should enjoy it. I like going to bed by myself.'

'Some do and some don't. Men seem to, more. They're not so proud, I don't think!'

'Well, I've never actually done it myself. But people do seem to like it. Particularly men do. It's funny.... Peg says, try anything once, so I suppose I shall…. Men don't seem to be proud in that way. They'll sometimes even *pay* to go to bed with someone. Pay money. I wouldn't do that, would you? I mean, I'd rather have the money. If I had enough money, I wouldn't want to waste time going to bed at all.'

Sir Barty Bun-Flanagan. Sir Barty was beautiful. He had a fine, pale, tanned *[sic]* face, a strong chin, a firm, full-lipped mouth, shrewd blue eyes looking narrowly from under hooded lids, smooth, thick brown hair going grey. He looked a masterful man, intelligent, kind, but wilful.

Lady Anne Bun-Flanagan: 'Bursting buxom! High heels make your ankles thick, push out your behind and your chest, give you that silly *swan* shape like a comic Edwardian landlady. Common.'

Sukey: 'But I'd sooner be swan-shaped and common, with a land-lady's bust and thick ankles and have the Women's Pages in the press call me smart and well shod, than have flat shoes and thin ankles and a straight behind and have them call me a frump.'

'I suppose you think *I* look a frump.'

'Oh no, Ma. *You* look so distinguished, even in tight frocks. I shall never look distinguished. All I can do is to try and not look odd. Even if my heels do stick in gratings. Byron wouldn't have liked me to look a frump, or odd. He'd rather I looked swan-shaped and bulgy and got stuck in gratings. So would Luigi and Dino, I'm sure.'

'Don't be silly, dear. Byron's more than enough without bring-ing in the gondoliers.'

Sukey sighed. 'Well, what with you looking so distinguished and Pa as handsome as Caligula or Hermes, and Emily so pretty and white and round, you surely don't mind my getting me a few nice men.'

Genealogy
Bibliography

Genealogy of Rose Macaulay

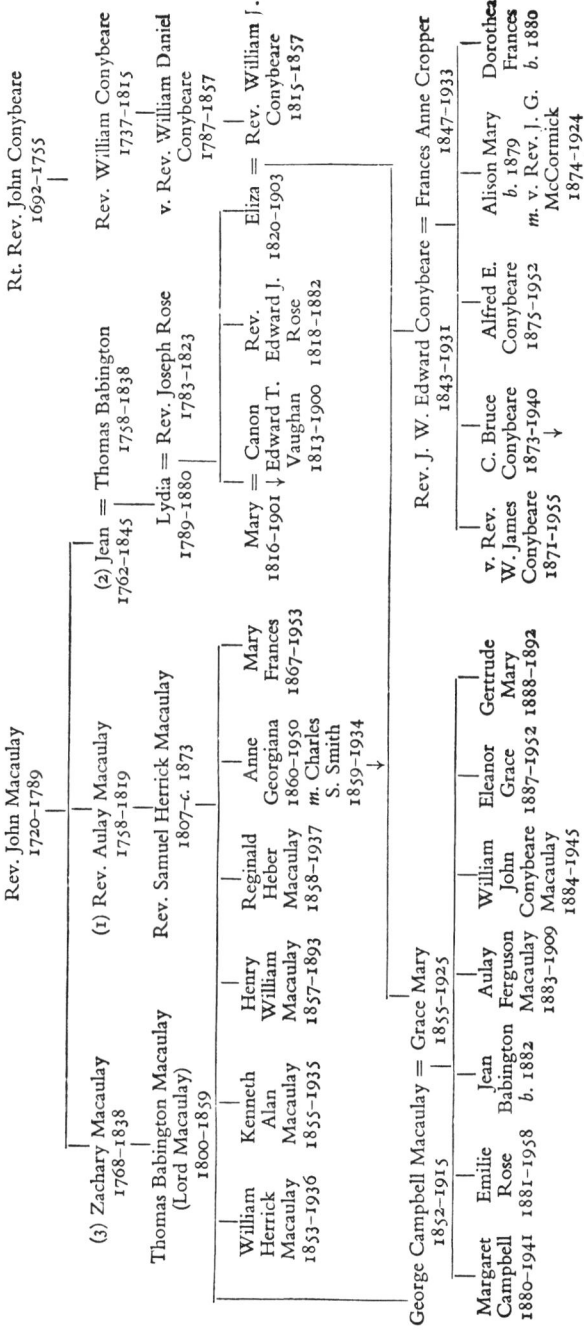

```
Rt. Rev. John Conybeare
        1692–1755
            |
   Rev. William Conybeare
        1737–1815
            |
   v. Rev. William Daniel
        Conybeare
        1787–1857
```

```
                    Rev. John Macaulay
                        1720–1789
                            |
                    (1) Rev. Aulay Macaulay        (2) Jean = Thomas Babington
                        1758–1819                      1762–1845   1758–1838
                            |
                    Rev. Samuel Herrick Macaulay        Lydia = Rev. Joseph Rose
                        1807–c. 1873                     1789–1880   1783–1823
```

```
(3) Zachary Macaulay                                                 Mary  = Canon      Rev.          Eliza = Rev. William J.
    1768–1838                                                     1816–1901 ↓ Edward T. Edward J.    1820–1903    Conybeare
        |                                                                    Vaughan    Rose                      1815–1857
Thomas Babington Macaulay                                                   1813–1900  1818–1882
    (Lord Macaulay)
    1800–1859
```

```
William      Kenneth    Henry      Reginald    Anne        Mary
Herrick      Alan       William    Heber       Georgiana   Frances
Macaulay     Macaulay   Macaulay   Macaulay    1860–1950   1867–1953
1853–1936    1855–1935  1857–1893  1858–1937   m. Charles
                                               S. Smith
                                               1859–1934
                                                   ↓
```

```
                                    Rev. J. W. Edward Conybeare = Frances Anne Cropper
                                            1843–1931                   1847–1933
```

```
George Campbell Macaulay = Grace Mary        v. Rev.      C. Bruce    Alfred E.   Alison Mary    Dorothea
    1852–1915              1855–1925          W. James     Conybeare   Conybeare   b. 1879        Frances
                                              Conybeare    1873–1940   1875–1952   m. v. Rev. J. G.  b. 1880
                                              1871–1955        ↓                   McCormick
                                                                                   1874–1924
```

```
Margaret     Emilie      Jean          Aulay        William      Eleanor      Gertrude
Campbell     Rose        Babington     Ferguson     John         Grace        Mary
1880–1941    1881–1958   b. 1882       Macaulay     Conybeare    1887–1952    1888–1892
                                       1883–1909    Macaulay
                                                    1884–1945
```

Select Bibliography

Novels

Abbots Verney	*John Murray*	1906
The Furnace	*John Murray*	1907
The Secret River	*John Murray*	1909
The Valley Captives	*John Murray*	1911
Views and Vagabonds	*John Murray*	1912
The Lee Shore	*Hodder & Stoughton*	1912
The Making of a Bigot	*Hodder & Stoughton*	1914
Non-Combatants and Others	*Hodder & Stoughton*	1916
What Not: A Prophetic Comedy	*Constable*	1918
Potterism: a Tragi-farcical Tract	*Collins*	1920
Dangerous Ages	*Collins*	1921
Mystery at Geneva	*Collins*	1922
Told by an Idiot	*Collins*	1923
Orphan Island	*Collins*	1924
Crewe Train	*Collins*	1926
Keeping up Appearances	*Collins*	1928
Staying with Relations	*Collins*	1930
They Were Defeated	*Collins*	1932
Going Abroad	*Collins*	1934
I Would be Private	*Collins*	1937
And No Man's Wit	*Collins*	1940
The World my Wilderness	*Collins*	1950
The Towers of Trebizond	*Collins*	1956

Poetry

The Two Blind Countries	*Sidgwick & Jackson*	1914
Three Days	*Constable*	1919

Essays, Criticism, Etc.

A Casual Commentary	*Methuen*	1925
Catchwords and Claptrap	*Hogarth Press*	1926
Some Religious Elements in English Literature	*Hogarth Press*	1931
Milton	*Duckworth*	1934

Personal Pleasures   *Gollancz*   1935
The Writings of E. M Forster   *Hogarth Press*   1938

Anthology

The Minor Pleasures of Life   *Gollancz*   1934

History and Travel

They Went to Portugal   *Jonathan Cape*   1946
Fabled Shore: from the Pyrenees to
   Portugal   *Hamish Hamilton*   1949
Pleasure of Ruins   *Weidenfeld & Nicolson*   1953

Letters

Letters to a Friend: 1950-1952   *Collins*   1961
Last Letters to a Friend: 1952-1958   *Collins*   1962

A NOTE ON THE AUTHOR

Rose Macaulay (1881–1958) was born in Rugby, Warwickshire but spent her early childhood in Italy. She was educated at Oxford High School for Girls and Somerville College, Oxford, where she read Modern History.

She wrote her first novel, *Abbots Verney*, in 1906, while living in Great Shelford, near Cambridge. Rose became an ardent Anglo-Catholic and, through her great childhood friendship with Rupert Brooks, was introduced to London literary society. After moving to London, in 1914 published her first book of poetry, *The Two Blind Countries*. In 1918 she met the novelist and former Catholic priest Gerald O'Donovan, the married man with whom she was to have an affair lasting until his death. Her final and most famous novel, *The Towers of Trebizond* (1956), was awarded a James Tait Black Memorial Prize and became a bestseller in America.

Rose Macaulay was made a Dame Commander of the British Empire in 1958, but seven months later suffered a heart attack and died at her home.

Leeds City Council

tem

Leeds City Council
Renewals Tel 0845 1207271
Enquiries Tel 0113